Tarascon Primary Care Pocketbook, First Edition

Tarascon Primary Care Pocketbook, First Edition

FOR TARASCON BOOKS/SOFTWARE, VISIT **WWW.TARASCON.COM**
See faxable order form on page 200

- Tarascon Primary Care Pocketbook
- Tarascon Pocket Pharmacopoeia® Classic Edition
- Tarascon Pocket Pharmacopoeia® Deluxe Edition
- Tarascon Pocket Pharmacopoeia® PDA software
- Tarascon Pocket Orthopaedica®
- Tarascon Pediatric Emergency Pocketbook
- Tarascon Adult Emergency Pocketbook
- Tarascon Internal Medicine & Critical Care Pocketbook
- How to be a Truly Excellent Junior Medical Student

"It's not how much you know, it's how fast you can find the answer."®

Important Caution Please Read This! The information in the *Tarascon Primary Care Pocketbook* is compiled from sources believed to be reliable, and exhaustive efforts have been put forth to make this book as accurate as possible. *However the accuracy and completeness of this work cannot be guaranteed.* Despite our best efforts this book may contain typographical errors and omissions. The *Tarascon Primary Care Pocketbook* is intended as a quick and convenient reminder of information you have already learned elsewhere. The contents are to be used as a guide only, and health care professionals should use sound clinical judgment and individualize patient care. This book is not meant to be a replacement for training, experience, continuing medical education, or studying the latest literature and drug information. This book is sold without warranties of any kind, express or implied, and the publisher and editors disclaim any liability, loss, or damage caused by the contents. *If you do not wish to be bound by the foregoing cautions and conditions, you may return your undamaged and unexpired book to our office for a full refund.*

Tarascon Primary Care Pocketbook
First Edition

ISBN 1-882742-33-8. Copyright ©2004 Joseph S. Esherick, MD. Published by Tarascon Publishing®, PO Box 517, Lompoc, California 93438. Printed in the USA. All rights reserved. No portion of this publication may be reproduced or stored in any form or by any means (including electronic, photocopying) without our prior written permission. Tarascon Publishing is a division of Tarascon Inc. *Tarascon Publishing* and *It's not how much you know, it's how fast you can find the answer* are registered trademarks of Tarascon Inc. CY1

Tarascon Primary Care Pocketbook
First Edition

Joseph S. Esherick, M.D.
Family Medicine, Ukiah, California

*Editorial Board**

Cover Artwork: *Vaccinating the Baby*, Ed Hamman, 1890. Courtesy of the National Library of Medicine, Images from the History of Medicine.

A Note from the Author

The Tarascon Primary Care Pocketbook is intended to be a quick reference guide for clinicians and students practicing primary care medicine. I have attempted to compile the core information in a concise fashion about most primary care topics. I have adapted the practice guidelines from nationally recognized medical associations and have footnoted the primary references when possible. I would like to thank all of my mentors and colleagues who have passed on to me countless clinical pearls many of which I have included in this book. I would also like to thank my brother Jonathon Mao for his help with formatting and book design. If you find an error or wish to make a suggestion, please let us know (e-mail: editor@tarascon.com). This book is dedicated to my wonderful wife Gina who constantly encouraged me and supported me through the entire project, and to my daughter Sophia who sacrificed a lot of "daddy time" over the past year.

↑ : increased/elevated	hgb: hemoglobin
↑↑ : very high	HIV: human immunodeficiency virus
↓ : decreased/depressed	HLA-B27: human leucocyte antigen-B27
+ : positive or present	HTN: hypertension
- : negative or absent	Hz: hertz
+/- : and/or	IU: international units
♂ : male	IV: intravenous
♀ : female	kcal: kilocalorie
> : greater than	kg: kilogram
≥ : greater than or equal to	l : liter
< : less than	Lb: pound
≤ : less than or equal to	lymph: lymphocytes
µL: microliter	m: meter
ACEI: angiotensin converting enzyme inhibitor	mcg: microgram
	MEq: milliequivalents
ACTH: adrenocorticotropin hormone	mg: milligram
AIDS: acquired immunodeficiency syndrome	MI: myocardial infarction
	min.: minute
ANA: antinuclear antibody	mL: milliliter
ARB: angiotensin receptor blocker	mm: millimeter
BP: blood pressure	mmol: millimole
CA: cancer	mmHg: millimeters of mercury
CA 15-3, CA 19-9, CA 27.29 and CA-125: cancer antibodies of that number	mo.: month
	monos: monocytes
CD4: helper T cells with CD4 receptors	mOsm: milliosmoles
CEA: carcinoembryonic antigen	MRI: magnetic resonance imaging
CHF: congestive heart failure	MRA: magnetic resonance angiogram
cm: centimeter	ng: nanogram
CNS: central nervous system	NSAID: nonsteroidal anti-inflammatory drug
COX-2: cyclooxygenase-2	pg: picogram
CT: computed tomography scan	PMN: polymorphonuclear neutrophil
CXR: chest x-ray	PPD: purified protein derivative
d: day	RPR: rapid plasma regain test
dB: decibels	SQ: subcutaneous
DC: direct current	t or tsp: teaspoon
dL: deciliter	U: units
ECG: electrocardiogram	URI: upper respiratory tract infection
fT4: free levothyroxine (T4) level	VDRL: venereal disease research laboratory
FTA: fluorescent treponemal antibody	WBC: white blood count
G6PD: glucose-6-phosphate dehydrogenase	wk: week
	yr: year
GI: gastrointestinal	
gm: gram	
GU: genitourinary	
h or hr: hour	

Adult Valvular Diseases

Category	Mitral Stenosis	Mitral Regurgitation	Aortic Stenosis	Aortic Regurgitation	IHSS	Innocent Murmur
Etiology	• Rheumatic • Congenital	• Rheumatic disease • Endocarditis • Mitral valve prolapse • Papillary muscle dysfunction	• Rheumatic disease • Bicuspid valve • Calcific stenosis	• Rheumatic • Bicuspid • Endocarditis • Aortic dissection • Marfans/syphilis aortitis	• Congenital	• Normal valves
♂ or ♀	♀ > ♂	♂ > ♀	♂ > ♀	♂ > ♀	♂ > ♀	♂ = ♀
Age	14 - 28 years	30 - 50 years	40 - 50 years	40 - 50 years	15 - 50 years	1 - 15 years
Clinical Features	• CHF symptoms • Hemophysis • Palpitations (atrial fibrillation)	• CHF symptoms • Palpitations (Atrial fibrillation) • Long latency	• Angina: 5 yr survival • CHF: 2 yr survival • Syncope: 3 yr survival • Sudden death	• CHF symptoms • Angina • Long latency	• Angina • CHF • Syncope • Sudden death • Long latency	• None

Adapted from American College of Cardiology practice guidelines and reproduced with permission from Daniel S. Clark, M.D., Director of Cardiology/ICU, Ventura County Medical Center, S₁ = first heart sound, S₂ = second heart sound, S₃ = third heart sound, S₄ = fourth heart sound, NYHA = New York Heart Association, ACEI = angiotensin converting enzyme inhibitor, IHSS = Idiopathic Hypertrophic Subaortic Stenosis

Adult Valvular Diseases

Category	Mitral Stenosis	Mitral Regurgitation	Aortic Stenosis	Aortic Regurgitation	IHSS	Innocent Murmur
Exam Findings	• ↑S₁ • Apical diastolic rumble • Presystolic accentuation • Opening snap (OS)	• ~ S₁ • ~ S₃ gallop • Apical systolic blowing murmur→ axilla • No increase after premature ventricular contraction (PVC)	• ↓S₂ • Harsh systolic murmur 2ⁿᵈ left intercostal space (ICS)→ carotids • ↑ after PVC • Paradoxical split S₂ • Gallavardin sign	• + S₃ gallop • Diastolic murmur • Quincke's sign • deMusset sign • Duroziez sign • Traube sign • Corrigan (water hammer pulse) • Bisferiens carotid pulse	• Harsh sys. murmur 3ʳᵈ left ICS • Lying → standing ↑ intensity • + S₄ • Bisferiens carotid pulse	• Soft systolic ejection murmur 2ⁿᵈ left intercostal space
Indicators of Severity	• Short S₂- OS interval • Long murmur	• None	• Long murmur • + S₄ gallop • Sustained PMI	• Wide pulse pressure • Austin-Flint murmur	• Bisferiens pulse	• None
Medical Therapy	• furosemide • digoxin • warfarin	• furosemide, digoxin & warfarin • ACEI (acute MR)	• No medical therapy. • AVR if	• ACEI or nifedipine • Add furosemide and digoxin for CHF	• β-blocker • verapamil	• None
Surgical Therapy When	• CHF NYHA class 3 on meds	• CHF NYHA 3 on meds • ESD > 45 mm • LVEF < 60%	• mild symptoms, AVA < 1.0 cm² or AV gradient > 60 mmHg	• NYHA 3 on meds • LVEF < 50% or ESD > 55 mm	• When symptoms start	• None

PMI = point of maximal impulse, ESD= end-systolic diameter, AVR = aortic valve replacement, AVA = aortic valve area, LVEF = left ventricular ejection fraction

General Management Guidelines for Atrial Fibrillation (Afib)
Rate control of Asymptomatic Hemodynamically Stable Patients
- Digoxin load with 0.25 mg PO q6h x 4 doses then 0.125–0.25 mg PO qd as maintenance)
  - ➢ Decrease dose in renal failure
  - ➢ Controls only resting ventricular rate
- Diltiazem 120 – 360 mg PO qd
- Metoprolol 25 – 100 mg PO bid (use only if normal cardiac contractility)
- Verapamil 240 – 480 mg PO daily (use only if normal cardiac contractility)
- Outpatient amiodarone load with 600 mg PO daily x 2 - 3 weeks → 200 mg PO daily maintenance (only for compliant patients at low risk for bradyarrhythmias)
  - ➢ Used for refractory Afib **only in consultation with a cardiologist**
  - ➢ Multiple drug interactions
  - ➢ Watch for heart block, pulmonary toxicity and hypo- or hyperthyroidism
- If hemodynamically unstable or symptomatic transport patient to ER.

Antithrombotic Therapy to Minimize Thromboembolic risk
- Therapy indicated for persistent or recurrent paroxysmal Afib
- Chronic anticoagulation with warfarin titrated to international normalized ratio (INR 2-3) indicated in most situations unless contraindicated (see below)
- Aspirin 325 mg qd if lone Afib or ischemic heart disease with no other risk factors (hypertension, CHF, left ventricular systolic dysfunction, diabetes mellitus and < 60 years old)
- Warfarin contraindications: noncompliance, active substance abuse, psychosis, hemorrhagic diathesis, blood dyscrasias, recent neurosurgery, ophthalmologic or trauma surgery, active bleeding, pericarditis, endocarditis or intracranial hemorrhage

Need for Synchronized Electrical or Chemical Cardioversion?
- Based on patients symptoms, need for atrial kick, duration and atrial size
  - ➢ Unlikely to stay in sinus rhythm if Afib > 6 mo. or left atrium > 5 cm
  - ➢ Cardioversion indicated for hypotension, angina or heart failure
- Timing of cardioversion
  - ➢ If duration < 48 hrs or negative transesophageal echocardiogram
  - ➢ After 3 weeks of adequate anticoagulation
- Continue warfarin for at least 4 weeks after successful cardioversion
- Choice of antiarrhythmic for chemical cardioversion and need for chronic antiarrhythmic therapy should be determined in consultation with cardiologist.

Special Circumstances
- Ventricular rate > 220 or increased rate after atrioventricular nodal blocking agent given suggests an accessory pathway
  - ➢ Transport to hospital for DC cardioversion, procainamide or ibutilide
  - ➢ Consider catheter ablation of accessory pathway
- Hyperthyroidism
  - ➢ β-blocker and anti-thyroid medications for rate control

References: J. Am. Coll. Cardiol., 2001; 38: 1266.

Etiologies

- Ischemic Heart Disease (40% of all cases)
- Valvular Heart Disease (12% of all cases)
- Hypertensive Heart Disease (11% of all cases)
- Nonischemic dilated cardiomyopathy (32% of all cases)
- Pericardial disease
- Chronic pulmonary disease → Cor pulmonale
- Myocarditis
- Hypertrophic cardiomyopathy
- Peripartum cardiomyopathy
- Toxin/medication-induced (e.g., alcohol or adriamycin)
- Infiltrative diseases (e.g., hemochromatosis, sarcoidosis or amyloidosis)
- High-output heart failure (e.g., thyrotoxicosis or beriberi)

Clinical Presentation of Heart Failure (CHF)

Left Heart Failure Symptoms	Left Heart Failure Signs	Right Heart Failure Symptoms	Right Heart Failure Signs
Exertional dyspnea	Pulmonary rales	Nocturia	Hepatomegaly
Orthopnea	S_3 gallop	Anorexia	Leg edema
PND	Displaced apical	Right upper	Jugular venous
Weakness	impulse	quadrant pain	distension
Nocturnal cough			
Exertional fatigue			
Exertional dizziness			

PND = paroxysmal nocturnal dyspnea and S_3 = 3rd heart sound

- Absence of exertional dyspnea makes heart failure very unlikely
- Displaced apical impulse, jugular venous distension and S_3 gallop are the most accurate signs of CHF

AHA/ACC Stages of Heart Failure (JACC, 2001; 38 (7): 2101-13)

Stage A	No structural heart disease. Has risk factors for CHF
Stage B	Has structural heart disease. No symptoms/signs of CHF
Stage C	Structural heart disease with mild-moderate CHF symptoms/signs
Stage D	Advanced heart disease with severe CHF symptoms/signs

New York Heart Association (NYHA) Classification of Heart Failure

Class 1	Asymptomatic except with very strenuous activity
Class 2	Symptoms with moderate exertion
Class 3	Symptoms with activites of daily living
Class 4	Symptoms at rest

General Measures for Heart Failure Management

- Lifestyle modification: ≤ 2 drinks alcohol daily, smoking cessation, aerobic exercise 2-3x/week, weight reduction in obese patients
- Diet: 2 gram sodium, low cholesterol diet
- Avoid: nonsteroidal anti-inflammatory agents, most anti-arrhythmics

- Vaccinations: pneumococcal and influenza vaccines

Evaluation of Patients with Congestive Heart Failure

- **Blood tests**: complete blood count, electrolytes and creatinine, urinalysis, brain natriuretic peptide (BNP) and thyroid stimulating hormone
- **BNP** > 100 pg/mL 90% sensitive, 76% specific, 83% positive predictive value for CHF and < 50 pg/mL 96% negative predictive value (not CHF)
- **Chest X-ray**: examine for cardiomegaly, cephalization of pulmonary vessels, Kerley B-lines, pleural effusions
- **Electrocardiogram**: evidence of ischemic heart disease, left ventricular hypertrophy, arrhythmias or low voltage
- **2-D Echocardiogram**: systolic dysfunction (ejection fraction<40%), diastolic compliance, segmental wall motion abnormalities and valvular abnormalities
- **Patients with angina**: need a coronary angiogram or noninvasive testing

Therapy for Heart Failure due to Systolic Dysfunction
Preload reduction
- Loop diuretics +/- PO metolazone (30 minutes prior)
  > Aggressive diuresis until patient euvolemic then maintenance dose

Maximize Afterload Reduction
- Angiotensin converting-enzyme inhibitor (ACEI) therapy with goal oral dosages: captopril 50 mg tid, enalapril 10 mg bid, ramipril 10 mg qd, lisinopril 20 mg qd, quinapril 20 mg bid, benazepril 20 mg bid or fosinopril 20 mg qd
- Angiotensin II Receptor Blocker if ACEI-induced cough or angioedema Titrate to goal dosages: losartan 50 mg PO bid or valsartan 160 mg PO qd
- Hydralazine + nitrates titrated to goal dosages: hydralazine 75-100 mg PO tid + isordil 40 mg PO tid

Spironolactone therapy (RALES trial)
- Initiate spironolactone 25 mg PO qd
- Definite benefit if history of NYHA Class 4 (probably helps Class 2-3 CHF)

Digoxin Therapy
- Titrate to improve symptoms but keep digoxin level < 1.1 ng/mL

Beta-blocker Therapy
- Start very low dose of carvedilol, metoprolol or bisoprolol
- Goal dosages: carvedilol 25-50 mg PO bid, metoprolol 75-100 mg PO bid and bisoprolol 5-10 mg PO qd

Wean off Diuretics (if possible)
- Long-term diuretic therapy decreases survival

Therapy for Heart Failure due to Diastolic Dysfunction
- Diuretic therapy as above until patient euvolemic
- Initiate a lusitropic agent (e.g., beta-blocker, verapamil or diltiazem)
- Addition of ACEI or ARB probably of benefit
- Wean off diuretics as soon as possible

References: JACC, 2001; 38 (7): 2101-13. Am J. Cardiol., 1999; 83(2A): 1A-38A. and NEJM, 2002; 347: 161

Classification of Hypertension in Adults

Normal	< 120/80 mmHg
Prehypertension	120-139/80-89 mmHg
Stage 1 hypertension	140-159/90-99 mmHg
Stage 2 hypertension	≥ 160/100 mmHg

Risk Stratification for Hypertensive Patients

Risk Factors	End-organ Damage
Cigarette smoking	Heart disease
Obesity (body mass index > 30 kg/m²)	• Left ventricular hypertrophy
Family history of cardiovascular disease ♀ < 65 years or ♂ < 55 years	• Coronary artery disease • Prior coronary artery bypass graft • Congestive heart failure
Dyslipidemia	Stroke/transient ischemic attack
Diabetes mellitus	Nephropathy (microalbuminuria or
Very sedentary lifestyle	creatinine clearance < 60 mL/minute)
Age > 55 yrs (♂) or > 65 yrs (♀)	Peripheral vascular disease
Men/postmenopausal women	Retinopathy

Lifestyle Modifications
- Weight reduction aiming for body mass index < 25 kg/m²)
- No more than 2 drinks of alcohol daily (♂) and ≤ 1 drink daily (♀)
- Regular aerobic activity (≥ 30 minutes/day for most days of the week)
- < 2.4 gram sodium diet
- Adequate potassium, magnesium and calcium in diet
- Smoking cessation
- Low saturated fat, high fiber and low cholesterol diet

Drug therapy
- Indicated for hypertension refractory to lifestyle modifications x 2-3 months
- Initial therapy in patients with no compelling indications for specific drug classes
  ➤ Thiazide diuretics (drug of choice for most patients if creatinine < 2 mg/dL)
  ➤ Alternative options are: ß-blockers, angiotensin converting enzyme inhibitors, calcium channel blockers or angiotensin receptor blockers
- Add second agent for inadequate response at goal dose
  ➤ Stage 2 hypertension usually requires at least 2 drugs
  ➤ Consider thiazide diuretic if not already taking
  ➤ Switch agents for unacceptable side effects to first agent
- Add third agent from a different class (see below) for inadequate response

Lab Evaluation
- Complete blood count, electrolytes, renal panel, calcium, lipid panel, urinalysis (+/- urinary albumin/creatinine ratio if proteinuria absent) and electrocardiogram

Features of Secondary Hypertension	Possible Etiologies
Sudden onset of severe hypertension or newly diagnosed in those < 30 or > 60 yr	Renal vascular/parenchymal disease
	Renal vascular/parenchymal disease
Abnormal urinalysis	Renal parenchymal/glomerular disease
Hypokalemia	Conn's syndrome
Hypercalcemia	Hyperparathyroidism
Paroxysmal severe hypertension	Pheochromocytoma
Abdominal mass	Polycystic kidney disease
Flank bruit	Renal artery stenosis
↑ glucose, striae, truncal obesity, etc.	Cushing's syndrome
Resistant hypertension on three meds	Renal vascular/parenchymal disease
Markedly decreased femoral pulses	Coarctation of aorta
Central obesity, loud snoring, daytime hypersomnolence, nonrestorative sleep	Obstructive sleep apnea

Specific Indications for Antihypertensive Drug Therapy

Indication	Drug class
Diabetes with proteinuria	ACEI* or ARB*
Congestive heart failure	ACEI*, ARB*, ß-blockers or diuretics
Isolated systolic hypertension	Diuretics and dihydropyridine CCB
Post-myocardial infarction	ß-blocker and ACEI*
Angina	ß-blocker and CCB
Atrial fibrillation	ß-blocker and nondihydropyridine CCB
Dyslipidemia	Alpha₁-blockers
Essential tremor	ß-blocker
Hyperthyroidism	ß-blocker
Migraine	ß-blocker and nondihydropyridine CCB
Osteoporosis	Thiazide diuretics
Benign prostatic hyperplasia	Alpha₁-blockers
Renal insufficiency	ACEI* or ARB*
Cerebrovascular disease	Thiazide diuretic or ACEI

ACEI = angiotensin converting enzyme inhibitor, CCB = calcium channel blocker, ARB = angiotensin receptor blocker and * caution with ACEI or ARB use if creatinine > 3 mg/dL)

Classes of Antihypertensive Medications

Diuretics	Negative Inotropic	Renin-angiotensin-aldosterone blockers	Vasodilators
thiazide diuretics (creatinine < 2 mg/dL)	ß-blockers	angiotensin converting enzyme inhibitors	hydralazine
	verapamil	angiotensin receptor blockers	alpha₁-blockers
furosemide (creatinine > 2mg/dL)	diltiazem	clonidine	dihydropyridine calcium channel blockers
		ß-blockers	minoxidil

Reference: Adapted from JNC VII, JAMA, 2003; 289: 2560 or NIH Publication No. 03-5231 (5/03).

National Cholesterol Education Program (Adult Treatment Panel III) Initiative
Step 1: Obtain fasting lipid panel (9-12 hours fasting)
Step 2: Presence of atherosclerotic disease?
- Coronary artery disease (diabetes is a risk equivalent), carotid artery disease, peripheral artery disease, abdominal aortic aneurysm

Step 3: Any major coronary artery disease (CAD) risk factors (other than LDL)?
- Cigarette smoking, hypertension ≥ 140/90, HDL< 40 mg/dl, family history premature CAD (♂ < 55 yrs or ♀ < 65 yrs), Age (♂ ≥ 45 yrs or ♀ ≥ 55 yrs)
- HDL ≥ 60 mg/dl removes one risk factor from total count

Step 4: If ≥ 2 risk factors and no atherosclerotic disease, assess 10-yr CAD risk based on Framingham risk score (see Ischemic Heart Disease section)
- High-risk group with 10-year risk of CAD > 20% = CAD risk equivalent

Step 5: Therapies in Different Risk Categories

Risk Category	LDL goal	LDL level to start TLC	LDL level to start meds
CAD or risk equivalent	<100 mg/dl	≥ 100 mg/dl	≥ 100 mg/dl with TLC
≥ 2 risk factors or 10-yr risk ≤ 20%	<130 mg/dl	≥ 130 mg/dl	10 yr risk ≥10%: ≥ 130 / 10 yr risk <10%: ≥ 160
0-1 risk factor	<160 mg/dl	≥ 160 mg/dl	≥ 190 mg/dl

Step 6: Initiate therapeutic lifestyle changes (TLC) if LDL above goal
- American Heart Association Type II diet (low saturated fat, high fiber), weight loss, aerobic exercise (30 minutes at least 3 times a week)

Step 7: Drug therapy to lower LDL

Medications	Daily doses	Lipid effects	Side effects	Contraindications
pravastatin simvastatin fluvastatin atorvastatin	20 - 40 mg 20 - 80 mg 20 – 80 mg 10 – 80 mg	LDL↓18-55% HDL↑5-15% TG↓7-30%	Myopathy Hepatitis	Significant liver disease. Use certain drugs with caution*
cholestyramine	8 – 24 gms	LDL↓15-30% HDL↑3-5% TG – 0%	GI upset ↓absorption of other meds	TG > 400 mg/dL
nicotinic acid	1.5 – 4 gms	LDL↓5-25% HDL↑15-35% TG ↓20-50%	Flushing Gout Hepatitis	Liver disease Gout +/- Diabetes
gemfibrozil fenofibrate clofibrate	600 mg bid 200 mg 1000 mg bid	LDL↓5-20% HDL↑10-20% TG ↓20-50%	Dyspepsia Gallstones Myopathy	Renal failure Severe liver disease

*Cyclosporin, macrolides, azole antifungals, fibrates, nicotinic acid and cytochrome P-450 inhibitors

- In general, first choice is a statin unless severe hypertriglyceridemia >500 mg/dL when fibrates or nicotinic acid preferable to prevent pancreatitis

Step 8: Identify and treat metabolic syndrome (≥ 3 risk factors): Abdominal obesity (♂ > 40 inches/♀ > 35 inches), TG ≥ 150 mg/dL, HDL < 40 mg/dL(♂)/< 50 mg/dL (♀), BP ≥ 130/85 or fasting glucose ≥ 110 mg/dL
- Weight loss, exercise, antihypertensives, aggressive lipid management
- Metformin 500 mg PO bid

Step 9: Treat hypertriglyceridemia and/or low HDL
- Add fibrate or nicotinic acid

LDL = low-density lipoprotein, HDL = high-density lipoprotein, TG = triglycerides
Reference: NCEP (ATP III) Guideline, 11/02 at www.nhlbi.nih.gov/guidelines/cholesterol/atglance.html

CORONARY ARTERY DISEASE 10-YEAR RISK

Framingham model for calculating 10-year risk for coronary artery disease (CAD) in patients without diabetes or clinically evident CAD. Diabetes is considered a CAD risk "equivalent", i.e., the prospective risk of CAD in diabetics is similar to those with established CAD.   (NCEP, *JAMA* 2001; 285:2497).

MEN			
Age	Points	Age	Points
20-34	-9	55-59	8
35-39	-4	60-64	10
40-44	0	65-69	11
45-49	3	70-74	12
50-54	6	75-79	13

WOMEN			
Age	Points	Age	Points
20-34	-7	55-59	8
35-39	-3	60-64	10
40-44	0	65-69	12
45-49	3	70-74	14
50-54	6	75-79	16

Choles-terol*	Age (years)				
	20-39	40-49	50-59	60-69	70-79
<160	0	0	0	0	0
160-199	4	3	2	1	0
200-239	7	5	3	1	0
240-279	9	6	4	2	1
280+	11	8	5	3	1

Choles-terol*	Age (years)				
	20-39	40-49	50-59	60-69	70-79
<160	0	0	0	0	0
160-199	4	3	2	1	1
200-239	8	6	4	2	1
240-279	11	8	5	3	2
280+	13	10	7	4	2

*Total in mg/dL

Age (years)	20-39	40-49	50-59	60-69	70-79
Nonsmoker	0	0	0	0	0
Smoker	8	5	3	1	1

Age (years)	20-39	40-49	50-59	60-69	70-79
Nonsmoker	0	0	0	0	0
Smoker	9	7	4	2	1

HDL mg/dL	Points	HDL mg/dL	Points
60+	-1	40-49	1
50-59	0	<40	2

HDL mg/dL	Points	HDL mg/dL	Points
60+	-1	40-49	1
50-59	0	<40	2

Systolic BP	If Untreated	If Treated
<120 mmHg	0	0
120-129 mmHg	0	1
130-139 mmHg	1	2
140-159 mmHg	1	2
160+ mmHg	2	3

Systolic BP	If Untreated	If Treated
<120 mmHg	0	0
120-129 mmHg	1	3
130-139 mmHg	2	4
140-159 mmHg	3	5
160+ mmHg	4	6

Point Total	10-Year Risk	Point Total	10-Year Risk
0	1%	9	5%
1	1%	10	6%
2	1%	11	8%
3	1%	12	10%
4	1%	13	12%
5	2%	14	16%
6	2%	15	20%
7	3%	16	25%
8	4%	17+	30+%

Point Total	10-Year Risk	Point Total	10-Year Risk
< 9	< 1%	17	5%
9	1%	18	6%
10	1%	19	8%
11	1%	20	11%
12	1%	21	14%
13	2%	22	17%
14	2%	23	22%
15	3%	24	27%
16	4%	25+	30+%

- See hyperlipidemia section for goal LDL based on Framingham risk score.

Cardiac Risk Factors

- Positive family history of premature coronary artery disease, diabetes, hypertension, hyperlipidemia, peripheral/carotid artery disease, Age > 60 years and cigarette smoking

ACC/AHA Guidelines for the Management of Chronic Stable Angina

- Aspirin 01 mg PO qd unless contraindicated
- β-blockers (especially in patients with a prior myocardial infarction)
- Angiotensin converting enzyme inhibitor in patients with coronary artery disease and diabetes or left ventricular ejection fraction ≤ 0.40
- Statin to achieve low-density lipoprotein < 100 mg/dL
- Smoking cessation
- Nitroglycerin 0.4 mg tablet sublingual or spray q 5 min x 3 prn angina

Indications for Coronary Angiography

- High-risk treadmill test (see below) at low workload
- Large reversible thallium defect during radionuclide testing
- High pretest probability when noninvasive testing not possible

High-risk Treadmill Features

- Symptom-limited treadmill at < 5 Mets exercise by Bruce protocol
- ST segment elevation or depression > 2 mm with exercise
- Diffuse ST segment depression with exercise
- ST segment changes last > 5 minutes into recovery period
- Hypotension with exercise
- Typical angina associated with ventricular arrhythmias

ACC/AHA Recommendations for Percutaneous Coronary Intervention (PCI)

- Single vessel coronary disease
- 2-3 vessel coronary disease in non-diabetics
- Failed medical therapy or high risk treadmill/radionuclide testing

ACC/AHA Recommendations for Coronary Artery Bypass Grafting (CABG)

- Significant left main disease > 50% occlusion
- 3 vessel coronary disease > 70% with left ventricular ejection fraction < 0.5
- 2 vessel coronary disease with significant proximal left anterior descending artery stenosis and left ventricular ejection fraction < 0.5
- 2-3 vessel coronary disease in diabetics

Follow-up Treadmill or Exercise Radionuclide Testing

- Annual treadmill test for stable angina (exercise prescription)
- Thallium treadmill 3-6 months after PCI/CABG (or earlier for symptoms)

Post-Myocardial Infarction (MI) Management

- Aspirin 81 mg qd
- β-blockers (even with concomitant heart failure)
- Angiotensin converting enzyme Inhibitor
- Statin (regardless of low-density lipoprotein level)
- No role for estrogen replacement therapy
- Follow-up symptom-limited treadmill test at 4-6 weeks post-MI
- Lipid panel q3months (aiming for low-density lipoprotein < 100 mg/dL and high-density lipoprotein level > 40 mg/dL)

The management of non-ST elevation acute coronary syndromes or acute ST elevation myocardial infarction requires hospitalization and is beyond the scope of this pocketbook. Refer to www.acc.org or www.americanheart.org for updated guidelines on the management of these areas.
References: Circulation, 1999; 100(9): 1016-30. Circulation, 2003; 107: 1-127 and Circulation, 1998; 97: 1837-47. Framingham risk table reproduced with permission from the Tarascon Pharmacopoeia, 2004, Tarascon publishing.

ACC/AHA Guidelines for Use of Pacemakers and Cardioverter-Defibrillators[1]

Indications for Pacemaker Insertion

- **Symptomatic bradycardia:** any documented bradyarrhythmia that is directly responsible for the development of syncope, near syncope, lightheadedness or transient confusional states from cerebral hypoperfusion
- **Pacing for Acquired Atrioventricular (AV) Block**
  - ➢ **Reversible causes of AV block have been ruled out**
  - ➢ Type II second-degree AV block (especially if a wide QRS or symptoms)
  - ➢ Third-degree AV block (complete heart block) – asymptomatic
  - ➢ Marked first-degree AV block (PR > 0.30 seconds) or Type I second-degree AV block with symptomatic bradycardia
- **Pacing for Chronic Bifascicular or Trifascicular Block**
  - ➢ If ambulatory ECG monitoring reveals intermittent Type II second-degree AV block or third-degree AV block
- **Pacing in Sinus Node Dysfunction**
  - ➢ Symptomatic sinus pauses (> 2 seconds)
  - ➢ Symptomatic chronotropic incompetence
- **Pacing in Carotid Sinus Syndrome and Neurocardiogenic Syncope**
  - ➢ Documented asystole > 3 seconds with minimal carotid sinus pressure
  - ➢ Recurrent neurocardiogenic syncope associated with bradycardia
- **Pacing in Tachy-Brady syndrome**
  - ➢ Pacemaker inserted to prevent symptomatic bradycardia when AV nodal blocking agents used to rate control rapid atrial fibrillation
- **Atrial Overdrive Pacing to Terminate Tachyarrhythmias**
  - ➢ For patients unresponsive to antiarrhythmic therapy, atrial overdrive pacing may be used for symptomatic, recurrent supraventricular tachycardia shown to be terminated by pacing

Pacemaker Follow-up via Transtelephonic Monitoring

- q2weeks x 1 mo.→ q1-2 mos. x 5 mos. → q2 mos. x 30 mos.→ qmonth

Indications for Implantable Cardioverter-Defibrillator (ICD) Insertion

- History of sustained ventricular tachycardia or ventricular fibrillation
  - ➢ Patients with left ventricular ejection fraction < 0.4 benefit the most
  - ➢ Best managed by a trained electrophysiologist.

All pacemaker decisions should be made in consultation with a cardiologist

References: Circulation, 10/15/2002 issue and J Am Coll Cardiol, 1998; 31: 1175-1209.

ACC/AHA Guideline for Perioperative Cardiovascular Eval. for Noncardiac Surgery[1]

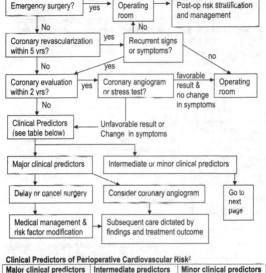

Clinical Predictors of Perioperative Cardiovascular Risk[2]

Major clinical predictors	Intermediate predictors	Minor clinical predictors
Unstable coronary syndrome[3]	Canadian class I/II angina	Advanced age
Decompensated CHF	Prior MI by history or ECG	Abnormal ECG[5]
Significant arrhythmias[4]	Compensated or prior congestive heart failure	Rhythm other than sinus
Severe valvular disease	Diabetes mellitus	Low functional capacity
		History of stroke
		Uncontrolled hypertension

ECG = electrocardiogram, CHF = congestive heart failure and MI = myocardial infarction

1. Circulation 2002; 105: 1257-67. Refer to www.acc.org for more specifics.
2. Increased risk for myocardial infarction, congestive heart failure or death.
3. Recent MI with ischemic risk, unstable or New York Heart Association class III/IV angina.
4. High-grade atrioventricular block, symptomatic ventricular arrhythmias with heart disease, supraventricular arrhythmias with rapid ventricular rate.
4. left ventricular hypertrophy, left bundle branch block or ST-T abnormalities

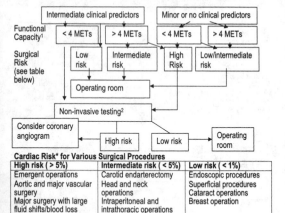

Cardiac Risk* for Various Surgical Procedures

High risk (> 5%)	Intermediate risk (< 5%)	Low risk (< 1%)
Emergent operations	Carotid endarterectomy	Endoscopic procedures
Aortic and major vascular surgery	Head and neck operations	Superficial procedures
Major surgery with large fluid shifts/blood loss	Intraperitoneal and intrathoracic operations	Cataract operations
	Orthopedic operations	Breast operation
	Prostate operations	

* combined risk of cardiac death and nonfatal myocardial infarction

Lee Cardiac Risk Index for Non-Cardiac Surgery[3]

Risk Factors: high-risk surgery[4], ischemic heart disease, history of congestive heart failure or cerebrovascular disease, insulin therapy and creatinine > 2 mg/dL.

Risk Class	# of risk factors	Rate of cardiac complications[5]
I	0	0.4 – 0.5%
II	1	0.9 – 1.3%
III	2	4 – 7%
IV	≥ 3	9 – 11%

Surgery in Specialized Situations

- Post-stroke/transient ischemic attack: preferable to wait 6-8 weeks
- Post-angioplasty: wait 4 weeks
- High-risk pulmonary disease: no smoking>8 wks + consider regional anesthesia

1. < 4 METs (metabolic equivalents): walking 1-2 blocks, light housework, activities of daily living
   4 METs: climb flight of stairs, heavy house work, bowling, dancing, golf or doubles tennis
2. Exercise or pharmacologic stress testing
3. Circulation, 1999; 100: 1043-49.
4. Intrathoracic, intraperitoneal or suprainguinal vascular operations
5. Combined MI, CHF, ventricular fibrillation, cardiac arrest or complete heart block
   Sections reproduced with permission from the Tarascon Internal Medicine & Critical Care Pocketbook, 2nd Edition, Tarascon Publishing.

Acute Arterial Insufficiency

- Most common cause is a cardioembolic event
- Ischemic complication rate rises dramatically if time from onset of symptoms to embolectomy is > 6 hrs: 10% if time < 6 hrs, 20% at 8 hrs & 33% at 24hrs
- Clinical features of arterial insufficiency (6 P's)
  ➢ Pain, pallor, pulseless, paresthesias, paralysis and poikilothermia (cold)
  ➢ Sudden onset of symptoms favors an embolic event
- Treatment
  ➢ Immediate heparinization
  ➢ Consult vascular surgeon for embolectomy

Chronic Arterial Insufficiency

- Clinical features of peripheral arteriosclerotic disease
  ➢ Intermittent claudication described as cramping discomfort of muscles with ambulation relieved by rest. Graded by blocks walked before symptoms.
  ➢ Aortoiliac disease: thigh/buttock claudication +/- impotence (Leriche syndrome).
  ➢ Femoropopliteal disease: calf claudication
  ➢ Signs: dystrophic nails, absent/weak peripheral pulses, loss of hair of distal extremity, cool distal extremity with shiny skin
- Risk Factors: smoking, positive family history, hyperlipidemia, diabetes, hypertension and vascular disease elsewhere

Evaluation of Claudication

- Ankle/Brachial index (ABI) 0.6 - 0.8 = mild arteriosclerotic disease, 0.4 - 0.6 = moderate disease and < 0.4 = severe disease (usually have rest pain).
  ➢ Measure first doppler sound as cuff is deflated at the radial artery and either the posterior tibial or dorsalis pedis artery. The ankle/brachial index is determined by dividing the ankle blood pressure by the wrist blood pressure.
  ➢ Diabetic patients with calcified arteries can have falsely elevated ABI.
- Duplex ultrasound of arterial system: good noninvasive study to estimate degree of arterial obstruction of iliac and femoropopliteal arteries.
- Aortogram with peripheral run-off is the gold standard test.

Treatment

- Lifestyle modification: smoking cessation and graded exercise program
- Lipid control: low-density lipoprotein < 100 mg/dL + high-density lipoprotein > 40 mg/dL
- Tight diabetic and blood pressure control (BP < 130/80)
- aspirin 325 mg PO qd
- pentoxifylline 400 mg PO tid or cilostazol 100 mg PO bid can improve claudication symptoms, but has no effect on natural history of disease.
- Arterial bypass indicated for disabling claudication, rest pain, gangrene, Leriche syndrome or nonhealing, ischemic ulcer
- No benefit of warfarin to decrease reocclusion rates of arterial grafts.

Reference: Chest, 1998; 114 (5): 666-82.

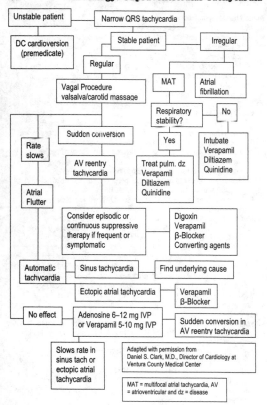

The flowchart contains the following elements:

- Unstable patient → DC cardioversion (premedicate)
- Narrow QRS tachycardia → Stable patient / Irregular
- Stable patient → Regular
- Irregular → MAT / Atrial fibrillation
- Regular → Vagal Procedure valsalva/carotid massage
- MAT → Respiratory stability?
  - Yes → Treat pulm. dz: Verapamil, Diltiazem, Quinidine
  - No → Intubate: Verapamil, Diltiazem, Quinidine
- Atrial fibrillation → No
- Vagal Procedure → Sudden conversion → AV reentry tachycardia → Consider episodic or continuous suppressive therapy if frequent or symptomatic → Digoxin, Verapamil, β-Blocker, Converting agents
- Rate slows
- Atrial Flutter
- Automatic tachycardia → Sinus tachycardia → Find underlying cause
- Ectopic atrial tachycardia → Verapamil, β-Blocker
- No effect → Adenosine 6–12 mg IVP or Verapamil 5-10 mg IVP
  - Sudden conversion in AV reentry tachycardia
  - Slows rate in sinus tach or ectopic atrial tachycardia

Adapted with permission from
Daniel S. Clark, M.D., Director of Cardiology at
Ventura County Medical Center

MAT = multifocal atrial tachycardia, AV
= atrioventricular and dz = disease

Etiologies of Syncope (mnemonic = SVNCOPE)

- **S**ituational – micturition, defecation, severe coughing, valsalva
- **V**ascular – subclavian steal, vertebrobasilar insufficiency or carotid sinus hypersensitivity
- **N**eurologic – neurocardiogenic, brainstem transient ischemic attacks or basilar migraines
- **C**ardiac – cardiac ischemia, obstructive valvular, arrhythmias or tumor
- **O**rthostatic hypotension
- **P**sychiatric
- **E**mbolism (pulmonary embolism)/Everything else (e.g., drug overdoses)

History

- Sudden onset suggests arrhythmia, pulmonary embolus or carotid sinus hypersensitivity
- Tonic-clonic movements, incontinence or tongue biting (seizure activity)
- Preceding events, precipitating factor (fear, pain, sight of blood), prodromal sensations (diaphoresis, nausea, dizziness, visual defects, weakness)
  - ➤ These and gradual onset suggest neurocardiogenic syncope
- Exercise-induced or occurred at rest?
  - ➤ Exertion-related often cardiac ischemia or obstructive valvular lesion
- Associated chest discomfort, palpitations or dyspnea?
  - ➤ Cardiac disease or psychiatric disorder
- Related to positional changes?
  - ➤ Orthostasis, atrial myxoma or carotid sinus hypersensitivity
- Postevent condition: confusion, fatigue, injury, duration of recovery
- History of arrhythmias, coronary artery disease, congestive heart failure, psychiatric history, pulmonary embolus or prior syncopal episodes?
- Family history of sudden cardiac death (suggests arrhythmic syncope)
- Age < 55 yrs, ♀, diaphoresis, palpitations, post-event fatigue and recovery > 1 minute all suggest neurally-mediated syncope and not arrhythmic syncope

Exam

- Check for orthostasis ($\downarrow \geq 20$ mmHg Systolic BP (SBP) supine to standing)
- Careful cardiac and neurologic examination
- Carotid massage (positive with $\downarrow$SBP ≥ 50 mmHg or asystole ≥ 3 seconds)

Diagnostic Evaluation

- ECG: evidence of structural heart disease or conduction disease?
- 2D-Echocardiogram if cardiac dysfunction or valvular anomalies suspected
- Ambulatory ECG if cardiac etiology suspected
  - ➤ Frequent symptoms (Holter monitor) & infrequent symptoms (Event monitor)
  - ➤ Positive if: symptoms and sinus pause > 2 sec., sinus bradycardia ≤ 40, supraventricular tachycardia > 180, Type II second-degree atrioventricular block, complete heart block or sustained ventricular tachycardia > 30 sec.
- Tilt-table testing: recurrent unexplained syncope with negative cardiac work-up
- Electrophysiologic testing not indicated for unexplained syncope if ECG normal.
- Rule out pregnancy in a young woman (? ruptured ectopic pregnancy)

References: Ann Int Med, 1997; 126: 989-96. Ann Int Med, 1997; 127: 76-86.

Condition	Clinical Features	Treatment
Atopic Dermatitis (or eczema) British Medical J, 1999; 318: 1600 Lancet. 1996; 348: 769.	• Pruritus and family history of atopy • Symmetric rash + propensity for flexural areas • Common findings: generalized xerosis, infraorbital darkening and skin folds (Dennie Morgan lines), hyperlinear palms • Infants: dry erythematous patches on cheeks and chin with fine scaling • Children: erythematous papules + plaques in flexural areas +/- lichenification • Adults: may present as childhood eczema • Nummular eczema: coin-shaped plaques • Dyshidrosis: hand erythema with scattered vesicles +/- peeling skin or lichenification	• Avoid frequent bathing, hot water, abrasive towels, wool or itchy fabrics and scented cleaning and cosmetic agents. • Avoid scratching • Moisturizing lotion applied to damp skin bid • Low-potency steroid cream to face or perineum bid • High potency steroid ointment for severe hand/nummular eczema • High potency steroid ointment for moderate eczema • Very high potency steroid ointment for lichenified plaques • Antistaphylococcal antibiotics for superimposed infections • 1% pimecrolimus cream bid for patients > 2 years • cyclosporine A 5 mg/kg/d to 150 mg/d x 12 weeks or 1 week course of PO prednisone for severe atopic dermatitis flare.
Acne J. Am. Acad. Dermatology, 1995; 32: 56. Amer. Fam. Physician, 1994; 50: 89. British J. Dermatol., 1997; 137: 563.	• Comedonal: red papules with a central black orifice (open) or white vesicle (closed) • Pustular: red papules with central pustules • Nodulocystic: red cystic and nodular lesions • Acne conglobata: communicating cysts, abscesses and draining sinuses • Distribution: face, upper back and neck. • Risk factors: oral steroids, exposure to industrial solvents or occlusive body gear use	• Comedonal acne: tretinoin, isotretinoin or adapalene cream • Pustular and nodulocystic acne: oral erythromycin or tetracyclines x 1-2 mo., topical retinoids + benzoyl peroxide • Benzomycin or topical clindamycin for maintenance therapy • Oral contraceptive pills with low androgenicity for women • Isotretinoin 10 mg bid titrated to 1 mg/kg/d divided bid for severe or refractory acne x 20 weeks. • Effective contraception, serial liver tests and lipid panels • Dermabrasion effective for pitted acne scars

Condition	Clinical Features	Treatment
Onychomycosis J. Amer. Academy Dermatology. 1999; 40: S21. Arch. Dermatology. 2002; 138: 811.	• Whitish, yellowish or brownish discoloration of the nail plate caused by dermatophyte infections. • Definitive diagnosis by identifying fungal hyphae on potassium hydroxide exam of nail bed scrapings.	• terbinafine 250 mg PO qd x 6 weeks (fingernails) and x 12 wks (toenails) • itraconazole 200 mg PO qd x 8 weeks or 400 mg qd x 1 week each month x 2 months (fingernails) • itraconazole 200 mg PO qd x 12 wks or 400 mg qd x 1 week each month x 3 months (toenails) • Monitor liver panel monthly while on azole antifungals.

Psoriasis
 	
J. Amer. Academy Dermatology. 2001; 45: 487 and 544.
J. Amer. Academy Dermatology. 1998; 38: 705.
British J. Dermatology. 2002; 146: 118.
	• 40% with positive family history
	• Plaque-type psoriasis
	  ▲ Erythematous, sharply demarcated plaques with silvery scale
	  ▲ Scalp, extensor elbows/knees, back
	• Guttate psoriasis
	  ▲ Multiple erythematous plaques < 1 cm with silvery scale on trunk
	  ▲ Frequently follows strep infection.
	• Pustular psoriasis
	  ▲ Erythroderma with scaling & pustules
	• Erythrodermic psoriasis
	  ▲ Diffuse erythroderma with scaling
	• Inverse psoriasis
	  ▲ Rash involves intertriginous areas
	• Nails frequently pitted
		• Mild plaque-type: high-potency topical corticosteroids
		• Moderate plaque-type or guttate psoriasis: high-potency topical corticosteroids and calcipotriene cream +/- topical tazarotene
		• Severe plaque-type, pustular or erythrodermic psoriasis:
		  ▲ Psoralen–ultraviolet A (PUVA) therapy, acitretin 25-50 mg PO qd, methotrexate 7.5-20 mg PO qweek or cyclosporine 3-5 mg/kg/day
		  ▲ acitretin is teratogenic and must monitor liver + lipid panels
		  ▲ Monitor renal function and blood pressure with cyclosporine
		  ▲ Monitor liver panel + use folate 1 mg qd with methotrexate
		• Inverse psoriasis: low-potency topical corticosteroids
		• Scalp psoriasis: tar shampoos or high-potency corticosteroids in an alcohol solution
		• Inhibitors of tumor necrosis factor-alpha (TNF-α) like infliximab or etanercept may be beneficial for severe plaque-type psoriasis or for psoriatic arthritis.

Condition	Clinical Features	Treatment
Rosacea J. Amer. Academy Dermatology, 2002; 46: 584. Arch Dermatology, 1998; 134: 679	• Affects middle-aged and elderly adults • Facial erythema and telangiectasias involving the nose, cheek, chin, eyelids and forehead • Erythema may become enhanced by hot or spicy foods, alcohol, heat or intense emotions. • Papules, pustules and nodules can develop • Rhinophyma is a late-stage complication involving papulonodular hyperplasia of the nose • Ocular rosacea with erythema & telangiectasias of lids, blepharitis +/- keratoconjunctivitis	• Use mild, nonscented soaps and strong sunscreen • 0.75% metronidazole cream bid initially • Can add 5% benzoyl peroxide cream qd or bid • tretinoin cream qhs added for recalcitrant cases • Tetracyclines or erythromycin bid x 4-8 weeks for nodular rosacea • Remission can usually be maintained with 0.75% metronidazole cream alone applied daily • National Rosacea Society at www.rosacea.org
Seborrheic Dermatitis	• "Cradle cap" in infants: erythema of scalp with a whitish-yellow thick scale • Tinea amiantacea develops in young children: thick, plates of white scale occur in patches on the scalp. • Adults develop erythematous patches with overlying fine, dry white scale. The involvement is on the scalp, nose, nasolabial folds, eyebrows, external ear canals and behind ears. • Skin and scalp is often oily • Frequent association with HIV disease	• Cradle cap treated with baby oil on scalp and combing with a fine bristle comb or toothbrush • Tinea amiantacea treated with warm 10% liquor carbonis detergens in Nivea oil qhs and washed off in morning. Tar shampoos for maintenance. • Adult seborrheic dermatitis treatment ▷ 2% ketoconazole **or** 2.5% selenium sulfide shampoo qod-qd for scalp involvement ▷ Low-potency topical steroid cream **or** Nizoral cream **or** 0.75% metronidazole cream applied qd effective for facial rash. ▷ Consider ketoconazole 400 mg PO x 1 prior to topical therapy for severe cases

Basal Cell Carcinoma (BCC)
- **Clinical Presentation of BCC**
  - ➤ Nodular BCC: nodule with a pearly, translucent surface and telangiectasias
    - o Typical location is on the head and neck
  - ➤ Sclerosing BCC: whitish, hard plaque with indistinct margins
  - ➤ Superficial BCC: reddish plaque with overlying scale usually on the back
- **Diagnosis** best made by a punch biopsy
- **Treatment Options**
  - ➤ Surgical excision with 5 mm margins
  - ➤ Consider Moh's micrographic surgery for BCC on the nose, ears, lips, eyelids, genitals and for recurrent BCCs.
  - ➤ 5% imiquimod cream bid x 12 weeks for superficial BCCs
  - ➤ Curettage and electrodessication for nodular BCCs not on the head
  - ➤ Radiation therapy or intralesional interferon-alpha therapy are options for very elderly patients or those unable to tolerate surgical excision.

Cutaneous Squamous Cell Carcinoma (SCC)
- **Clinical Presentation**
  - ➤ Typically nontender papule or plaque with a dark, hyperkeratotic, adherent scale and/or overlying ulceration
  - ➤ 2/3 arise from a pre-existing actinic keratosis or cutaneous horn
  - ➤ Commonly on scalp, face, lips, forearms or dorsum of hands
- **Diagnosis** best made by a punch biopsy
- **High-risk Features for Metastasis**
  - ➤ Depth > 4 mm, poorly differentiated SCC, perineural or intravascular invasion, size > 2 cm, recurrent SCC or location on ear, lips or genitals
- **Treatment Options**
  - ➤ Surgical excision with 4-5 mm margins is the treatment of choice
  - ➤ Consider Moh's micrographic surgery for SCC on the nose, ears, lips, eyelids, genitals, fingers and for recurrent SCCs.
  - ➤ 5% imiquimod cream bid or 5% 5-fluorouracil cream bid x 4-8 weeks can be used for Bowen's disease (SCC *in situ*)
  - ➤ Radiation therapy for well-delineated, primary SCCs < 2 cm

Melanoma
- **Clinical Presentation**
  - ➤ Superficial spreading melanoma: brown or black macules or patches usually with irregular borders and color variation
  - ➤ Nodular melanoma: nodules that may be black, brown, red or hypopigmented (amelanotic melanomas)
  - ➤ Acral lentiginous: hyperpigmented patch on the palms, soles or subungual
  - ➤ Lentigo maligna: arises from melanoma *in situ* usually on the head or neck
- **Diagnosis**: excisional biopsy if lesion small or incisional biopsy if large
- **Staging**: sentinel lymph node biopsy, chest x-ray, lactate dehydrogenase and liver panel
- **Treatment Options**
  - ➤ Definitive treatment is surgical excision with the following surgical margins based on the microscopic depth of the melanoma found by biopsy

Melanoma depth	In situ melanoma	< 2 mm depth	2-4 mm depth	>4 mm depth
Margin	5 mm margin	1 cm margin	2-3 cm margin	3-5 cm margin

References: NEJM, 2001; 344: 975, Cancer, 1995; 75: 699 and Lancet, 1996; 347: 803.

Etiologies of Adrenal Insufficiency

Primary Adrenal Insufficiency	Secondary Adrenal Insufficiency
• Metastatic carcinoma of lung, breast or renal cell carcinoma or lymphoma • Miliary tuberculosis • AIDS-associated infections* • Waterhouse-Friedrichsen syndrome • Autoimmune adrenalitis • Adrenal hemorrhage • Antiphospholipid syndrome	• Systemic glucocorticoid therapy > 2 weeks within the last year • Pituitary or hypothalamic tumors • Sarcoidosis • Lymphocytic hypophisitis • Sheehan's syndrome

*most commonly HIV or cytomegalovirus infections

Symptoms of Adrenal Insufficiency
• Fatigue, weakness, cognitive slowing, anorexia, orthostatic dizziness, nausea/vomiting, diffuse abdominal pain
• Salt craving in primary adrenal insufficiency
• Decreased libido can occur with pituitary lesions

Signs and Typical Labs in Adrenal Insufficiency (AI)

Both Types of AI	Primary AI	Secondary AI
• Unexplained fever • Orthostatic hypotension • Hyponatremia • Hypoglycemia • Normocytic anemia • Eosinophilia	• Hyperpigmentation of palmar creases, extensor surfaces and buccal mucosa • Hyperkalemia • Non-anion gap acidosis	Pituitary lesions may exhibit: • Amenorrhea • Secondary hypothyroidism • Diabetes insipidus • Sexual dysfunction

Diagnosis of Adrenal Insufficiency
• Fasting serum cortisol level $\leq$ 3 mcg/dL
• Cosyntropin stimulation test using 250 mcg cosyntropin (synthetic ACTH)
• Measure serum cortisol levels at time 0 and 60 minutes post-cosyntropin
  ➢ Any cortisol level $\geq$ 19 mcg/dL signifies adequate adrenal reserve

Treatment of Adrenal Insufficiency
• Airway/Breathing/Circulation assessment
• 5% dextrose in isotonic saline until normotensive
• dexamethasone 4 mg IV bolus then 2 mg IV q8h until results of cosyntropin stimulation test known (dexamethasone only steroid that will not interfere with cosyntropin test)
• Treat underlying cause
• Maintenance dose hydrocortisone 15 mg PO qAM/10 mg PO qPM
• Recommend Medic Alert bracelet

Reference: NEJM, 1996; 335: 1206-12.

Hypercalcemia

Etiologies (hyperparathyroidism and cancer account for 90% of all cases)

- Hyperparathyroidism (~80% of cases from isolated parathyroid adenoma)
  - ➢ Urinary cyclic adenosine monophosphate (cAMP) high, serum chloride/bicarbonate ratio high, hypercalcemia not too elevated
- Malignancy (bony mets or humoral hypercalcemia of malignancy)
  - ➢ Breast, prostate, lung, kidney, bladder cancers or multiple myeloma
  - ➢ Urinary cAMP usually low normal, serum chloride/bicarbonate ratio usually low and hypercalcemia often very high
- Other causes include: milk-alkali syndrome, vitamin D intoxication, tuberculosis, sarcoidosis, thyrotoxicosis, familial hypocalciuric hypercalcemia, Paget's disease, adrenal insufficiency, pheochromocytoma, prolonged immobilization and medications (thiazide diuretics, lithium, tamoxifen & ↑↑ calcium ingestion).

Clinical Presentation ("bones, stones, moans and groans")

- Bony pain
- Nephrolithiasis or nephrocalcinosis
- Constipation, nausea/vomiting, anorexia and diffuse abdominal pain (predisposes patients to peptic ulcer disease and pancreatitis)
- Lethargy, fatigue, depression, cognitive impairment, confusion and depressed level of consciousness
- Electrocardiogram changes: shortened QT and prolonged PR intervals

Treatment

- Acute treatment of severe hypercalcemia in hospital
  - ➢ Hydration with isotonic saline +/- furosemide diuresis
- Chronic treatment of hypercalcemia
  - ➢ Bisphosphonates (e.g., pamidronate 60-90 mg IV qmonth)

Hypocalcemia Etiologies

Renal failure	Rhabdomyolysis	Severe hypomagnesemia
Hypoparathyroidism	Respiratory alkalosis	Massive transfusion
Tumor lysis	Acute pancreatitis	Vitamin D deficiency
Furosemide, phenytoin, phenobarbital, steroids, aminoglycosides & cisplatinum

Corrected Calcium Calculation (gm/dL)

- Calcium(corrected) (gm/dL) = calcium + [0.8 x (4 – serum albumin in gm/dL)]
- Pseudohypocalcemia from hypoalbuminemia is the most common cause of low serum calcium

Clinical Presentation

- Neuromuscular irritability (Chvostek's sign and Trousseau's sign), tetany, paresthesias, muscle cramps and seizures
- Psychiatric disorders: psychosis, depression and cognitive impairment
- Electrocardiogram changes: prolonged QT interval +/- heart block

Treatment of Hypocalcemia

- Search and treat underlying etiology
- 1 – 2 grams of elemental calcium with meals daily divided bid – tid
- Add calcitriol 0.25 mg PO qd for hypoparathyroidism or vitamin D deficiency

Reference: NEJM, 2000; 343: 1863-75. Critical Care Clinics, 2001; 17(1): 139-53.

Clinical Features of Cushing's Syndrome
- Centripetal obesity involving the face, neck, trunk and abdomen
  - "Moon facies"
  - "Buffalo hump" or dorsocervical fat pad
- Skin changes: atrophy, easy bruisability and purple striae
  - Hyperpigmentation occurs with ↑↑ adrenocorticotropin (ACTH) secretion.
- Menstrual irregularities
- Adrenal tumors can cause premature puberty in boys and hirsutism, virilization, acne and decreased libido in women.
- Proximal muscle wasting
- Osteoporosis
- Secondary diabetes mellitus
- Hypertension and hypokalemia
- Mood disorders and emotional lability common
- Relative immunosuppression with increased infection rate

Diagnosing Cushing's Syndrome
- Exclude use of exogenous glucocorticoids or medroxyprogesterone acetate.
- 24 hour urine for cortisol and creatinine
  - 24 hr creatinine: 20-25 mg/kg lean body weight (♂) and 15-20 mg/kg (♀).
  - Cushing's syndrome if urinary cortisol is more than 3x upper limit of normal.
- Hypercortisolism can occur in people with polycystic ovary syndrome, severe depression, morbid obesity and rarely chronic alcohol abuse, but levels are usually less than 3 times the upper limit of normal.
- If a 24 hour urine cortisol level is equivocal, a low-dose dexamethasone suppression test can be done.
  - 1 mg dexamethasone at 11 P.M.-12 A.M. & check serum cortisol at 8 A.M.
  - Normal if serum cortisol < 5 mcg/dL (rules out Cushing's syndrome).

Determining the Cause of Cushing's syndrome
- 2-3 measurements of ACTH + serum cortisol between 11 P.M. and 12 A.M.
  - Cortisol >15 mcg/dL and ACTH < 5 pg/mL = primary adrenal disease
  - ACTH >15 pg/mL = definite ACTH-dependent disease
  - ACTH 5-15 pg/mL = probable ACTH-dependent disease
- For ACTH-independent disease, proceed with a CT scan or MRI with thin cuts through the adrenal glands to rule out an adrenal tumor.
- High-dose dexamethasone suppression test in ACTH-dependent diseases
  - Dexamethasone 2 mg PO q6h x 8 doses
  - Collect a 24 hour urine collection for cortisol + 17-hydroxycorticosteroids.
  - > 90% suppression of urinary cortisol or > 69% decrease of 17-hydroxycorticosteroids indicates Cushing's disease.
  - If ectopic ACTH-secreting tumor suspected, perform a In[111]-octreotide or In[111]-pentetreotide scintigraphy scan for localization.

Treatment of Cushing's Syndrome
- Regardless of the cause, surgical excision is the treatment of choice.

References: NEJM, 1995; 332 (12): 791-803.

Diagnosis of Diabetes Mellitus (DM) in Nonpregnant State

- Symptoms of DM + random plasma glucose ≥ 200 mg/dL
- Fasting plasma glucose ≥ 126 mg/dL
- 2-hour postglucola glucose > 200 mg/dL (after 75 gm oral anhydrous glucose)
- Confirm by a separate test on a different day
- Impaired glucose tolerance if fasting glucose 110-125 mg/dL or 2 hr glucose 140-199 mg/dL after 75 gm anhydrous glucose load

Criteria for Screening Asymptomatic Patients

- All people > 45 years of age at least q3 years
- Can start screening at a younger age and more frequently for the following:
  - ➢ Overweight (body mass index ≥ 25 kg/m²)
  - ➢ First-degree relative with diabetes
  - ➢ High-risk ethnic population (e.g., African-American, Hispanic, Native American or Pacific Islander)
  - ➢ History of baby weighing > 9 pound or history of gestational DM
  - ➢ Hypertensive patients
  - ➢ HDL ≤ 35 mg/dL or triglyceride level ≥ 250 mg/dL
  - ➢ History of glucose intolerance
  - ➢ History of acanthosis nigricans or polycystic ovary syndrome

Glycemic Goals for Nonpregnant Patients with DM

	AC plasma	qhs plasma	AC CBG	qhs CBG	HgbA1c (%)
Goal range	90-130	110-150	80-120	100-140	< 7.0
Adjustment	<90 - >150	<110->180	<80->140	<100->160	>8.0

AC = preprandial plasma glucose, qhs = bedtime plasma glucose, CBG = capillary blood glucose (mg/dL) and HgbA1c=hemoglobinA1c

Classification of DM

Characteristics	Type 1	Type 2	MODY
Age at onset	Usually < 20 years	Usually > 30 years	< 25 years
Family history	10-15%	Very common	Common
DKA	Common	Very rare	Rare
Symptom onset	Sudden	Insidious	Insidious
Body habitus	Thin-normal weight	Usually obese	Usually obese
C-peptide	Low	High	Low normal
Islet cell/insulin Ab	Present	Absent	Absent
Autoimmune dzs	Often present	Rare	Rare

MODY = maturity-onset diabetes of youth, DKA = diabetic ketoacidosis, Ab = antibodies, dzs = diseases

General Management Guidelines for DM patients

- Every visit: check blood pressure (BP), DM diary, weight and review meds
  - ➢ Check feet each visit for all neuropathic patients
- Every 3 months: check Hemoglobin A1c

- Annual: fasting lipid panel, creatinine, thyroid stimulating hormone (in Type I diabetics), electrocardiogram, comprehensive foot exam, dental exam, assess for nephropathy, monofilament testing for peripheral neuropathy, dilated eye exam by an eye specialist, influenza vaccination if > 6 months of age and adult pneumococcal vaccine once
- Tight glycemic control as above, lipid control (LDL< 100, HDL>40 and triglycerides < 150) and BP<130/80 significantly reduces the risk of microvascular complications: retinopathy, nephropathy and neuropathy.
- Consider baby aspirin PO daily for primary prevention of cardiovascular disease if any evidence of macrovascular disease or ≥ 40 years + ≥ 1 cardiac risk factor
- Smoking cessation counseling and dietary reminders

Diabetic Nephropathy

- Initiate screening: at diagnosis for Type 2 and ≥ 5 years for Type 1 DM
- Consider other causes of nephropathy in absence of retinopathy.
- Screening for microalbuminuria:
  ➢ Spot urine albumin/creatinine ratio (mcg/mg creatinine)
  ➢ Microalbuminuria = 30-299 mcg/mg and overt nephropathy = ≥ 300 mcg/mg
- 24h urine for creatinine clearance yearly once nephropathy diagnosed.
- Methods to delay progression of nephropathy
  ➢ Maintain BP<130/80 for microalbuminuria, <120/75 for overt nephropathy
    o Preferred order: angiotensin converting enzyme inhibitors, angiotensin receptor blockers, β-blockers and verapamil or diltiazem
  ➢ Restrict protein to ≤ 0.8 gm/kg ideal body weight/day
- Referral to nephrologist when creatinine clearance < 70 mL/minute

Diabetic Retinopathy

- Screening guidelines are the same as for diabetic nephropathy.
- Laser photocoagulaton surgery indicated for macular edema, severe nonproliferative diabetic retinopathy or any proliferative diabetic retinopathy.

Diabetic Neuropathy

- May present as burning, tingling, numbness or aching in hands or feet.
- Best screening tool is use of a 5.07 U monofilament tool tested at 6 areas on each foot: plantar skin over the 1st and 5th toes, the skin over the 1st, 3rd and 5th metatarsal heads and the area over the heel.
- Avoid prolonged walking, jogging and step exercises.
- Treatment of neuropathic pain: gabapentin, tricylic antidepressants, carbamazepine, paroxetine, venlafaxine, clonidine and valproic acid
- Rule out other causes: alcohol, B12 deficiency, hypothyroidism, uremia, paraneoplastic, amyloidosis, dysproteinemias, sarcoidosis and meds (e.g.: isoniazid, vincristine, cisplatin, didanosine, zalcitabine and stavudine)

Cardiovascular Disease

- Treadmill test for abnormal electrocardiogram, typical or atypical chest pain, peripheral or carotid arterial disease, $\geq$ 2 cardiac risk factors or age > 35 years, sedentary lifestyle and plans to begin vigorous exercise program
- Aspirin 81 mg PO qd as primary prevention for criteria as described above

Insulins

Time (hr)	lispro	aspart	regular	NPH	lente	ultralente	glargine
Onset	0.25	0.5	0.5-1	1-1.5	1-2.5	4-8	1
Peak	0.5-1.5	1-3	2.5-5	4-12	7-15	10-30	N/A
Duration	6-8	3-5	8-12	24	22-24	>36	24-30

N/A = not applicable

Oral Medications for Type 2 Diabetes Mellitus

Classes	Examples	Fall in HgbA$_{1c}$	Mechanism	Contra-indications	Side effects
Sulfonylurea	glipizide glimepiride	1.5-2.0	Insulin secretagogue	Sulfa allergy	Weight gain Hypoglycemia SIADH
Biguanide	metformin	1.5-2.0	Insulin sensitizer and $\downarrow$ gluconeo-genesis	crt >1.4 ($\female$) crt >1.5 ($\male$) acute CHF cirrhosis IV contrast alcoholic	Nausea, Anorexia, Metallic taste, B$_{12}$ deficiency
Alpha-glucosidase inhibitor	acarbose miglitol	0.5-1.0	α-glucosidase inhibitor	crt > 2	Nausea, Diarrhea, Flatulence
Thiazolidine-diones	pioglitazone rosiglitazone	1.5	Insulin sensitizer	CHF Cirrhosis	Hepatitis Edema Anemia
Meglitinides	repaglinide nateglinide	1.5-2.0	Insulin secretagogue	Hypersensi-tivity	Weight gain Hypoglycemia Headache

crt = creatinine, SIADH = syndrome of inappropriate antidiuretic hormone secretion, CHF = congestive heart failure and IV = intravenous

Prevention of Type II Diabetes in Patients at Risk

- High-risk patients: those with the metabolic syndrome (see hyperlipidemia section), impaired glucose tolerance or a history of gestational diabetes
- The diabetes prevention program has found two effective methods:
  - Lifestyle modification is the best method available and consists of aerobic exercise $\geq$ 30 minutes most days of the week & diet $\rightarrow$ $\geq$ 10% weight loss
  - metformin 500 mg PO bid effective but not as much as lifestyle modification

References: adapted from American Diabetes Association Clinical Practice Recommendations 2003 in Diabetes Care, 2003, 20 (Supplement 1). Guidelines available at http://care.diabetesjournals.org.

Etiologies of Hyperthyroidism
- Graves disease: TSH receptor antibody/thyroid stimulating immunoglobulin +
- Toxic multinodular goiter or toxic thyroid nodule
- Hyperthyroid phase of thyroiditis (Hashimoto's, postpartum, lymphocytic or de Quervain's/Subacute thyroiditis)
- Thyroid stimulating hormone-secreting pituitary adenoma (very rare)
- Struma ovarii
- Thyrotoxicosis factitia (from exogenous thyroid hormone ingestion)
- Thyrotoxicosis of gestational trophoblastic disease
- Amiodarone-induced hyperthyroidism

Clinical Presentation of Hyperthyroidism
- Signs: diaphoresis, fine resting tremor, diarrhea, muscle weakness, diffuse goiter, irregular menses, infertility, insomnia, exophthalmos, lid retraction, lid lag, weight loss despite good appetite, mental slowing, moist skin + hair loss
- Symptoms: nervousness, irritability, heat intolerance and fatigue
- Complications: atrial fibrillation and periodic paralysis

An Approach to Patients with Suspected Hyperthyroidism

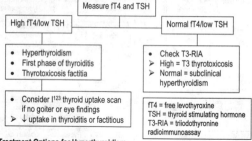

Measure fT4 and TSH

High fT4/low TSH
- Hyperthyroidism
- First phase of thyroiditis
- Thyrotoxicosis factitia

- Consider I^{123} thyroid uptake scan if no goiter or eye findings
  - ➢ ↓ uptake in thyroiditis or factitious

Normal fT4/low TSH
- Check T3-RIA
  - ➢ High = T3 thyrotoxicosis
  - ➢ Normal = subclinical hyperthyroidism

fT4 = free levothyroxine
TSH = thyroid stimulating hormone
T3-RIA = triiodothyronine radioimmunoassay

Treatment Options for Hyperthyroidism
- If thyroid gland <2x normal and soft, recommend antithyroid drugs.
  - ➢ methimazole 10-40 mg PO qd or propylthiouracil 50-200 mg PO tid
- If thyroid gland > 2x normal, multinodular or hard, severe exophthalmos or atrial fibrillation, recommend radioiodine ablation (pretreat with antithyroid drugs).
- Thyroidectomy for pregnant patients intolerant of antithyroid drugs, pediatric Graves disease or patients refusing I^{131} therapy.
- Propranolol is an adjunctive agent for tachycardia, tremors & nervousness.
- Graves' ophthalmopathy followed with exophthalmometer. Use artificial tears & severe cases may need prednisone therapy (especially prior to I^{131}).

Subclinical Hyperthyroidism
- Asymptomatic patient and non-nodular thyroid disease → no treatment.
- Symptomatic patient or nodular thyroid disease → consider low-dose antithyroid drugs for 6 month trial.
- If symptoms resolve with therapy, can consider I^{131} radioiodine ablation.

References: NEJM, 2000; 343 (17): 1236-48 and NEJM, 2001; 345 (7): 512-6.

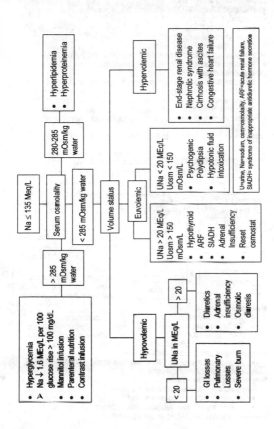

Na ≤ 135 Meq/L

Serum osmolality

> 285 mOsm/kg water

- Hyperglycemia
- Na ↓ 1.6 MEq/L per 100 glucose rise > 100 mg/dl
- Mannitol infusion
- Parenteral nutrition
- Contrast infusion

280–285 mOsm/kg water

- Hyperlipidemia
- Hyperproteinemia

< 285 mOsm/kg water

Volume status

Hypovolemic

UNa in MEq/L

< 20
- GI losses
- Pulmonary Losses
- Severe burn

> 20
- Diuretics
- Adrenal insufficiency
- Osmotic diuresis

Euvolemic

UNa > 20 MEq/L
Uosm > 150 mOsm/L
- Hypothyroid
- ARF
- SIADH
- Adrenal Insufficiency
- Reset osmostat

UNa < 20 MEq/L
Uosm < 150 mOsm/L
- Psychogenic Polydipsia
- Hypotonic fluid intoxication

Hypervolemic

- End-stage renal disease
- Nephrotic syndrome
- Cirrhosis with ascites
- Congestive heart failure

U=urine, Na=sodium, osm=osmolality, ARF=acute renal failure, SIADH= syndrome of inappropriate antidiuretic hormone secretion

Etiologies of Hypothyroidism
- Hashimoto's thyroiditis (95% with + anti-thyroid peroxidase antibody)
- Postpartum thyroiditis
- Lymphocytic thyroiditis
- deQuervain's/Subacute thyroiditis
- Post-thyroidectomy or post-radioablation
- Panhypopituitarism: consider if low or low normal TSH and low FT4
- Medication-induced: antithyroid drugs, lithium, interferon or amiodarone

Clinical Presentation
- Signs: dry skin, coarse hair, hair thinning, delayed relaxation of reflexes, irregular menses, infertility, hypothermia, bradycardia, myxedema, mental slowing, eyebrow loss, deep, hoarse voice, constipation, weight gain
- Symptoms: cold intolerance, fatigue, weakness, myalgias, confusion
- Complications: myxedema coma, pericardial effusion, heart block or hyponatremia

An Approach to the Patient with Suspected Hypothyroidism

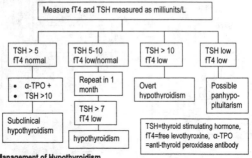

Management of Hypothyroidism
- Mean replacement dose of levothyroxine = 1.7 mcg/kg/day
- If > 50 years old or cardiac disease, start with levothyroxine 50 mcg qd
- If < 50 years old + no cardiac disease, start with levothyroxine 100 mcg qd
- Check TSH level q6 weeks and adjust dose until TSH normalizes

Management of Subclinical Hypothyroidism
- Recommend therapy for TSH > 10 or +anti-thyroid peroxidase antibody
- Desire TSH 0.3 – 3.0 milliunits/L

Screening for Hypothyroidism
- All women > 60 years and at least q5years
- All patients with suspicious symptoms
- Unexplained infertility, depression, dementia or hyperlipidemia

References: NEJM, 2001; 345: 260-5. NEJM, 1996; 335: 99-107.

Obesity Equations and Definitions
- **Body Mass Index** (BMI) = weight (kg)/(height in meters)^2
- **Normal weight** = BMI 20 – 25
- **Overweight** = BMI 25.1 – 29.9
- **Obese** = BMI 30 – 39.9
- **Morbidly obese** = BMI $\geq$ 40
- **Waist-to-hip ratio** $\geq$ 1.0 in men and $\geq$ 0.9 in women is another measure of obesity that portends an increased risk of obesity-related medical problems.

Relative Risk (RR) of Developing Medical Complications Because of Obesity

Category	RR in Women*	RR in Men‡
Coronary Artery Disease	3.56	2.9
Type 2 Diabetes	61 (if BMI $\geq$ 35)	11.2
Hypertension	4.2	3.2
Cardiovascular mortality	4.1	2.9
Cancer mortality	2.1	1.6
Cholelithiasis	3.5	3.2
Osteoarthritis	18	Not available
Congestive heart failure	2	1.8
Stroke	2.4	2.1

* data from the Nurses' Health Study and is the relative risk for ♀ with BMI $\geq$ 32 vs BMI < 21

‡ data from the Framingham Heart Study or the Health Professionals Follow-up Study: BMI$\geq$30 vs BMI<21

- Swedish Obese Subjects Study followed obese patients (average BMI = 38) for 2 years and they developed these complications: hypertension (13.6%), diabetes (6.3%), insulin resistance (6.3%), hypertriglyceridemia (7.7%), low high-density lipoprotein (8.6%) and hypercholesterolemia (12.1%)
- Obesity caused 11% CHF in ♂ and 14% in ♀ in Framingham Heart Study
- Obesity increases the risk of: gout, obstructive sleep apnea, hyperlipidemia, obesity-hypoventilation syndrome, cancers of the breast, endometrium, colorectum & prostate, anovulatory cycles, abdominal striae & depression.

Nonpharmacologic Interventions for the Management of Obesity
- Maintenance calories = caloric intake to maintain weight = 22 kcal/kg/day
- Maintenance calories – 500 kcal/day → weight loss about 0.5 kg/week.
- Reduce daily fat intake to 30 grams for each 1,000 kcal
- Increase fiber in diet and avoid soda, juices, alcohol and sweets.
- 30-45 minutes of aerobic exercise 3 - 5 times a week
- Behavioral treatments to develop adaptive thinking & increase self-esteem

Pharmacologic Interventions for the Management of Obesity
- Indicated for BMI $\geq$ 30 or $\geq$ 27 + two obesity-related medical problems
- sibutramine 5 – 15 mg/day (side effects: hypertension, insomnia, headache)
- orlistat 120 mg tid within 1 hour of meals (side effects: flatulence, fecal incontinence, steatorrhea and oily spotting)
- phentermine 15 – 37.5 mg/day (side effects: insomnia, dry mouth, palpitations and hypertension)

Candidates for Bariatric Surgery
- BMI $\geq$ 40 or $\geq$ 35 + 1 obesity-related medical problems
- Failed medical & dietary therapy
- Compliant and no history of substance abuse
- Mentally stable and has realistic expectations.

References: NEJM, 2002; 346 (8): 591. NEJM, 1999; 341: 427 and Obesity Research, 1998; 6 (S2): 51S.
A website for details on obesity treatment is www.nhlbi.nih.gov/guidelines/obesity/ob_gdlns.htm

Risk Factors for Osteoporosis

- Menopausal women
- Low calcium intake
- Alcohol and tobacco abuse
- Chronic medications: glucocorticoids, anticonvulsants, heparin or cyclosporin A
- Sedentary lifestyle
- Chronic amenorrhea
- Caucasion or Asian ethnicity
- Family history of osteoporosis
- Medical conditions: hyperthyroidism, hyperparathyroidism, Cushing's syndrome, hyperprolactinemia, chronic renal failure and myeloma

Who to screen for osteoporosis

- All women 65 years or older at 2-year intervals
- Postmenopausal women with any of the following:
  - History of fractures with minimal trauma
  - Family history of osteoporosis
  - Active tobacco users
  - History of frequent falls
  - Thin women < 70 kg.

Diagnosis of Osteoporosis

- Dual-energy x-ray absorptiometry scans to assess bone mineral density.
  - Osteoporosis if the T-score is > 2.5 standard deviations below the mean.
  - Osteopenia if the T-score is 1-2.5 standard deviations below the mean.

Management of Osteoporosis

- Elemental calcium 1,200-1,500 mg/day and Vitamin D 800 IU/day
- Weight-bearing exercise for 30 minutes at least 3 times/week.
- Smoking and alcohol cessation
- Bisphosphonates (alendronate 70 mg PO or risedronate 35 mg PO qweek)
- Hormone replacement therapy for < 5 years an option (see corresponding chapter for potential risks to women)
- Selective estrogen receptor modulators like raloxifene excellent for prevention and second-line to bisphosphonates for osteoporosis treatment
  - Increases bone mineral density, reduces cholesterol and does not increase the breast or endometrial cancer risks.
- Parathyroid hormone (Forteo) 20 mcg subcutaneously daily for patients at high risk for fracture.
- Thiazide diuretics may ↓ bone loss in hypertensive menopausal women.
- Nasal calcitonin 200 IU/day is not very effective at ↑ bone mineral density, but it provides good analgesia for acute vertebral compression fractures.

Follow-up of Patients on Therapy

- Repeat Dual-energy x-ray absorptiometry (DEXA) scan every 2 years.
- May follow biochemical markers of bone turnover such as urinary N-telopeptide or deoxypyridinoline at baseline and after 3 months of therapy to guide therapy.

References: JAMA, 2001; 285: 785. NEJM, 1998; 338: 736 and Arch Int. Med., 2002; 162: 2297.

Causes of Hypokalemia

- Decreased potassium intake (extremely rare)
- Increased intestinal losses (vomiting, diarrhea, laxative abuse)
- Increased renal losses (diuretics, hyperaldosteronism, hypomagnesomia, amphotericin B therapy, steroid therapy, high-dose penicillin therapy, toluene intoxication ("glue sniffing") and Bartter's syndrome)
- Type I (distal) or II (proximal) renal tubular acidosis
- Increased cellular shift into cells: alkalosis, insulin use, high-dose β-agonist use, chloroquine intoxication and severe hypothermia.
- Hypokalemic periodic paralysis
- Increased blood cell production: Post-therapy with vitamin B_{12}, folate or granulocyte-macrophage colony-stimulating factor (GM-CSF).

Clues to Certain Etiologies of Hypokalemia

- Primary hyperaldosteronism presents as refractory hypertension.
- Renal tubular acidosis: normal anion gap metabolic acidosis.
  Type I (urine pH > 5.5) and Type II (urine pH < 5.5)
- Hypokalemic periodic paralysis: normal potassium between paralytic episodes.
  ➢ May have thyrotoxicosis (especially in young Asian men)
- Bartter's syndrome: ↑ serum renin + aldosterone in normotensive patient

Causes of Hyperkalemia

- Increased transcellular shift out of cells: metabolic acidosis, insulin deficiency, increased tissue catabolism, $β_2$-blockade or digitalis intoxication.
- Cellular breakdown: crush injury, severe burns, rhabdomyolysis, hemolysis
- Pseudohyperkalemia from hemolyzed blood specimen, marked leukocytosis or marked thrombocytosis.
- Decreased urinary potassium excretion: hypoaldosteronism, renal failure and ureterojejunostomy.
- Type IV renal tubular acidosis
- Excessive potassium ingestion/administration
- Tumor lysis syndrome

Electrocardiogram Changes with Hypokalemia and Hyperkalemia

- Hypokalemia: ST depression → U waves
- Hyperkalemia: peaked T waves → PR prolongation → QRS widening → sinusoidal pattern

Treatment of Hyperkalemia (mnemonic CBIGKDrop)

C – calcium (1 ampule calcium gluconate IV for ECG changes from hyperkalemia)
B – bicarbonate (1 ampule sodium bicarbonate IV)
I – insulin (10 units regular insulin subcutaneous or IV)
G – glucose (1 ampule of 50% dextrose unless patient already hyperglycemic)
K – kayexalate (15-30 grams PO or PR)
D(rop) – Dialysis

References: NEJM, 1998; 339: 451-8.

Syndrome of Inappropriate Antidiuretic Hormone Secretion (SIADH)
- Diagnosis of exclusion
- Frequently associated with a low serum uric acid
- Causes: post-operative, central nervous system disorder, lung process (pneumonia, pulmonary embolus, lung cancer), delirium tremens, psychosis, cancer, medications (e.g., cyclophosphamide, opiates, chlorpropramide, phenothiazines, tricyclic antidepressants, vincristine, neuroleptics, nonsteroidal anti-inflammatory drugs, carbamazepine or general anesthesia)
- Treatment: remove any offending meds and treat underlying condition
  - ➤ Can add demeclocycline 600 mg PO bid for chronic SIADH

Reset Osmostat (or "sick cell syndrome")
- Generally in patients with severe malnutrition, tuberculosis, AIDS, alcoholics, terminal cancer or pregnancy.
- Patients appropriately regulate serum osmolality around a reduced set point.

General Guidelines for the Treatment of Hyponatremia
- Hypovolemic, hypotonic hyponatremia: use isotonic saline until euvolemic
- Hypervolemic or hypotonic, euvolemic hyponatremia: free water restrict to 800-1000 mL daily in severe cases and 1500-2000 mL daily in mild cases.
- Consider hypertonic saline +/- furosemide in the intensive care unit only for severe, symptomatic hyponatremia
- Maximum correction of 1 mEq/L/hr and 8 mEq/L over 24 hours.
  - ➤ More rapid correction can lead to osmotic demyelination syndrome

Hypernatremia
- **Etiologies**
  - ➤ Extrarenal free water losses (skin, pulmonary)
  - ➤ Diabetes insipidus (central or nephrogenic)
  - ➤ Hypothalamic disorders (cancer, granulomatous diseases or cerebrovascular accidents)
  - ➤ Osmotic diuresis (e.g., mannitol or glycosuria)
  - ➤ Conn's or Cushing's syndromes
  - ➤ Excessive sodium administration
- **Clinical features**
  - ➤ Confusion, decreased level of consciousness and in severe cases seizures
- **Treatment**
  - ➤ Initially volume replete dehydrated patients with isotonic saline
  - ➤ Once euvolemic, give water by mouth or 5% dextrose in water IV infusion at a rate based on free water deficit
  - ➤ Free water deficit (liters) calculated as follows:
    Deficit = patient's body weight (kg) x 0.6 x (Serum Na [mEq/L] – 140)/140
  - ➤ Replace ½ of free water deficit in first 12 hours and remaining over the following 24 hours.
  - ➤ Too rapid correction can lead to cerebral edema.

References: NEJM, 2000; 21: 1581-9 and Ann Intern. Med, 1997: 126: 57-62.

Epidemiology
- Palpable thyroid nodule ≥ 1 cm in 4-7% of U.S. population
- < 5% of all thyroid nodules are malignant

Risk Factors for malignancy
- Male sex, age less than 20 or greater than 60 years, history of radiation therapy to the neck, positive family history of thyroid cancer, hoarseness, dysphagia, cervical lymphadenopathy and a firm, hard, nontender or fixed nodule

Management of the Solitary Thyroid Nodule [1]

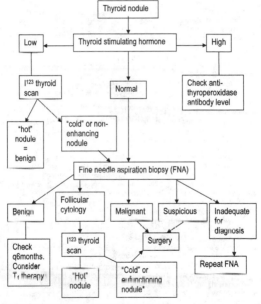

* levothyroxine (T4) suppression therapy also an option if nodules < 2 cm

Adapted from the American Association of Clinical Endocrinologist guidelines for the management of thyroid nodules. References: Arch Int Med., 1996; 156: 2165-72. Endocrine Practice, 1996; 2: 78-84.

Etiologies of Ascites

- Classification based on serum-ascites albumin gradient (SAAG)
- SAAG ≥ 1.1 gm/dL = portal hypertension (97% accuracy)

High SAAG (≥ 1.1 gm/dL)	Low SAAG (< 1.1 gm/dL)
• Cirrhotic ascites	• Peritoneal carcinomatosis
• Alcoholic hepatitis	• Peritoneal tuberculosis
• Right-sided congestive heart failure	• Pancreatic ascites
• Multiple liver metastases	• Biliary ascities
• Fulminant hepatic failure	• Nephrotic syndrome
• Budd-Chiari syndrome	• Lupus serositis
• Portal vein thrombosis	• Bowel infarction/obstruction
• Veno-occlusive disease	• Postoperative lymphatic leak
• Fatty liver of pregnancy	
• Myxedema	

Evaluation of Ascites

- Diagnostic paracentesis for all new-onset ascites
- Peritoneal fluid for protein, albumin, glucose, cell count, lactate dehydrogenase (LDH) and culture.
  - ➢ Place peritoneal fluid directly into blood culture bottles for optimal yield.
  - ➢ If SAAG low, consider placing a PPD test and sending fluid for cytology

Management of Cirrhotic Ascites

- Dietary restriction to < 2 grams sodium daily essential to successful control
- No role for bed rest
- No need for fluid restriction unless severe hyponatremia present
- Diuretic therapy (keep spironolactone/furosemide ratio approximately 5:2)
  - ➢ Begin spironolactone 100 mg PO qAM and furosemide 40 mg PO qAM
  - ➢ Double dosages q3days until urine sodium>40 MEq/L + weight loss 1 lb/d or maximal doses of spironolactone 400 mg/furosemide 160 mg PO qAM.
  - ➢ Monitor for encephalopathy, renal insufficiency and electrolyte imbalances.
- Serial therapeutic paracenteses in diuretic-resistant ascites
- Third-line therapy is a peritoneovenous shunt or a transjugular intrahepatic portosystemic shunt (TIPS procedure).
- Evaluation for liver transplantation if patient is a good candidate.

Spontaneous Bacterial Peritonitis (SBP)

- **Clinical Features:** abdominal pain, fever, encephalopathy or asymptomatic
- **Diagnosis:** ascitic fluid neutrophils ≥ 250 or monomicrobial bacterial growth
  - ➢ Secondary bacterial peritonitis likely if ascitic white blood count >10,000/μL, glucose<50 mg/dL, LDH>250 U/L, protein>1 gm/dL or polymicrobial growth.
- **Treatment:** cefotaxime for inpatients or ofloxacin in outpatients x 5 days.
- **Prophylaxis:** norfloxacin 400 PO mg qd or trimethoprim-sulfamethoxazole DS 1 tablet PO qd.
  - ➢ Indicated for previous bout of SBP or if ascitic fluid protein < 1 gm/dL.

References: CID, 1998; 27: 669-76. NEJM, 1994; 330: 337-42. Mayo Clin Proc, 2000; 75: 501-9.

Definition: increased frequency (>3/day) and liquidity of stools for ≥ 4 weeks.
History
- Family history of diarrhea (inflammatory bowel disease or celiac disease)
- Follows ingestion of dairy products (lactose intolerance) or "sugar-free" foods (sorbitol-induced osmotic diarrhea)
- Recent travel (aeromonas, giardiasis, cryptosporidiosis or amebiasis)
- Previous intestinal surgery (consider "dumping syndrome")
- Abdominopelvic radiation (radiation enteritis)
- Systemic illnesses (hyperthyroidism, diabetic enteropathy, Whipple's disease or systemic mastocytosis)
- AIDS (opportunistic infections of colon)
- Abdominal pain out-of-proportion to tenderness (ischemic colitis)
- Crampy lower quadrant pain with altered bowel habits (irritable bowel syn.)
- Voluminous, malodorous stool (malabsorption)
- Nocturnal diarrhea (consider secretory process)
- Bloody stools (infectious or ischemic colitis or inflammatory bowel disease)
- Antibiotic usage in last 6 weeks (consider *Clostridium difficile* colitis)

Categories of Chronic Diarrhea

Category	Malabsorption	Inflammatory	Secretory	Osmotic
Stool osmotic gap (mOsm/kg)*	Not Applicable	Not Applicable	< 50	>125
Fecal leukocytes	Absent	Present	Absent	Absent
Hemoccult	Negative	+ or -	Negative	Negative
Nocturnal BMs	No	Possible	Yes	No

* stool osmotic gap = 290 − 2 x($stool_{Na}$ + $stool_K$), BM = bowel movement

Work-up of Chronic Diarrhea
- **Malabsorptive diarrhea**
  - ➤ Typical findings: anemia, decreased serum iron, folate, calcium, magnesium, cholesterol, albumin and carotene +/- vitamin B_{12}.
  - ➤ 72 hour quantitative stool fat > 6 grams diagnostic of steatorrhea
  - ➤ Etiologies: pancreatic exocrine insufficiency (screen with Bentiromide or Pancreolauryl tests), celiac disease (screen with IgA antiendomysial or anti-gliadin antibodies) or lactose intolerance (check Lactose tolerance test with 50 gram test dose and measure serum glucose at 0, 60 and 120 minutes).
- **Inflammatory diarrhea**
  - ➤ Stool for ova and parasites on 3 consecutive days
  - ➤ Stool for clostridium difficile toxin if recent antibiotic use
  - ➤ If no infectious cause, consider flexible sigmoidoscopy or colonoscopy
- **Secretory diarrhea**
  - ➤ Stool for aeromonas, microsporidia, cryptosporidia and ova + parasites
  - ➤ Check stool for giardia antigen by enzyme-linked immunoassay test.
  - ➤ Rule out thyrotoxicosis or diabetic enteropathy
- **Osmotic diarrhea**
  - ➤ Stool for laxatives
  - ➤ D-xylose test positive for carbohydrate malabsorption
  - ➤ Examine diet/meds for magnesium- or sorbitol-containing substances.
- Diagnosis of exclusion is irritable bowel syndrome (see page 47)

References: Gastroenterology, 1999; 116: 1464. NEJM, 1995; 332: 725.

Definition: cirrhosis is the end stage of liver injury characterized by diffuse, hepatic fibrosis and replacement of the normal lobular architecture with abnormal nodules.

Etiologies of Cirrhosis in the U.S.
- Hepatitis C Virus (HCV) infection (26%)
- Alcoholic liver disease (21%)
- Hepatitis C Virus infection + Alcoholic liver disease (15%)
- Cryptogenic (mostly nonalcoholic steatohepatitis) (18%)
- Hepatitis B Virus (HBV) +/- delta agent (15%)
- Miscellaneous (5%): Wilson's disease, hemochromatosis, autoimmune hepatitis or alpha₁-antitrypsin deficiency

Diagnosis of Cirrhosis
- Gold standard is a percutaneous liver biopsy
- Presumptive diagnosis by abnormal labs, imaging studies or exam findings
  ➤ Imaging studies: ultrasound or radionuclide liver/spleen scan

Child-Pugh Classification of Cirrhosis

Categories	1 point	2 points	3 points
Albumin (gm/dL)	>3.5	2.8-3.5	<2.8
Bilirubin (mg/dL)	<2.0	2.0-3.0	>3.0
Prolongation of prothrombin time (seconds)	1-4	4-6	>6
Presence of ascites	None	Diuretic-controlled	Diuretic-resistant
Encephalopathy	None	Mild	Severe
Class A = 5-6 points, Class B = 7-9 points, Class C = >9 points			

Clinical Features that May be Present in Cirrhosis
- General: muscle wasting, hepatic fetor
- Skin: jaundice, spider angiomata, palmar erythema
- Thorax: gynecomastia, pleural effusion (hepatic hydrothorax)
- Extremities: Dupuytren's contracture, white nails, clubbing
- Abdomen: ascites, caput medusae, splenomegaly
- Genitourinary: testicular atrophy
- Neurologic: confusion, decreased level of consciousness, asterixis

Work-up of Cirrhosis
- Labs: complete blood count, chem. 7, liver panel, prothrombin time
- Labs to consider: Hepatitis B and C virus serologies, iron studies, antimitochondrial and anti-smooth muscle antibodies, serum ceruloplasmin, alpha₁-antitrypsin level & a percutaneous liver biopsy if diagnosis equivocal
- Imaging studies: abdominal ultrasound +/- duplex of portal vein blood flow

Complications of Cirrhosis
- **Gastroesophageal varices**
  ➤ Prophylaxis with oral propranolol titrated to decrease resting pulse 25%
  ➤ Portosystemic shunts can be used as a bridge to transplantation
- **Ascites and spontaneous bacterial peritonitis** (see ascites page)
- **Hepatic Encephalopathy**
  ➤ Precipitants: intestinal bleed, medications, high protein intake or infection
  ➤ Treatments: lactulose, oral neomycin or oral metronidazole
- **Hepatorenal syndrome:** diagnosis of exclusion and urinary indices mimic prerenal azotemia
- **Hepatopulmonary syndrome:** diagnosis with radioisotope perfusion scan

Treatment of Cirrhosis. The cure for cirrhosis is orthotopic liver transplantation

References: American Family Physician, 2001; 64 (9): 155-62. NEJM, 2001; 345 (9): 669-81.

Clinical presentation

- Acute diarrheal illness (< 2 weeks duration)
- Most cases are self-limited, of viral etiology, and last less than 48 hours.
- Bacterial etiology more likely if any of the following are present:
  - ➢ Profuse watery diarrhea with dehydration
  - ➢ Passage of stool containing blood and mucus
  - ➢ Fever > 101°F
  - ➢ Passage of ≥ 6 unformed stools/day for > 48 hours
  - ➢ Diarrhea in patients who are over 65 years or immunocompromised
  - ➢ Presence of occult blood or fecal leukocytes

History

- Recent ill contacts
- Recent travel
- Ingestion of undercooked beef, pork, shellfish, eggs, poultry, unpasteurized dairy products or fried rice
- Pet turtles, reptiles or ducklings (Salmonella)
- Recent use of antibiotics (*Clostridium difficile* colitis)
- Attends day care
- Immunocompromised patient
- Medication side effect

Work-up

- Stool studies for occult blood, fecal leukocytes and routine cultures if bacterial etiology likely or host immunocompromised.
- Stool for clostridium difficile toxin if recent antibiotic use, recent chemotherapy or recent hospitalization
- Consider sigmoidoscopy in young, acutely-ill patient when infectious etiology has been ruled out to examine for inflammatory bowel disease.
- Consider endoscopy in patients > 50 with vascular disease, severe abdominal pain and blood in stool to rule out ischemic colitis.

Treatment

- Oral rehydration solutions
  - ➢ WHO-ORS or Rehydralyte solutions contain the optimal compositions.
  - ➢ Home mix: ½ tsp salt, ½ tsp baking soda, 8 tsp sugar in 1 liter of water.
  - ➢ Products like Gatorade, soda or dilute juices have less optimal formulations.
- Antimotility agents if patients are nontoxic and there is absence of fever, blood in stool or fecal leukocytes (e.g., loperamide or diphenoxylate).
- Consider empiric antibiotic therapy if bacterial etiology likely (based on criteria above)
  - ➢ Oral quinolone x 5 days (7 days for *Yersinia enterocolitica*) is first choice
  - ➢ Doxycycline good second choice (covers all bacteria except shigella)

Adapted from the Guidelines on acute infectious diarrhea in adults by the American College of Gastroenterology (Reference: Am J Gastroenterology, 1997; 92: 1962.)

Indications for Testing and Treatment
- Peptic ulcer disease
- Ulcer-like dyspepsia
- Chronic active gastritis
- Mucosa-associated lymphoid tissue lymphoma
- Controversial for nonulcer dyspepsia

Noninvasive Testing for Helicobacter pylori (H. pylori)

Test	Sensitivity	Specificity	Test for cure
Urea breath test	95%	95%	Yes
H. pylori serum IgG by ELISA	90-93%	95-96%	No
H. pylori whole blood IgG by ELISA	50-85%	75-100%	No
H. pylori stool antigen test‡	95-98%	92-95%	Yes

ELISA = Enzyme Linked Immunosorbent Assay, IgG = immunoglobulins

‡ = Test of cure should be done 4 weeks post-therapy and off proton pump inhibitor for ≥ 1 week

Treatment Regimens for Helicobacter pylori
- Favor treatment with any regimen for a 14 day course

Treatment regimen	Cure rate (%)
PPI bid + metronidazole 500 mg bid + clarithromycin 500 mg bid	90-95%
PPI bid + amoxicillin 1000 mg bid + clarithromycin 500 mg bid	86-91%
RBC 400 mg bid + clarithromycin 500 mg bid + tetracycline 500 mg bid **or** amoxicillin 1000 mg bid **or** metronidazole 500 mg bid	82-94%
PPI qd + bismuth subsalicylate 525 mg qid + metronidazole 500 mg tid + tetracycline 500 mg qid	94-98%
bismuth subsalicylate 525 mg qid + metronidazole 250 mg qid + tetracycline 500 mg qid + H$_2$-blocker	84-95%

PPI = proton pump inhibitor: omeprazole 20 mg or lansoprazole 30 mg or esomeprazole 20 mg are the only PPIs FDA-approved for H. pylori therapy

RBC = ranitidine bismuth subsalicylate

Bismuth subsalicylate = Pepto Bismol

PPI or H$_2$ blockers therapy generally continues for at least 2 weeks beyond antibiotic treatment

Indications for Esophagogastroduodenoscopy
- New-onset dyspepsia of patients ≥ 45 years of age
- Alarm signs: unintentional weight loss, anemia, early satiety, dysphagia
- Dyspepsia refractory to appropriate medical therapy
- Dyspepsia which recurs within 3 months of a complete 2 month treatment course for ulcer-like dyspepsia

References: Ann. Intern. Med., 2002; 136: 280-7. Am J. Gastroenterology, 1998; 93 (12): 2330-8. Amer. Fam. Physician, 2002; 65 (7):1327-36.

Adapted from the American Gastroenterological Association Guidelines for the Evaluation of Occult or Obscure GI Bleeding

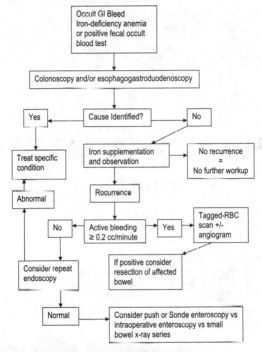

Tagged-RBC scan is a technetium 99m-labeled red blood cell scintigraphy scan

Reference: Gastroenterology, 2000; 118: 201

Hepatitis, or inflammation of the liver, can be subclassified into one of three categories: cholestatic, hepatocellular injury or infiltrative patterns.

- **Cholestasis**: alkaline phosphatase and gamma-glutamyl transpeptidase elevated more so than the elevation of the liver transaminases.
- **Hepatocellular injury**: liver transaminase $\uparrow$ > alkaline phosphatase $\uparrow$.
- **Infiltrative diseases of the liver**: usually cause marked elevations of alkaline phosphatase with disproportionately low bilirubin levels.

Cholestatic Pattern	Hepatocellular injury	Infiltrative Diseases
• Gallstones	• Alcoholic hepatitis	• Sarcoidosis
• Hepatocellular carcinoma	• Autoimmune hepatitis	• Tuberculosis
• Primary biliary cirrhosis	• Chronic viral hepatitis	• Deep fungal infections
• Primary sclerosing cholangitis	• Nonalcoholic steatohepatitis (diabetes and obesity)	• Hepatocellular carcinoma
• Venoocclusive disease	• Congestive hepatopathy	• Metastatic carcinoma to the liver
• Budd-Chiari syndrome	• Wilson's disease	• Leukemic infiltrate
Medications	• Hemochromatosis	• Lymphoma
• haloperidol	• Alpha$_1$-antitrypsin deficiency	
• benzodiazepines	• Ischemic hepatitis	
• estrogens	• Rhabdomyolysis	
• sulfonylureas		
• androgenic steroids	**Medications**	
• erythromycin	• acetaminophen	
• phenothiazines	• penicillins	
• Darvon	• valproic acid	
• propylthiouracil	• halothane	
• nitrofurantoin	• phenytoin	
• carbamazepine	• procainamide	
• gold	• quinidine	
• penicillamine	• diclofenac	
• chlorpromazine	• sulfonamides	
• amoxicillin-clavulanate	• allopurinol	
• azathioprine	• hydralazine	
• cyclosporin A	• methotrexate	
• mercaptopurine	• verapamil	
• niacin	• angiotensin-converting enzyme inhibitors	
• sulindac	• fluconazole	
	• griseofulvin	
	• amiodarone	
	• ketoconazole	
	• rifampin	
	• isoniazid	
	• methyldopa	

Rome II Criteria for Irritable Bowel Syndrome (IBS)
- At least 12 weeks of the preceding year with abdominal discomfort characterized by 2 or 3 of the following features:
  - Relieved with defecation
  - Change in the frequency of defecation
  - Change in consistency of the stool
- IBS is a diagnosis of exclusion after all organic etiologies have been ruled out.

Criteria to subtype IBS and increase the diagnostic accuracy
- Abnormal stool frequency
  - > 3 times per day or < 3 times per week
- Abnormal stool consistency
  - Hard/lumpy or loose/watery in > 25% of defecations
- Abnormal stool passage
  - Straining, urgency or sensation of incomplete evacuation in >25% of defecations
- Passage of mucus in > 25% of defecations
- Abdominal bloating > 25% of the time

Diagnostic Studies for IBS
- In the absence of "alarm signs" (see below), routine labs, thyroid function tests, stool for culture, ova and parasites, fecal occult blood test and lower endoscopy are NOT INDICATED.
- For severe diarrhea, consider thyroid function tests, IgA anti-endomysial or anti-gliadin antibodies (celiac sprue), stool for ova and parasites +/- colonoscopy.
- Sigmoidoscopy or colonoscopy for patients > 50 yrs or those with "alarm signs"

"Alarm" Signs and Clinical Features that Make the Diagnosis of IBS Unlikely
- Weight loss, fever, anorexia, dysphagia, anemia, chronic and severe diarrhea, melena or hematochezia
- Pain that is progressive, awakens the patient from sleep or prevents sleep
- Presence of an abdominal mass or organomegaly

Principles of Treatment
- Dietary modification
  - Eliminate dairy products and foods that increase gas (e.g., beans, onions, celery, carrots, raisins, bananas, apricots, prunes, wheat germ and bagels).
- Psychotherapy can be very helpful if an associated mood disorder is present.
- Validate patient's symptoms and remain non-judgemental

Medications for Irritable Bowel Syndrome
- Abdominal cramps
  - Antispasmodic agents may offer marginal benefit. Use with caution if patient constipated.
  - dicyclomine 10-40 mg PO qid or hyoscyamine 0.125 – 0.25 mg PO q4h prn.
- IBS with Diarrhea
  - loperamide can ↓ diarrhea, but no effect on pain or global IBS symptoms
  - alosetron hydrochloride 1 mg PO qd-bid for women with severe symptoms
    - Observe carefully for obstipation or ischemic colitis
  - Low-dose tricyclic antidepressants can ↓ pain and global IBS symptoms.
- Women that have IBS with Constipation
  - Fiber may help constipation, but little benefit for pain or bloating
  - tegaserod 6 mg PO bid for short-term treatment

References: Gut, 1999; 45 (supplement 2): 43. NEJM, 1993; 329: 1940. Amer. J. Gastroenterology, 2002; 97 (11) Supplement: S1-S5.

Categories	Peptic Ulcer Disease	Biliary Colic	Gastritis	GERD
Character of pain	• Burning • Sharp	• Crampy • Sharp	• Dull • Burning	• Burning
Radiation of pain	• Penetrating ulcers radiate to back	• Right scapula	• None	• Retrosternal chest to throat
Exacerbating factors	• Alcohol	• Fatty foods	• Alcohol	• Supine • Fatty foods, chocolate • Alcohol
Alleviating factors	• Antacids	• None	• Antacids	• Upright • Antacids
Risk Factors	• Smoking • NSAIDS • Salicylates • Steroids • Stress • Alcohol • Age > 60 y • H. pylori infection • + Family history	• Female • Middle age • Obese • Positive family history	• Same as in ulcer disease • Risk of H. pylori infection controversial	• Obese • Pregnancy • Alcohol • Smoking
Nocturnal pain	• DU usually 12 – 2 AM	• No	• No	• Yes if supine
Relationship with meals	• DU 2-5 hrs after meal • GU pain 30-60 min. after meals	• Pain 30 - 180 min. after meals	• Pain soothed by bland meals	• Postprandial pain in supine position
Antacids help	• Yes	• No	• Yes	• Yes
Associated symptoms	• Anorexia • Nausea • Bloating • Belching	• Nausea • Vomiting • Anorexia	• Nausea	• Acid taste in mouth • Hoarseness • Dry cough
Diagnostic tests	• EGD is optimal	• Abdominal ultrasound	• EGD is optimal	• EGD • Esophageal pH probe

H. pylori = Helicobacter pylori, DU = duodenal ulcer, GU = gastric ulcer,

EGD = esophagogastroduodenoscopy and GERD = gastroesophageal reflux disease

Recommended Guidelines for Periodic Health Examinations

Age group(s)	Condition(s)	Screening/treatment
Newborns	Phenyketonuria, Hypothyroidism Hemoglobinopathies and more	Newborn screen
Newborns	Gonococcal/chlamydia ophthalmia neonatorum	Ophthalmic ointment following birth
Newborns	Hemorrhagic disease newborn	Vitamin K .5-1 mg IM
All children unless contraindicated	Diphtheria, pertussis, tetanus, poliomyelitis, measles, mumps, rubella, haemophilus influenzae type b, pneumococcal disease, hepatitis B, varicella	Immunize using American Academy of Family Physicians or American Academy of Pediatrics recommendations
By age 3-4	Visual problems or misaligned eyes	Screen for amblyopia and strabismus
6 months – 16 years with water fluoride < 0.6 parts per million	Dental caries	Supplemental fluoride
9-12 months	Iron-deficiency anemia	Hemoglobin
12 months	Lead poisoning	Lead level
All ♀ ≥ 13 years	Osteoporosis	Calcium 1,200 mg qd
Adolescents/adults	Drug addiction	Screening for substance abuse/dependence
Adolescents/adults	Sexually-transmitted diseases	Safe sex counseling
Adults and children	Obesity	Regular weight check
♀ ≥ 18 yrs or sexually active	Cervical dysplasia/cancer	Annual pap smear until age 65 years (if normal)
Adults ≥ 18 years	Hypertension	Blood pressure check q2 years
♀ ≥ 25 yrs or sexually active	Chlamydia	Cervical swab for chlamydia testing
Preconception ♀	Neural tube defects	Folic acid 0.4-0.8 mg qd
Preconception or pregnant ♀	Congenital rubella syndrome	Rubella titers and vaccinate nonimmune ♀
New mothers	Nutrition/immunologic benefits	Encourage breast feeding
Smoking parents	Asthma, allergies, otitis media	Smoking cessation
♂ > 35 yrs and ♀ > 45 yrs	Hyperlipidemia	Total cholesterol and high-density lipoprotein check q1-2 years
20 < ♀ < 40 years	Breast cancer	Clinical breast exam q3yr
♀ ≥ 40 years	Breast cancer	Annual clinical breast exam and mammogram
Adults	Tetanus and Diphtheria	Tetanus toxoid q10 years

Recommended Guidelines for Periodic Health Examinations

Age group(s)	Condition(s)	Screening/treatment
Adults	Coronary artery disease, obesity, hypertension and diabetes	Regular aerobic exercise for at least 30 minutes 2-3 x/week
Adults	Depression	Periodic Yale or Beck Depression screening
Adults ≥ 45 years	Diabetes	Fasting glucose
♀ ≥ 65 years	Osteoporosis	Dual-energy bone mineral densitometry study q2 yrs
Tb contacts, health care workers, immigrants, immunosuppressed, injection drug users or institutionalized	Tuberculosis (Tb)	Apply Mantoux (PPD) test annually
Sexually promiscuous + homosexual men	Syphilis, gonorrhea, HIV, chlamydia	Venereal Disease Research Laboratory test, HIV, gonococcal and chlamydia tests q1-2 yrs
♀ ≥ 50 years	Apathetic hypothyroidism	Thyroid stimulating hormone level q1-2 years
People ≥ 50 years	Colorectal cancer	Annual fecal occult blood test and flexible sigmoidoscopy q5yrs **or** colonoscopy q10yrs
≥ 50 years, cardiac or pulmonary disease, diabetes, asplenia immunosuppressed, sickle cell disease or pregnancy	Influenza	Annual influenza shot
≥ 65 years, cardiac or pulmonary disease, diabetes, asplenia or institutionalized	Pneumococcal disease	Pneumococcal vaccine
People ≥ 65 years	Visual impairment	Snellen acuity test q1-3 yr
People ≥ 65 years	Hearing impairment	Screening audiogram for all in question
≥ 70-75 years	Falls	Get-up-and-go test and fall prevention testing

References: United States Preventive Services Task Force Guide to Clinical Preventive Services, 3rd Ed., 2003 (website at www.ahcpr.gov/clinic/uspstfix.htm) American Academy of Family Physicians Policy Recommendations for Periodic Health Examinations, 2002 and the National Cancer Institute guidelines at the website www.cancer.gov

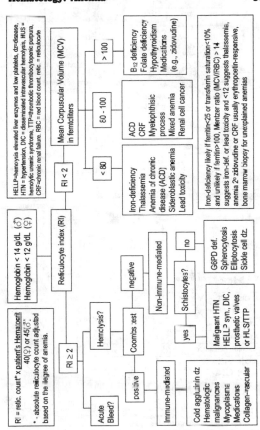

HELLP=hemolysis elevated liver enzymes and low platelets, dz=disease, HTN = hypertension, DIC = disseminated intravascular hemolysis, HUS = hemolytic uremic syndrome, TTP=thrombotic thrombocytopenic purpura, CRF=chronic renal failure. RBC = red blood count. retic. = reticulocyte

Hemoglobin < 14 g/dL (♂)
Hemoglobin < 12 g/dL (♀)

RI = retic. count × patient's Hematocrit / 40(♀) or 45(♂)*
* - absolute reticulocyte count adjusted based on the degree of anemia.

Reticulocyte index (RI)

RI < 2

Mean Corpuscular Volume (MCV) in femtoliters

< 80
Iron-deficiency
Thalassemia
Anemia of chronic disease (ACD)
Sideroblastic anemia
Lead toxicity

80 - 100
ACD
CRF
Myelophthisic process
Mixed anemia
Renal cell cancer

> 100
B$_{12}$ deficiency
Folate deficiency
Hypothyroidism
Medications
(e.g., zidovudine)

Iron-deficiency likely if ferritin<25 or transferrin saturation<10% and unlikely if ferritin>100, Mentzer ratio (MCV/RBC) > 14 suggests iron-def. or lead toxicity and <12 suggests thalassemia, anemia 2° zidovudine or CRF usually erythropoietin-responsive, bone marrow biopsy for unexplained anemias

RI ≥ 2

Hemolysis?

negative → Coombs test ← positive

Immune-mediated
Cold agglutinin dz
Hematologic malignances
Mycoplasma
Medications
Collagen-vascular

Non-immune-mediated
Schistocytes?

yes →
Malignant HTN
HELLP syn., DIC, prosthetic valves or HLS/TTP

no →
G6PD def.
Spherocytosis
Elliptocytosis
Sickle cell dz

Acute Bleed?

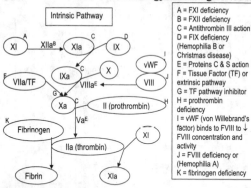

A = FXI deficiency
B = FXII deficiency
C = Antithrombin III action
D = FIX deficiency
(Hemophilia B or
Christmas disease)
E = Proteins C & S action
F = Tissue Factor (TF) or
extrinsic pathway
G = TF pathway inhibitor
H = prothrombin
deficiency
I = vWF (von Willebrand's
factor) binds to FVIII to ↓
FVIII concentration and
activity
J = FVIII deficiency or
(Hemophilia A)
K = fibrinogen deficiency

Coagulation Studies for Various Bleeding Diatheses

Disorder	PTT	PTT with mixing study	PT	Other tests
vWD	↑	NL	NL	RCA + RIPA ↓ ↑ BT
Hemophilia A	↑	NL	NL	RCA NL and FVIII ↓
Hemophilia B	↑	NL	NL	↓ FIX
Inhibitors to fibrinogen, II, V or X	↑	NL	↑	PT NL with mixing study
Inhibitors to VIII, IX, XI or XII	↑	↑	NL	
TF inhibitor or FVIII deficiency	NL	NL	↑	↓ FVIII
FXI deficiency	↑	NL	NL	↓ FXI
FXII deficiency	↑	NL	NL	↓ FXII
Prothrombin deficiency	↑	NL	↑	↓ prothrombin
Fibrinogen deficiency	↑	NL	↑	↓ fibrinogen
Vitamin K deficiency	↑	NL	NL/↑	Normal TT
DIC	↑	NL	↑	↓ PLT, ↑ TT, ↓ fib, ↑ FSP

vWD = von Willebrand's disease, Roman numerals refer to specific clotting factors, RCA = ristocetin cofactor activity, RIPA = ristocetin-induced platelet aggregation, PTT = partial thromboplastin time, PT = prothrombin time, TT = thrombin time, NL = normal, BT = bleeding time, PLT = platelets, Fib = fibrinogen, FSP = fibrin split products, DIC = disseminated intravascular coagulation

General Points About Cancer of Unknown Primary
- Primary site identified by work-up in only 20% of patients
- Extensive search for the primary site should be undertaken only if it is expected to alter the overall management of the patient.
- Identifying the cell type is more important than identifying the site of origin as this may alter the chemotherapy regimen used.
- **Work-up of all patients**: a thorough history and exam, complete blood count, chemistry panel, chest x-ray & immunohistochemistry when possible

Histologic Categories of Cancer of Unknown Primary Site
- Adenocarcinoma – 80% of all cases
- Poorly-differentiated carcinoma (non-adenocarcinoma) – 5-10%
- Poorly-differentiated neoplasm - < 5%
- Squamous cell carcinoma – 5%
- Neuroendocrine carcinoma - < 5%

Adenocarcinoma of Unknown Primary Site (AUP)
- Pancreas, hepatobiliary, lung, gastric and colon are all relatively common
- Breast and prostate uncommon
- **Work-up of AUP in Addition to General Work-up Above**
  - ➤ Urinalysis, FOBT and prostate specific antigen (♂). Mammogram (♀).
  - ➤ Abdominal CT scan with careful assessment of stomach, pancreas and liver
  - ➤ Positron emission tomography scan using 18-F-fluorodeoxyglucose has proven to be of additional benefit **if results would alter management**.
  - ➤ No role for CEA, CA 19-9, CA 15-3, CA 125, human chorionic gonadotrophin or alpha-fetoprotein in diagnostic work-up of AUP

Poorly-differentiated Carcinoma of Unknown Primary Site (PDCUP)
- Melanoma 10%, lymphoma 5%, neuroendocrine tumor 4%, prostate CA 1%
- **Work-up of PDCUP in Addition to General Work-up Above**
  - ➤ CT scan of the chest and abdomen, human chorionic gonadotrophin and alpha-fetoprotein (extragonadal germ cell tumor) and immunohistochemistry

Poorly-differentiated Neoplasms of Unknown Primary Site (PDNUP)
- Non-Hodgkin's lymphomas account for 34-66% of all PDNUP
- Most of the other cases are from poorly-differentiated carcinomas and a small percentage are from melanomas and sarcomas
- **Work-up of PDNUP in Addition to General Work-up Above**
  - ➤ Immunohistochemical staining, electron microscopy +/- cytogenetic analysis of tissue can differentiate lymphoma, sarcoma, melanoma or carcinoma

Squamous Cell Carcinoma of Unknown Primary Site (SCCUP)
- Upper or mid-cervical lymph node involvement
  - ➤ Fiberoptic nasopharyngolaryngoscopy to rule out primary head/neck cancer Chest/neck CT scan. Fine needle aspiration of involved lymph nodes.
- Lower cervical or supraclavicular lymph node involvement
  - ➤ Primary lung cancer more likely than head and neck cancer
  - ➤ CT scan of thorax and neck and if unrevealing a bronchoscopy
- Inguinal lymph node involvement
  - ➤ 99% are primary in anorectal or genital areas
  - ➤ Anoscopy and careful exam of either penis or vulva/vagina/cervix.

FOBT = fecal occult blood test, CEA = carcinoembryonic antigen, CA = cancer antibody

References: Ann Oncol., 1990; 1: 119. J Clin. Oncol., 1991; 9: 1931. J. Clin Oncol., 1995; 13: 274.

Clinical Features of Deep Venous Thrombosis (DVT)
- Extremity swelling, pain, warmth +/- mild erythema

Diagnosis of DVT
- Use clinical prediction tool algorithm below to guide work-up.
- The diagnosis can be made by duplex ultrasonagraphy for deep venous thromboses in the deep venous systems of the extremities.
- MRI scanning is superior to ultrasound for diagnosis of pelvic vein thrombosis.
- D-Dimer < 500 ng/mL by enzyme-linked immunoassay has a 98% negative predictive value for ruling out deep venous thrombosis

Clinical Prediction Tool for Venous Thromboembolic Event (VTE)

Clinical feature	Points	Pretest probability
Active cancer (treatment within last 6 months)	1	Low = 0 points
Paralysis, paresis or recent extremity casting	1	Intermediate = 1-2
Bedridden ≥ 3 days or major surgery within 4 wks	1	High = ≥ 3 points
Tenderness along deep venous system	1	
Entire extremity swollen	1	
Calf swelling > 3 cm over asymptomatic leg	1	
Pitting edema	1	
Prominent non-varicose collateral superficial veins	1	
Alternative diagnosis likely	-2	

Pretest Probability	Chance of Venous Thromboembolic Event (VTE)	Duplex Ultrasound (UTZ) Normal	Duplex Ultrasound Abnormal
High (≥ 3 points)	75%	Venography	DVT
Intermediate (1-2)	17%	Duplex UTZ qwk	DVT
Low (0 points)	3%	No DVT	DVT or artifact

Treatment Options for Proximal DVT
- Unfractionated heparin 80 units/kg bolus → 18 units/kg/hr titrated to PTT **or**
- enoxaparin 1 mg/kg SQ q12h (or other low molecular weight heparin)
  > Outpatient therapy if: > 18 years, hemodynamically stable, compliant and no exclusion criteria
- Begin warfarin and overlap heparin/warfarin for ≥ 5 days + INR 2-3 x 2 days
- D-Dimer < 500 ng/mL by enzyme-linked immunoassay after anticoagulation has 95% negative predictive value for a recurrent venous thromboembolic event.
- +/- thrombolysis if massive ileofemoral DVT or phlegmasia cerulea dolens
- Inferior vena caval filter for proximal DVT and contraindications to warfarin

Prophylaxis Against VTE after Major Knee or Hip Surgery
- enoxaparin 30 SQ bid starting 6 hours preoperatively.
- fondaparinux 2.5 mg SQ qd: 55% risk reduction for VTE in all orthopedic surgeries compared to enoxaparin, but slightly ↑ risk of major bleeding.

Duration of Anticoagulation

Underlying Condition or Risk Factor(s)	Duration
First episode with reversible risk factors*	3-6 mo.
Idiopathic (first episode)	6-12 mo.
First episode‡ with: active cancer, antiphospholipid syndrome or antithrombin III deficiency or for recurrent DVT	12 mo.-life

* trauma, immobilization, estrogen use, pregnancy, recent surgery.
‡ duration unclear for Factor V Leiden, Protein C or S deficiency, prothrombin gene mutation or↑ Factor VIII

References: JAMA, 1998; 279: 1094-9. NEJM, 1996; 334: 677-87. Lancet, 1998; 351: 571-2.

Screening for Hypercoagulable States in Patients with a Venous Thrombosis
- No consensus recommendations for screening
- Recommend screening *after* course of anticoagulation completed
- Reasonable approach is to screen high-risk individuals:
  - Idiopathic venous thromboembolic event (VTE)
  - Second episode of a venous thromboembolic event
  - Venous thrombosis in an unusual location (upper extremity, cerebral vein, portal vein or mesenteric vein)
  - Family history of a deep venous thrombosis (DVT) or a pulmonary embolus (PE) is strong evidence for a heritable condition.
  - VTE associated with oral contraceptive use or pregnancy
  - History of warfarin-induced skin necrosis

Heritable Conditions Predisposing to Venous Thrombosis
- Antithrombin III deficiency
  - Screen with serum antithrombin III level
- Protein C deficiency
  - Screen with serum Protein C level
- Protein S deficiency
  - Screen with serum Protein S level
- Activated protein C resistance
  - Incidence is 5% in Caucasians, 2% Hispanics, 1.5% African-Americans
  - Screen for Factor V Leiden mutation
- Antiphospholipid syndrome
  - Screen for anticardiolipin antibody and Lupus anticoagulant assays
  - Patients may have history of premature vascular disease, recurrent second-trimester abortions or digital ulcerations
- Prothrombin gene mutation
  - Genetic analysis for the prothrombin 20210A mutation
- Increased Factor VIII activity
  - Assay for increased Factor VIII coagulant activity

Heritable Conditions Associated with Premature Arterial Thrombosis
- Antiphospholipid syndrome
- Hyperhomocysteinemia
  - Can either test patient after an overnight fast or empirically treat them with folate 1 mg PO daily.

Malignancy-associated Thrombosis
- Lymphomas, pancreatic, gastric, lung, ovary, prostate and brain cancers
- In patients with an idiopathic DVT/PE, perform good history, exam, routine labs and chest x-ray looking for malignancy. NO role for full body CT scan.

Indefinite Anticoagulation in High-Risk Patients with Thrombophilia
- ≥ Two venous thromboembolic events
- One spontaneous life-threatening thrombotic event
- One spontaneous thrombosis at an unusual site (see above)

References: Ann Int Med, 1997; 126: 638-44. Ann Intern Med., 2001; 135: 367. Medicine, 1999; 78: 285.

Definition: any white blood count >11,000 per μL is elevated, but typical work-ups are not initiated unless white blood count persistently elevated > 15-20,000 per μL.

Causes of Leukocytosis
Spurious
- Platelet clumping (0.1% of blood draws)
- Cryoglobulinemia

Primary
- Chronic idiopathic neutrophilia (diagnosis of exclusion)
- Myeloproliferative disorders (chronic myelogenous leukemia, polycythemia vera, essential thrombocythemia and agnogenic myeloid metaplasia)

Secondary
- Infection
- Stress reaction
- Chronic anxiety or post-traumatic stress disorder
- Severe burn, electric shock
- Major operation or trauma
- Myocardial infarction
- Cigarette smoking
- Meds (glucocorticoids, lithium, epinephrine, β-agonists, granulocyte/macrophage-colony stimulating factor (GM-CSF) and all-trans retinoic acid)
- Solid tumors (e.g., lung, renal cell and breast cancer)
- Heat stroke
- Chronic hemolysis (e.g., sickle cell or hemoglobin SC disease)
- Asplenia
- Recent vaccination
- Pregnancy

Causes of Severe Leukocytosis > 50,000/ μL
- **Chronic myelogenous leukemia**
  - Leukocyte alkaline phosphatase low, positive Philadelphia chromosome (or positive serum test for bcr-abl translocation) and more myelocytes than metamyelocytes
- **Leukemoid reaction** from sepsis, all-trans retinoic acid or GM-CSF therapy
  - Serum leukocyte alkaline phosphatase normal or high

How the Complete Blood Count Differential Can Narrow the Possibilities
- Presence of Dohle bodies, toxic granulations or cytoplasmic vacuoles
  - 80% sensitivity for chronic inflammatory or infectious process
- Presence of polycythemia suggests polycythemia vera especially with eosinophilia, thrombocytosis and microcytic indices
- Thrombocytosis:
  - Infection, chronic inflammation, malignancy or essential thrombocythemia
- Monocytosis can be from steroid use, pregnancy, asplenia or tuberculosis
- Eosinophilia can be from neoplasms (e.g., lymphomas and lung cancer), helminthic infections (ascariasis or tapeworms), allergic reactions, chronic infections (e.g., tuberculosis, HIV, aspergillus or coccidiomycosis), adrenal insufficiency, collagen-vascular disease or a parasitic infection.

Absolute Neutrophil Count (cells/mm³)	Risk of Bacterial Infection
>1500	None
1000-1500	No significant risk
500-1000	Some infection risk if ANC<750. Often outpatient therapy
200-500	Significant risk of infection. Usually inpatient management
<200	Very high risk of infection

Etiologies of Neutropenia

Acquired			Congenital
Bacterial infection	Rickettsial infection	Viral: HBV, HCV, HIV, EBV	Chediak-Higashi syndrome
Felty's syndrome*	Drug-induced	Hemodialysis	Cyclic neutropenia
Adult respiratory distress syndrome	Systemic lupus erythematosus	Myelodysplastic syndrome	Reticular dysgenesis
Autoimmune	Chronic idiopathic	Alcoholism	Severe infantile agranulocytosis
B₁₂ deficiency	Folate deficiency	Chemotherapy	Shwachman-Diamond-Oski syn.
Aplastic anemia	Leukemia	Transfusion reaction	

HBV/HCV = Hepatitis B or C virus, HIV = human immunodeficiency virus, EBV = Epstein Barr virus, *Felty's syndrome = rheumatoid arthritis with splenomegaly and neutropenia

Drug-Induced Neutropenia			
amiodarone	dapsone	NSAIDS	spironolactone
amphotericin B	flucainido	penicillamine	sulfasalazine
angiotensin converting enzyme inhibitors	furosemide	semisynthetic penicillins	sulfonamides
	gold salts		thiazides
carbamazepine	H₂-antagonists	phenothiazines	ticlopidine
cephalosporins	isotretinoin	phenytoin	tolbutamide
chloroquine	macrolides	procainamide	tricyclic antidepressants
chlorpropamide	methimazole	propylthiouracil	valproic acid
clozapine		quinine	

Drug-induced neutropenia usually resolves 1-3 weeks after stopping offending drug, NSAIDS = nonsteroidal anti-inflammatory drugs, H₂-antagonists = Histamine₂-antagonists

Outpatient Management of Fever and Neutropenia in Patients with Cancer

- Empiric antibiotics if ANC < 500 cells/mm³ and fever ≥ 38.3°C (101 °F)
- Check blood, urine and sputum (if cough) cultures and check a chest x-ray
- Outpatient management if patient at "low risk" for serious infection: nontoxic, age < 60 years, absolute neutrophil and monocyte counts both ≥ 100 cells/mm³, normal chest x-ray, liver and renal panels, no intravenous catheter site infection, abdominal pain, hypotension, hypoxia, vomiting, diarrhea, chronic lung disease, neurologic or mental status changes, malignancy in remission, neutropenia duration < 7 days, signs of early bone marrow recovery & temperature < 39.0°C
- Ciprofloxacin 500 mg PO bid + amoxicillin clavulanate 875 mg PO bid
- If an etiologic agent is identified, tailor antibiotics based on culture sensitivities
- Antibiotics are continued for 48 hours after patient afebrile if ANC ≥ 500 and when afebrile for 5-7 days if ANC < 500 cells/mm³ on day 7 of antibiotics.

References: Arch Int. Med., 1992; 152. 1475. JAMA, 1994; 271: 935 and CID, 2002; 34: 730-51.

Clinical Features for Pulmonary Embolus in the PIOPED study
- Symptoms: dyspnea (73%), pleuritic chest pain (66%), cough (37%) and less likely hemoptysis
- Signs include tachypnea (70%), pulmonary rales (51%), tachycardia (30%), an S_4 (24%), a loud S_2, fever < 102º(14%) or pleural rub.

Risk Factors for Pulmonary Embolus (use to determine pretest probability)
- Recent immobilization, abdominal/orthopedic/pelvic surgery in the last month, stroke, personal or family history of prior venous thromboembolic event, active cancer, hypercoagulable state, recent shock, congestive heart failure, severe burn, pregnancy and estrogen-based contraception.

Clinical Pretest Probability for Pulmonary Embolus

Low Pretest Probability	Intermediate Pretest Probability	High Pretest Probability
• No risk factors	• 1-2 risk factors	• > 2 risk factors
• Alternative diagnosis more likely	• Alternative diagnosis of similar likelihood	• Chest x-ray with oligemia or pulmonary infarct
• No leg swelling	• No $S_1Q_3T_3$ on ECG	• $S_1Q_3T_3$ pattern on ECG
• Normal vital signs	• Fairly normal chest x-ray	• Pleuritic chest pain
		• Sudden dyspnea

Suggested Work-up to Diagnose Pulmonary Embolus

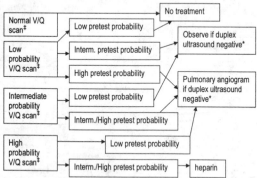

Note: consider empiric heparinization while work-up in progress. Interm. = intermediate
* all positive duplex ultrasound tests are treated with anticoagulation
‡ V/Q scan = ventilation perfusion scan (a spiral CT scan is an alternative imaging study)

Laboratory Evaluation for Possible Pulmonary Embolism
- Oxygen saturation can be normal or low with a pulmonary embolus
- ECG findings: sinus tachycardia, nonspecific ST/T wave changes +/- $S_1Q_3T_3$.
- Chest X-ray: normal or atelectasis +/- pleural effusion +/- a Hampton's hump
- Enzyme-linked immunosorbent assay D-Dimer ≤ 500 ng/mL carries a 98% negative predictive value to rule out a pulmonary embolus.

Methods to Exclude Pulmonary Emboli on Initial Presentation
- Normal pulmonary angiogram
- Normal ventilation/perfusion lung scan
- Normal spiral CT lung scan
- Normal D-Dimer level by enzyme-linked immunosorbent assay in all patients*
- Normal D-Dimer level by enzyme-linked immunosorbent assay, whole blood agglutination assay or latex-enhanced photometric immunoassay in a patient with low pretest probability

Methods to Exclude Pulmonary Emboli With an Indeterminate V/Q Scan
- Normal pulmonary angiogram
- Normal serial impedance plethysmography or serial compression ultrasonography (2-3 tests over a 2 week period) in patients with a low-intermediate pretest probability
- Normal D-Dimer level in patients with a low pretest probability

Excluding Pulmonary Emboli with Intermediate-High Pretest Probability
- Normal V/Q scan
- Normal spiral CT scan and normal compression ultrasonography scan
- Normal pulmonary angiogram

Methods to Exclude Pulmonary Emboli with an Elevated D-Dimer Test
- Normal V/Q scan
- Normal spiral CT scan and normal compression ultrasonography scan
- Normal pulmonary angiogram

Excluding Pulmonary Emboli with an Indeterminate V/Q Scan and an Elevated D-Dimer Test
- Normal pulmonary angiogram
- Serial compression ultrasonography scans with a low-intermediate pretest probability

References: JAMA, 1990; 263: 2753. Ann Intern Med, 1998; 129: 997, Annals Internal Med, 2001; 135: 08 and Annals Internal Medicine, 2003; 138: 941-51.
* study only had 201 patients so if patients have intermediate-high pretest probability would consider a secondary test to fully exclude a pulmonary embolism.

Definition: Platelet count < 150,000 cells/μL (abbreviated as 150K)

Clinical Presentation
- Asymptomatic, petechiae, purpura, ecchymoses, epistaxis, menorrhagia, hematuria, hematochezia or spontaneous intracranial bleeds

Risks of Complications at Different Platelet Counts
- > 50K: major surgery safe
- 20 – 50K: risk of major bleeding low
- 10 – 20K: risk of mild-mod. bleeding (low risk for spontaneous hemorrhage)
- <10K: high risk for spontaneous hemorrhage (especially if < 5K)
- Consider platelet transfusion if platelets < 5-10K or active bleeding (avoid in hemolytic uremic syndrome, thrombotic thrombocytopenic purpura +/- for severe idiopathic thrombocytopenic purpura).
  - ➢ 1 unit platelets usually increases platelet count ~10K

Etiologies
- **Pseudothrombocytopenia** (platelet clumping in 0.1% of all blood draws)
- **Decreased Platelet Production**
  - ➢ Congenital causes (May-Hegglin, Bernard-Soulier, aplastic anemia)
  - ➢ Myelodysplasia (> 60 years) or lymphoproliferative disorders
  - ➢ Meds/Toxins: alcohol, thiazides, estrogens, chemo-/radiation therapy
  - ➢ Vitamin deficiencies: B_{12} or folate
  - ➢ Infection: sepsis, tuberculosis, measles, HIV, rubella, mumps, parvovirus
- **Increased Platelet Destruction** (most common mechanism)

Immune-mediated
- ➢ Idiopathic thrombocytopenic purpura (ITP - diagnosis of exclusion)
- ➢ Systemic lupus erythematosus or transfusion reaction
- ➢ Meds: heparin, gold, quinine, quinidine, sulfa, valproate, carbamazepine, aspirin, nonsteroidal anti-inflammatory drugs, penicillin, digoxin, rifampin, cephalosporins, amphotericin B, amiodarone, indinavir, spironolactone, procainamide, ranitidine and allopurinol
- ➢ Infection: cytomegalovirus, hepatitis viruses, toxoplasmosis, HIV, varicella

Non-immune-mediated
- ➢ Disseminated intravascular coagulopathy, hemolytic uremic syndrome/ thrombotic thrombocytopenic purpura, vasculitis, prosthetic valve, Hemolysis Elevated Liver enzymes Low Platelets (HELLP syndrome) or malignant hypertension
- **Splenic sequestration** (platelets usually > 20K)
  - ➢ Portal hypertension, Gaucher's disease, lymphoma/leukemias, congestive right heart failure
- **Gestational** (5% of all pregnancies in late 3rd trimester. Platelets > 80 K)
- **Dilutional**: Usually follows massive blood transfusion

Work-up
- Good history/exam assessing spleen size, any lymphadenopathy & med list
- Examine peripheral blood smear for platelet clumping and schistocytes
- Are other cell lines and differential normal?
- Check mean platelet volume (MPV) – usually high with platelet destruction
- Labs: complete blood count with differential and coagulation studies (other labs will depend on most likely etiologies as above)
- Anti-platelet antibodies **not** useful for diagnosing ITP
- Consider bone marrow biopsy if etiology unclear or patient > 60 years

References: NEJM, 1994; 331: 1202-11. Ann Int Med, 1997; 126: 319-26. Lancet, 1997; 349: 1531-6.

Diagnosis
- Acute symptoms (cough +/- sputum, dyspnea, +/- fever, +/- chest pain)
- Exam: pulmonary rales or ronchi +/- egophony or tactile fremitus
- Chest x-ray almost always with an infiltrate (unless severe dehydration)

Pneumonia Patient Outcome Research Team (PORT) Prediction Rule
- Exclusion criteria: Age < 18, HIV+, admission within last 7 days

Characteristic	score	Comorbid Disease	score	Exam Findings	score	Laboratory Findings	score
Age	Age	Cancer	+30	AMS	+20	pH < 7.35*	+30
Female	-10	Liver disease	+20	RR ≥ 30	+20	BUN ≥ 30	+20
Nursing home resident	+10	CHF	+10	SBP < 90	+20	Na < 130	+20
		Cerebrovas-cular disease	+10	T ≤ 35ºC or T ≥ 40ºC	+15	Glucose > 250 mg/dL	+10
		Renal disease	+10	Pulse≥ 125	+10	Hct< 30%	+10
						PaO₂< 60	+10
						Pl. effusion	+10

CHF = congestive heart failure, AMS = altered mental status, RR = respiratory rate, SBP=systolic blood pressure, Pl. = pleural, Na = sodium, PaO₂ = partial pressure arterial oxygen, * pH from arterial blood sample, BUN = blood urea nitrogen, T = temperature and Hct = hematocrit

Risk Class	PORT score	Mortality (%)	Recommended care	* patient
I*	N/A	0.1	Outpatient	< 50 years &
II	≤ 70	0.6	Outpatient	no worrisome
III	71-90	0.9 - 2.8	Outpatient or inpatient	predictors as
IV	91-130	8.2 – 9.3	Inpatient	in table
V	>130	27.0 – 29.2	Inpatient	above

Recommended Diagnostic Studies for Outpatient treatment
- PA/Lateral Chest radiograph – examine for infiltrate/effusion
- Pulse oximetry
- Complete blood count, electrolytes, renal panel, +/- sputum culture & gram stain +/- pretreatment blood cultures x 2

Empiric Antibiotic Treatment for Community-acquired Pneumonia
- Outpatient therapy (patient < 65 years, no recent antibiotics or steroid use)
  - Macrolide (azithromycin 500 mg PO qd or clarithromycin 500 mg PO bid)
  - Doxycycline 100 mg PO bid
- Outpatient therapy (patient > 65 years or recent antibiotic or steroid use)
  - Respiratory fluoroquinolone (levofloxacin 500 mg PO qd, gatifloxacin 400 mg PO qd, moxifloxacin 400 mg PO qd, sparfloxacin 400 mg PO x 1→ 200 mg PO qd or ofloxacin 400 mg PO bid)
  - Amoxicillin-clavulanate 875 mg PO bid + either macrolide or doxycycline
- Duration of therapy typically 10-14 days.

References: CID, 2000; 31: 347-82. and Am J Respir Crit Care Med, 2001; 163: 1703-26.

Condition	Clinical Features	Diagnosis	Empiric Therapy
Amebiasis: diarrhea *Entamoeba histolytica*	Chronic diarrhea or dysentery	Stool ova and parasites examination positive *E. histolytica* titers positive	metronidazole 750 mg PO tid x 10 days followed by either paromomycin 500 mg PO tid x 7days **or** iodoquinol 650 mg PO tid x 20 days.
Amebiasis: Extraintestinal *Entamoeba histolytica* CID,1992; 15: 974-82	Right upper quadrant abdominal pain, fevers, chills, anorexia, nausea, (hepatic abscess usually right lobe & solitary)	*E. histolytica* titers positive Abscess aspirate "anchovy paste" appearance + sterile	Abscess drainage for: size > 5 cm, left hepatic lobe or refractory to antibiotics at 5 d
Balanitis	Multiple red papules and thick white exudate on glans of penis	Clinical diagnosis. potassium hydroxide prep of exudate positive for hyphae check blood sugar	Topical antifungal cream to penile glans bid **or** fluconazole 150 mg PO x 1 for refractory cases
Bites (animal)	Historical evidence of animal bite	Thorough cleansing and debridement of wound(s). Amoxicillin-clavulanate 875 mg PO bid x 5 days (prophylaxis) **or** doxycycline 100 mg PO bid x 10 days (if penicillin-allergic). Give tetanus shot if none in last 5 years.	
Blepharitis	Inflammation of the lid margin with erythema, scaling and yellow crusting	Clinical diagnosis. Exclude seborrheic blepharitis or ocular rosacea	Use 50:50 solution of baby shampoo to lid margin followed by warm compresses bid-tid. No role for antibiotics.

Condition	Clinical Features	Diagnosis	Empiric Therapy
Acute Bronchitis Ann Intern Med, 2001 134: 518-20	Acute cough < 3 weeks, +/- sputum production. Majority of cases from respiratory viruses including influenza. Rarely pertussis.	Exclude cough asthma and pneumonia. **Unlikely if** pulse <100, respiratory rate < 24, temperature < 38°C and no consolidative findings on exam	No role for antibiotics unless pertussis suspected. Consider empiric antivirals if influenza suspected & < 48hours of symptoms (see influenza)
Brucellosis **(Notifiable infection to state)** MMWR, 2001; 50(RR-2): 1-72	Fevers, chills, diaphoresis, weakness, headache, myalgias, arthralgias, bloody diarrhea Incubation period: 7-21 days	Ingestion of unpasteurized milk, goat cheese or contaminated meats. Positive blood culture or brucella serologies	doxycycline 100 mg PO bid – rifampin 600-900 mg PO qd x 6 weeks (>8 years) **or** trimethoprim-sulfamethoxasole 5 mg/kg trimethoprim IV q12h x 6 weeks + gentamicin 2 mg/kg IV/ qd x 2 weeks (< 8 years)
Cat Scratch Disease *(Bartonella henselae)* Ped. Infect. Dis. 1997; 16: 163-79	Papular/pustular lesion forms at puncture site with regional lymphadenopathy, infrequent fevers, nausea, splenomegaly. Usually self-limited disease	Clinical diagnosis. Positive serology by immunofixation or by polymerase chain reaction testing	Generally antibiotics not needed. In severe cases can use azithromycin 500 mg PO x 1 then 250 mg PO qd x 4 days.
Cellulitis Immunocompetent patient	Erythema, warmth, tenderness and swelling of affected area. Often fever, chills, leukocytosis and indistinct borders	Clinical diagnosis. Risk factors include chronic edematous states, morbid obesity, venous/lymphatic obstruction and skin puncture	dicloxacillin 250-500 mg PO bid **or** cephalexin 250-500 mg PO qid **or** erythromycin 500 mg PO qid **or** levaquin 500 mg FO qd x 10 days & extremity

Condition	Clinical Features	Diagnosis	Empiric Therapy
Cellulitis Immunosuppressed by Diabetes, alcohol abuse, AIDS or malignancy	Erythema, warmth, swelling and tenderness of affected area. +/- fever, chills, leukocytosis or systemic toxicity	Clinical diagnosis Deep venous thrombosis can mimic signs of cellulitis and may need to be excluded	amoxicillin-clavulanate 875 mg PO bid **or** clindamycin 600 mg PO tid + levofloxacin 500 mg PO qd x 10-14 days. Extremity elevation.
Cellulitis Erysipelas	Bright red, marked swelling, tenderness of affected area and sharp demarcation. 85% involves legs. ↑ Lymphatic involvement	Clinical diagnosis. Streptococcal cellulitis is frequently rapidly spreading	amoxicillin-clavulanate 875 mg PO bid **or** dicloxacillin 500 mg PO qid **or** erythromycin 500 mg PO qid x 10-14 days.
Chancroid *(Haemophilus ducreyi)* MMWR, 2002; 51 (RR-6): 1-80.	Small papule of genital area → a painful ulcer with grayish exudate. 2/3 with painful inguinal lymphadenitis. Sexually transmitted	Pleomorphic gram negative coccobacilli. Positive culture, polymerase chain reaction (PCR) or antibody tests	ceftriaxone 250 mg IM x 1 **or** azithromycin 1 gm PO x 1 **or** ciprofloxacin 500 mg PO bid x 3↑. Treat sex partners as well.
Chlamydia (urethritis or cervicitis) AFP, 2002; 65 (4): 673-6	Asymptomatic. Dysuria and urinary frequency or cervical discharge. Sexually transmitted.	PCR test on urine or enzyme immunoassay test on endocervical/urethral swab.	doxycycline 100 mg PO bid x 7d **or** azithromycin 1 gm PO x 1.
Cholera *(Vibrio cholerae)* Notifiable to state (Adapted from the CDC guidelines for the management of cholera)	Profuse watery diarrhea, vomiting, often severe dehydration. Source: contaminated water, fish/shellfish.	Stool culture	**If >12 yrs**, use ciprofloxacin 1 gm PO x1 **or** doxycycline 300 mg PO x 1. **If < 12 yrs**, trimethoprim-sulfamethoxazole 5 mg/kg based on trimethoprim PO bid x 3 days.

Condition	Clinical Features	Diagnosis	Empiric Therapy
Coccidiomycosis (Pulmonary)	High risk: African-American, pregnant, Southeast Asian, immunosuppressed patients. Subclinical infection 50-65%, 30% have self-limited pneumonitis with fatigue, **cough**, headache, myalgias, and 5% with reticulonodular or cavitary pneumonia.	Elevated coccidiomycosis complement fixation (CF) titers. Eosinophilia in 25%. Chest x-ray with interstitial or reticulonodular infiltrates, cavities or effusions	**Mild** pneumonia: supportive care **Moderate** pneumonia: fluconazole 400 mg PO qd x 1 month. **Severe** pneumonia: Amphotericin B 1 gram IV total dose then fluconazole 400 mg PO qd x 10-12 months.
Coccidiomycosis (Extrapulmonary)	Nonmeningeal: maculopapular, erythema multiforme or erythema nodosum rash, arthritis, osteomyelitis meningitis	Elevated coccidiomycosis CF titers (usually >1:32), Cocci spherules in tissue biopsy, positive bone scan or cerebrospinal fluid with lymphocytic pleocytosis and high protein/low glucose.	fluconazole 400 mg PO qd for lifetime. For meningitis, may use fluconazole 800–1,000 mg PO qd initially. Amphotericin B 1-2 grams total IV load initially for very severe cases
Cystitis CID 1999; 28: 745-58	Dysuria, urinary frequency, suprapubic pain and no fever or significant flank pain	midstream urine with significant pyuria or >10^3 bacteria/mm^3 + symptoms or ≥10^5 bacteria/mm^3	trimethoprim-sulfamethoxazole double-strength 1 tab PO bid **or** nitrofurantoin 100 mg PO qid x 7d **or** fluoroquinolone PO **or** nitrofurantoin 100 mg PO qid x 7d
Cystitis/Bacteriuria in Pregnancy	Same presentation and diagnostic criteria as cystitis		nitrofurantoin 100 mg PO qid **or** cephalexin 250 mg PO qid **or** trimethoprim-sulfamethoxazole double-strength 1 tab PO bid (14-36 wks pregnant) **or** amoxicillin 250 mg PO tid x 5-7days

Condition	Clinical Features	Diagnosis	Empiric Therapy
Diverticulitis (mild-moderate) Dis Col Rectum 2000; 43:289 Am J Gastro 1999; 94: 3110	Left>>right lower quadrant abdominal pain +/- fever, nausea, vomiting, anorexia or constipation	Clinical diagnosis, often leukocytosis, mild-moderate tenderness on exam. CT scan with diverticula	ciprofloxacin 500 mg PO bid + metronidazole 500mg PO qid **or** amoxicillin-clavulanate 875 mg PO bid x 7-10 d + clears
Epididymo-orchitis MMWR. 2002; 51 (RR-6): 1-80. J. Urology. 1995; 154: 209-13.	Scrotal pain, testicular and epididymal swelling & tenderness +/- dysuria and/or urinary frequency. Usually a sexually-transmitted disease if < 35 years old.	Clinical diagnosis. Urine may show sterile pyuria. Urethral discharge may test positive for gonorrhea or chlamydia.	**Age < 35:** ceftriaxone 250 mg IM + doxycycline 100mg PO bid x 10 days **or** ofloxacin 300 mg PO bid x 10 days. **Age > 35:** oral fluoroquinolone x 10-14 days
Gastroenteritis (mild)	≥3 unformed stools daily, duration <14 days, recent travel, ill contacts. Usually viral in etiology.	+/- fecal leukocytes +/- occult blood +/- stool cultures	Oral rehydration solutions + antimotility agents if afebrile and mild symptoms
Gastroenteritis (moderate-severe) CID 2001; 32: 331-51. Am J Gastro 1997; 92: 1962	≥3 unformed stools qd,duration<14d, recent travel, ill contacts, fever, abdominal cramps, anorexia, nausea and/or vomiting	fecal leukocytes present, +/- tenesmus, bloody diarrhea or dehydration. Positive stool cultures	ciprofloxacin 500 mg PO bid x 3 - 5 days. For severe symptoms, oral/IV rehydration and avoid antimotility agents
Giardiasis (Giardia lamblia) CID, 1997; 25: 545-50.	Transmission person-to-person or waterborne. Asymptomatic carriers or chronic watery diarrhea, nausea, steatorrhea + abdominal cramps	Positive stool ova and parasites exam or fecal enzyme-linked immunosor-bent assay for giardia antigen	metronidazole 250 mg PO tid **or** albendazole 400 mg PO qd x 5 days **or** furazolidone 100 mg PO qid x 7-10 days.

Condition	Clinical Features	Diagnosis	Empiric Therapy
Gonorrhea (Neisseria gonorrhea) urethritis/cervicitis	Asymptomatic carrier or urethral or cervical discharge. +/- dysuria, urinary frequency or pelvic pain	endocervical or urethral swab culture or enzyme-linked immunosorbent assay positive	ceftriaxone 125 mg IM x 1 or ofloxacin 400 mg PO x 1 or ciprofloxacin 500 mg PO x 1
Disseminated Gonococcal Infection MMWR, 2002; 51 (RR-6): 1-80.	Monoarticular arthritis, fever, tender skin vesiculopustules. Rarely heart, bone, liver or meninges involved	As above or isolating organism from joint, skin or blood	ceftriaxone 1 gm IV/IM qd or ciprofloxacin 400 mg IV q12h until improved x 24-48hrs then ciprofloxacin 500 mg PO bid x 7d
Granuloma inguinale (Calymmatobacterium granulomatis)	Subcutaneous nodules/papules in genital area erode into painless ulcers or become verrucous lesions	Wright stain of tissue smear or biopsy with Donovan bodies or culture of organism	trimethoprim-sulfamethoxazole DS 1 tab PO bid or doxycycline 100 mg PO bid x 3-4 weeks
Hordeolum (stye)	Infection of superficial sebaceous glands → mass along lid margin	Clinical diagnosis	Warm compresses bid-tid. Rarely excision required
Herpes Simplex Virus (labialis or gingivostomatitis)	painful vesicles or shallow ulcers of lip and/or mouth. Self-resolve in 7-14 days.	Tzanck prep of blister fluid with multi-nucleated giant cells or culture positive	Symptomatic relief with topical anesthetics or 5% acyclovir or 1% penciclovir ointment prn
Herpes Simplex Virus (genitalis) MMWR, 2002; 5ˡ (RR-6): 1-80.	Usually asymptomatic or painful vesicles or ulcers in genital area. Primary episode may have fever, myalgias and lymphadenopathy	**Primary outbreak:** acyclovir 400 mg PO tid or valacyclovir 1 gm PO bid or famciclovir 250 mg PO tid x 7-10 days. Diagnosis as above	**Recurrent outbreaks:** acyclovir 400 mg PO tid or famciclovir 125 mg PO bid or valacyclovir 500 mg PO bid x 5 days **Prophylaxis:** acyclovir 400 mg PO bid or valacyclovir 500 mg PO qd if ≥ 10 episodes/year.

Condition	Clinical Features	Diagnosis	Empiric Therapy
Impetigo	Contagious, skin infection. Primary lesion bullous or vesicular and usually with golden crust +/- itching	Clinical diagnosis. Lesions may become superinfected and if so appropriate therapy for cellulitis needed	Mupirocin ointment tid until lesions resolve **or** dicloxacillin 250 mg PO qid **or** cephalexin 250 mg PO qid x 10 days and antibacterial soap.
Influenza Prevention NEJM, 1999; 341: 1387	Abrupt onset of fever, headache, myalgias, malaise, cough, sore throat during winter months. Mild cases self-resolve in 5-7 days. Severe cases with influenza pneumonia or secondary bacterial pneumonia	Disease occurs in outbreaks. Isolation of virus in tissue culture or rapid detection of viral antigens by immunologic assays from throat/nasal swabs or sputum.	Influenza vaccination for high-risk: > 50, diabetes, renal failure, pregnancy, immunosuppressed, institutionalized, heart and lung disease. zanamivir 2 puffs inhaled qd **or** oseltamivir 75 mg PO qd during peak influenza season or in household contacts of index cases. **Avoid zanamivir in asthma**
Influenza Treatment Lancet, 2000; 355: 1845	Clinical features and diagnosis are same as above. All treatment should be started ≤ 48h of symptoms Influenza A treatment: amantadine **or** rimantadine 100 mg PO bid or 5 mg/kg/d (>1 year) x 7 days. Influenza A/B treatment: zanamivir 2 puffs inhaled bid **or** oseltamivir 75 mg PO bid x 5 days.		
Leptospirosis (*Leptospira interrogans*) CID, 1995; 21: 1. (Severe icteric form is Weil's disease)	Ingestion of contaminated water or infected animal tissue. Abrupt fever, rigors, myalgias, cough, headache, nausea, diarrhea **Weil's disease:** severe icteric form with acute renal failure.	Risk groups: farmers, ranchers, military, trappers. Positive blood/cerebrospinal fluid cultures or serologies. Polymerase chain reaction testing of fluids under investigation	**Mild infection:** doxycycline 100 mg PO bic **or** ampicillin 500 mg PO qid x 7 days **Weil's disease:** penicillin G 4 million units IV q4h x 7 days.

Condition	Clinical Features	Diagnosis	Empiric Therapy
Listeriosis (*Listeria monocytogenes*) CID, 1997; 24: 1.	Fever, chills, meningitis symptoms, gastroenteritis or shock. In pregnancy with intact membranes can cause chorioamnionitis or preterm labor.	Positive culture from cerebrospinal fluid, blood or amniotic fluid.	ampicillin 2 gm IV q4-6h **or** trimethoprim-sulfamethoxazole 20 mg/kg/d IV ÷ qid x 14 days (immunocompetent) or x 3-6 weeks (immunocompromised or meningitis).
Lyme Disease= (*Borrelia burgdorferi*) Early disease CID, 200; 31(S1):S1-14.	After tick bite, erythema chronicum migrans, 1st or 2nd-degree heart block, Bell's palsy, headache, arthralgias, fever, lymphadenopathy	Antibody positive by enzyme-linked immunoassay after 2-4 weeks, polymerase chain reaction testing in joint fluid or culture from skin biopsy.	doxycycline 100 mg PO bid **or** amoxicillin 500 mg PO tid x 14-21d. In endemic areas consider doxycycline 200 mg PO x 1 after a worrisome tick bite.
Lyme Disease (*Borrelia burgdorferi*) Late disease NEJM, 2001; 344: 115-25.	Lyme arthritis: large joints affected and arthritis is oligoarticular. Neuroborreliosis: meningitis, acute radiculopathy or encephalopathy Carditis: complete heart block	As above	Oral regimen as above x 28 days ceftriaxone 2 gm IV qd **or** penicillin G 4 million units IV q4h x 14-28 d for Lyme arthritis ceftriaxone 2 gm IV qd **or** penicillin G 4 million units IV q4h x 21-28 days
Lymphogranuloma venereum (*Chlamydia trachomatis*) MMWR, 2002; 51(RR-6): 1-80.	Incubation period 3-30 d. Painless papule/pustule→ small shallow ulcer→ painful inguinal lymph nodes (buboes)→ proctocolitis (late stage)	Positive culture of lymph node aspirate or infected tissue. > 1:64 complement fixation antibody titer	doxycycline 100 mg PO bid x 2* days **or** erythromycin 500 mg PO qid x 21 days. May need incision and drainage of buboes.

Condition	Clinical Features	Diagnosis	Empiric Therapy
Odontogenic infections	Uncomplicated dental infections present as dental caries and periodontitis with tooth pain and sensitivity to cold	Clinical diagnosis. Rule out parapharyngeal or other dental abscess. X-rays can rule out periapical abscess	Extract tooth + give amoxicillin-clavulanate 875 mg PO bid **or** penicillin VK 500 mg PO qid **or** clindamycin 450 mg PO qid x 10 days
Otitis Externa	Otalgia, ear pruritus +/- hearing impairment. Ear canal swollen & erythematous with yellowish debris. Risks: swimming and ear devices	Clinical diagnosis. Treat otitis suspension 4 drops qid **or** cipro/hydrocortisone suspension 3 drops bid x 5-7 days. If severe in a diabetic patient, ciprofloxacin 500-750 mg PO bid x 7-10 days. Ear wick for very edematous ear canals.	
Acute Otitis Media (AOM) NEJM, 2002; 347(15): 1169-74	Most cases are in children < 5 years and follow a viral upper respiratory infection. Otalgia, fever, irritability, ↓ hearing. Red, bulging tympanic membrane suggests bacterial cause	Red tympanic membrane with ↓ mobility. If tympanic membrane not bulging, many will use antibiotics only if patient unimproved in 2-3 days.	amoxicillin 80 mg/kg/d PO ÷tid x 10 d **or** azithromycin 10mg/kg PO x 1d then 5 mg/kg/d PO x 4d **or** clarithromycin 7.5 mg/kg PO bid x 10 days.
Otitis Media with effusion (OME)	Patient usually has no systemic symptoms, but may have decreased hearing.	Fluid behind non-inflammed tympanic membrane whose mobility is decreased. Fluid persisting > 3 months after AOM	Consider tympanostomy tubes if hearing impaired and speech delayed. No role for antibiotics.
Resistant otitis media	Resistant otitis media if AOM with unimproved symptoms ≥ 5 days on appropriate antibiotics	Symptoms of AOM should be much improved within 72 hrs on antibiotics. Uninfected fluid may persist in middle ear for 3 months	amoxicillin-clavulanate 90 mg/kg/d PO ÷ tid **or** cefuroxime 30 mg/kg/d PO ÷ bid x 10 d **or** ceftriaxone 50 mg/kg/d IM x 3d

Condition	Clinical Features	Diagnosis	Empiric Therapy
Recurrent otitis media (recurrent OM)	≥ 3 episodes acute otitis media (AOM) in 6 months or ≥ 4 episodes acute otitis media in 12 months.	Patient must have proven resolution after each episode of AOM to make diagnosis of recurrent OM	Suppressive antibiotics with amoxicillin 40 mg/kg PO qd **or** sulfisoxazole 50 mg/kg PO chs. May need tympanostomy tubes
Pelvic inflammatory disease (PID) MMWR, 2002; 51(RR-6).	**Risk factors:** multiple sexual partners, prior history, no condoms and poor. Lower abdominal pain < 2 weeks, onset during or just after menses, dyspareunia, cervical motion and adnexal tenderness +/- fever or purulent vaginal discharge	Clinical. +/- leukocytosis, high sedimentation rate, positive chlamydia or gonorrhea test or laparoscopic evidence of salpingitis	levofloxacin 500 mg PO qd + metronidazole 500 mg PO bid **or** ceftriaxone 250 mg IM x 1 + doxycycline 100 mg PO bid x 14 days. **Partner(s) must be evaluated**
Streptococcal pharyngitis Ann Int Med, 2001; 134: 509.	Sudden sore throat, tonsillar exudates, tender cervical lymphadenopathy and fever. Absent cough or rhinorrhea	Gold standard is throat culture. Rapid antigen test 20-30% false negative rate	Bicillin LA 1.2 MU IM x 1 **or** penicillin VK 500 mg bid **or** erythromycin 500 mg qid x 10 d
Acute prostatitis JAMA, 1999; 282: 236.	Suprapubic, perineal and/or testicular pain, irritative and/or obstructive urinary symptoms, fever and/or hematospermia	Tender, edematous prostate, pyuria and leukocytosis. No cystitis.	< 35 yrs: Treat as per PID > 35 yrs: PO fluoroquinolone **or** trimethoprim-sulfamethoxazole DS 1 tab PO bid x 14 days
Acute pyelonephritis CID 1999; 29: 745-58.	Cystitis symptoms, fever, flank pain and tenderness, abdominal pain, nausea, vomiting, and anorexia	Urine with marked pyuria usually with leukocyte casts, leukocytosis, positive urine culture	14 days of PO fluoroquinolone, trimethoprim-sulfamethoxazole DS 1 tab PO bid **or** amoxicillin-clavulanate 875 mg PO bid +/- ceftriaxone 2 gm IV/IM x 1

Condition	Clinical Features	Diagnosis	Empiric Therapy
Scabies and Head lice	Scabies: severely pruritic papules, worse at night in finger web spaces, wrists, elbows, knees, axillae, penis and umbilicus Head lice: itchy scalp	Scabies: Clinical diagnosis. Microscopic exam of skin scraping: mites/eggs/feces. Head lice: nits on hairshafts (comb out nits after meds)	For scabies: 5% permethrin cream apply from neck down → wash off in 8-12h. For head lice: 1% permethrin liquid x 10 minutes then wash off. lindane reserved for refractory cases.
Acute rhinosinusitis J All Clin Immun, 1998; 102 (6): 1-69	Purulent rhinorrhea, postnasal drip, facial pain, "sinus" headache, sinus tenderness and opaque transillumination of affected sinus Symptoms/signs ≤ 4 weeks	Clinical. Coronal sinus CT scan with mucosal thickening or sinus fluid or Waters view sinus x-rays with air/fluid levels	amoxicillin 250-500 mg PO tid or TMP/SMX DS 1 tab PO bid x 10 days. If refractory: amoxicillin-clavulanate 875 mg PO bid or cefuroxime 250 mg PO bid x 10-14 days.
Syphilis (1=Primary and 2=secondary) MMWR, 2002; 51 (RR-6): 1-80.	Sexually-transmitted disease. Primary syphilis: genital area papule → painless ulcer (chancre) Secondary syphilis: maculopapular rash on body with palms/soles +/- condylomata lata, lymphadenopathy or "moth-eaten" alopecia	Darkfield microscopy or direct fluorescent antibody testing of chancre or skin/genital lesions or positive VDRL or RPR test confirmed by positive FTA test	Primary syphilis or non-neuro secondary syphilis < 1 year : benzathine penicillin 2.4 million units IM x 1. Latent syphilis (secondary syphilis > 1 year): benzathine penicillin 2.4 million units IM qweek x 3.
Syphilis (tertiary) NEJM, 1992; 326: 1060	Cutaneous or visceral gummas (mass lesions in brain or viscera), aortitis or neurosyphilis (stroke, meningitis or asymptomatic)	Serologic testing as above. Cerebrospinal fluid (CSF) with lymphocytes, + protein VDRL +/- ↓glucose/↑protein	Neurosyphilis: penicillin G 4 million units IV q4h x 10 – 14 days. Gummas or aortitis: benzathine penicillin 2.4 million units IM qweek x 3

VDRL = venereal disease research laboratory, RPR = rapid plasma regain, FTA = fluorescent treponemal antibody test, TMP/SMX = trimethoprim-sulfamethoxazole

Condition	Clinical Features	Diagnosis	Empiric Therapy
Trichinosis (*Trichinella spiralis*) Prog Clin Parasitol, 1994; 4: 117.	Eating undercooked infected pork. **Intestinal stage:** asymptomatic or abdominal cramps, vomiting, diarrhea. **Muscle stage:** subungual splinter, conjunctival & retinal hemorrhages, chemosis, myalgias, weakness. **Late complications:** arrhythmias, myocarditis, meningoencephalitis or pneumonia	Positive antibody enzyme-linked immunoassay test after > 3 weeks infestation or biopsy of symptomatic muscle near tendinous insertion identifying trichinella larvae.	Mild infections self-limited and do not require meds. Infection of brain, heart or lungs: albendazole 400 mg PO bid **or** mebendazole 400 mg PO tid x 14 days + prednisone 40-60 mg PO qd x 7 days then taper off over 7 days
Vaginitis (*Bacterial vaginosis*) MMWR, 2002; 51 (RR-6): 1-80.	Asymptomatic: vaginal discharge or occasionally vaginal and/or vulvar pruritus	Any 3 of the following: • watery vaginal discharge • "clue cells" on wet mount • "fishy" odor when discharge mixed with potassium hydroxide • vaginal pH >4.5	metronidazole 500 mg PO bid **or** clindamycin 300 mg PO bid x 7 days. **or** 0.75% metronidazole cream 1 applicator intravaginally qhs x 5 days. Treat partner if he has balanitis or exudate on glans.
Vaginitis (Yeast)	Asymptomatic or commonly a pruritic, thick, "cheesy", white vaginal discharge	potassium hydroxide prep of discharge with fungal hyphae	Antifungal cream qhs x 7 c **or** fluconazole 150 mg PO x 1
Vaginitis (*Trichomonas vaginalis*) MMWR, 2002; 51 (RR-6): 1-80.	Asymptomatic or commonly with frothy, malodorous vaginal discharge', "strawberry cervix" and/or vaginal/vulvar pruritus	Wet prep of discharge with trichomonads. Vaginal pH > 5	metronidazole 2 gm PO x 1 **or** 500 mg PO bid x 7 days. Must treat patient and partner.

Condition	Clinical Features	Diagnosis	Empiric Therapy
Warts Anogenital MMWR, 2002; 51 (RR-6): 1-80.	Sexually-transmitted. Human papilloma virus-related. Appearance pink, painless, verrucous growths often coalescing in anogenital area	Clinical diagnosis. 5% acetic acid applied to penis/scrotum can identify subclinical flat warts that can transmit human papilloma virus	**Patient applied:** podofilox cream bid x 3 consecutive days/week x 4 wks or imiquimod cream applied for 6-10 hours 3x/week x 16 weeks. **Physician-applied:** 25% podophyllin x 4 hr qweek or cryotherapy q2week
Warts Cutaneous	Dome-shaped gray-brown hyperkeratotic papules on extremities. Flat or filiform growths on face. Cut edge reveals black dots representing thrombosed capillaries	Clinical diagnosis. Differential diagnosis includes calluses or corns (which retain their skin lines). Warts lack skin lines.	Topical salicylic acid, electrocautery or cryotherapy for common and filiform warts. 0.025% Retin A or 5% Efudex cream qhs for flat facial warts

Complications of HIV Infection by CD4 count

CD4 count	Infectious	Non-infectious
> 500	Acute retroviral syndrome, vaginal candidiasis	Lymphadenopathy, Guillain-Barre, aseptic meningitis
200-500	Pneumonia, sinusitis, pulmonary tuberculosis (Tb), thrush, zoster, Kaposi's sarcoma, cryptosporidiosis, Oral Hairy Leukoplakia	B-cell or Hodgkin's lymphoma, anemia, idiopathic thrombocytopenic purpura, cervical dysplasia/cancer, mononeuritis multiplex
50-200	Pneumocystis carinii pneumonia, disseminated herpes simplex, toxoplasmosis, cryptococcosis, histoplasmosis, coccidiomycosis or Tb, microsporidiosis & prog. multifocal leukoencephalopathy	HIV wasting, HIV dementia, Central Nervous System or immunoblastic lymphoma, HIV cardiomyopathy, peripheral neuropathy, myelopathy or polyradiculopathy
< 50	Disseminated cytomegalovirus/Mycobacterium avium complex	

Estimated Risk of Infective Endocarditis with Various Cardiac Conditions

High Risk	Moderate Risk	Negligible Risk
• Prosthetic valve • Prior bacterial endocarditis • Cyanotic congenital heart disease • Systemic - pulmonary shunts or conduits	• Noncyanotic congenital ht. disease • Mitral valve prolapse & mitral regurgitation • Acquired valvular heart disease • Hypertrophic cardiomyopathy	• Mitral valve prolapses & no mitral regurgitation • Innocent murmur • Prior coronary bypass • Prior rheumatic fever • Cardiac pacemaker • Atrial septal defect • Post-op ASD, VSD or PDA

ASD = Atrial septal defect, VSD = ventricular septal defect, PDA = patent ductus arteriosus

Bacterial Endocarditis Prophylaxis for Various Procedures

Endocarditis Prophylaxis Indicated	Endocarditis Prophylaxis Not Indicated

• Dental extractions or cleaning
• Dental implants
• Periodontal procedures
• Cleaning with gingival/mucosal bleeding
• Subgingival surgery
• Orthodontic banding
• Root canal operations
• Tonsillectomy/adenoidectomy
• Rigid bronchoscopy
• Surgery involving respiratory mucosa
• Variceal sclerotherapy
• Esophageal stricture dilatation
• Endoscopic retrograde cholangiopancreatography
• Biliary tract surgery
• Surgery involving GI mucosa
• Prostate surgery
• Cystoscopy
• Urethral dilatation
• Open heart surgery
• Urethral catheterization if urinary tract infection present
• Vaginal delivery with chorioamnionitis
	• Restorative dentistry
	• Placement of oral appliances
	• Suture removal from mouth
	• Cardiac catheterization or angioplasty
	• Endotracheal intubation
	• Flexible bronchoscopy *
	• Tympanostomy tubes
	• Trans-esophageal echocardiogram*
	• Upper/Lower endoscopy*
	• Vaginal hysterectomy*
	• Uncomplicated vaginal delivery*
	• In absence of infection:
	  ➤ Sterilization operations
	  ➤ Cesarean section
	  ➤ Intrauterine device insertion or removal
	  ➤ Therapeutic abortion
	  ➤ Uterine dilatation and curettage
	  ➤ Skin biopsy
	  ➤ Circumcision
	  ➤ Laparoscopy
	• Defibrillator or pacemaker insertion

* prophylaxis may be given to high-risk patients

References: JAMA, 1997; 277: 1794-1801 and NEJM, 1995; 332 (1): 38-44.

Prophylaxis for Bacterial Endocarditis in Adults

For dental, oral, respiratory tract or esophageal procedures	
Standard prophylaxis	amoxicillin 2 gm PO 1 hour before procedure
Unable to take oral meds	ampicillin 2 gm IM/IV 30 minutes before procedure
penicillin-allergic	clindamycin 600 mg PO **or** cephalexin 2 gm PO **or** azithromycin 500 mg PO **or** clarithromycin 500 mg PO 1 hour before procedure
penicillin-allergic and unable to take oral meds	clindamycin 600 mg IV **or** cefazolin 1 gm IM/IV 30 minutes before procedure
For genitourinary and gastrointestinal procedures (excluding the esophagus)	
High-risk patients	ampicillin 2 gm IV/IM plus gentamicin 1.5 mg/kg (up to 120 mg) IV/IM 30 minutes before procedure; ampicillin 1 gm IV/IM or amoxicillin 1 gm PO 6 hrs after procedure
High-risk patients allergic to penicillin	vancomycin 1 gm IV over 1-2 hours plus gentamicin 1.5 mg/kg (up to 120 mg) IV 30 minutes before procedure.
Intermediate-risk patients	amoxicillin 2 gm PO or ampicillin 2 gm IV/IM 30 minutes before procedure
Intermediate-risk patients allergic to penicillin	vancomycin 1 gm IV over 1-2 hours completed within 30 minutes of procedure.

Prophylaxis for Bacterial Endocarditis in Children

For dental, oral, respiratory tract or esophageal procedures	
Standard prophylaxis	amoxicillin 50 mg/kg PO 1 hour before procedure
Unable to take oral meds	ampicillin 50 mg/kg IM/IV 30 minutes before procedure
penicillin-allergic	clindamycin 20 mg/kg PO **or** cephalexin 50 mg/kg PO **or** azithromycin 15 mg/kg PO **or** clarithromycin 15 mg/kg PO 1 hour before procedure
penicillin-allergic and unable to take oral meds	clindamycin 20 mg/kg IV **or** cefazolin 25 mg/kg IM/IV within 30 minutes of procedure
For genitourinary and gastrointestinal procedures (excluding the esophagus)	
High-risk patients	ampicillin 50 mg/kg IV/IM plus gentamicin 1.5 mg/kg (up to 120 mg) IV/IM 30 minutes before procedure. Then, ampicillin 25 mg/kg IV/IM or amoxicillin 25 mg/kg PO 6 hours after procedure
High-risk patients allergic to penicillin	vancomycin 20 mg/kg IV over 1-2 hours plus gentamicin 1.5 mg/kg (up to 120 mg) IV both completed within 30 minutes of procedure.
Intermediate-risk patients	amoxicillin 50 mg/kg PO or ampicillin 50 mg/kg IV/IM 30 minutes before procedure
Intermediate-risk patients allergic to penicillin	vancomycin 20 mg/kg IV over 1-2 hours completed within 30 minutes of procedure.

References: JAMA, 1997; 277: 1794-1801 and NEJM, 1995; 332 (1): 38-44.

Baseline Diagnostic Studies

Test	Whom to test	Frequency of testing
HIV-1 serology	All patients	Baseline only
Total CD4 count	All patients	Every 3-4 months
HIV-1 RNA by PCR	All patients	Every 3-4 months
Complete blood count with differential	All patients	As needed
Full chemistry panel	All patients	As needed
VDRL	All patients	Annually
Purified protein derivative (PPD) skin test	If no history of positive PPD or tuberculosis	Annually
Toxoplasma antibody titer	Sulfa-allergic patients	Baseline if CD4 <200 cells/µL
Varicella zoster antibody titer	Unknown history of chickenpox infection	Baseline
Hepatitis B virus antigen and antibody tests	All patients	Baseline
Hepatitis C virus antibody	History of intravenous drug use or transfusion	Baseline
G6PD level	African-Americans	Baseline
Pap smear	All women	Consider every 6 months

G6PD = Glucose-6-phosphate dehydrogenase, VDRL = venereal disease research laboratory, RNA = ribonucleic acid and PCR = polymerase chain reaction

Vaccinations

- Influenza vaccine yearly
- Pneumovax q10 years
- HBV vaccine series
- Hepatitis A Virus vaccine series
- Tetanus q10 years

When to Consider Initiation of Highly-Active Antiretroviral Therapy

- Symptomatic HIV infection regardless of CD4 count/viral load
- Asymptomatic HIV infection if < 350 CD4 T cells/mm³
- Asymptomatic HIV infection if quantitative HIV-1 ribonucleic acid (RNA) > 55,000 copies/mL by b-deoxyribonucleic acid (bDNA) or reverse transcriptase-polymerase chain reaction assays
- Needlestick prophylaxis
- Compliant, motivated and capable individuals

Prophylaxis for Opportunistic Infections

Infection	CD4 count	Preferred medication prophylaxis
Pneumocystis carinii pneumonia	< 200 cells/ µL	trimethoprim-sulfamethoxazole DS 1 tablet PO qd or dapsone 100 mg PO qd
Toxoplasma gondii	< 100 cells/ µL	trimethoprim-sulfamethoxazole DS 1 tablet PO qd or (dapsone 50 mg PO qd + pyrimethamine 50 mg PO qwk + leucovorin 25 mg PO qwk)
Mycobacterium avium complex	< 50 cells/ µL	azithromycin 1200 mg PO qwk or clarithromycin 500 mg PO bid or rifabutin 300 mg PO qd
History of salmonellosis	Any	Consider chronic ciprofloxacin 500 mg PO qd for history of severe salmonella septicemia
Varicella zoster	Any	Varicella zoster immune globulin 1.25 mL x 5 vials IM by 96 hours of exposure
+ PPD skin test	Any	Isoniazid 300 mg PO qd + pyridoxine 50 mg PO qd x 9 months

Note: Would recommend that HIV-positive patients be cared for in collaboration with an HIV specialist as the spectrum of disease is broad & rapidly changing. Check www.hivatis.org or www.aidsinfo.nih.gov/guidelines.

Adapted from 2003 Department of Health and Human Services Clinical Practices for HIV treatment

Drug	Side Effect	%	Side Effect	%
Abacavir[1] Ziagen	Nausea vomiting	5-15%	Insomnia	2-7%
	Fever, Rash	3 & 7%	Diarrhea	1-12%
	Dizziness	5-10%	Hypersensitivity	3-5%
Adefovir dipivoxil	Prox tube dysfunction	18-38%	Diarrhea	5%
	AST/ALT/CK elevation	2-4%	Nausea	5-8%
Amprenavir[3] Agenerase	Rash	18%	Headache	7-44%
	Nausea	10-33%	Vomiting	15%
Delavirdine[2] Rescriptor	Rash	10-18%	Fatigue	3-5%
	Headache	3-11%	Diarrhea	4%
Didanosine[1] Videx, ddI	Diarrhea	15-28%	Periph. Neuropathy	2-20%
	Pancreatitis	5-9%	AST/ALT elevation	6-10%
Efavirenz[2] Sustiva	CNS effects	52%	AST/ALT elevation	2%
	Rash	5-10%		
Hydroxyurea Hydrea, Doxia	↓ WBC, platelets, Hgb	15%each	Stomatitis, rash	8 & 6%
	Nausea, headache	5&12%	AST/ALT elevation	2%
Indinavir[3] Crixivan	Nephrolithiasis	3-5%	Abdominal pain	9%
	Elevated bilirubin	10%	Headache	6%
	Nausea	12%	Vomiting, diarrhea	4 & 5%
Lamuvidine[1] Epivir, 3TC	Headache, fatigue	8 & 4%	Nausea, insomnia	4% each
Nelfinavir[3] Viracept	Diarrhea	14-32%	Nausea	3-7%
Nevirapine[2] Viramune	Rash	17-24%	Fever	5-10%
	Nausea	7-11%	AST/ALT/GGT high	3-8%
	Headache	7-10%	Steven Johnson's	0.5%
Ritonavir[3] Norvir	Nausea, Headache	26 & 5%	Asthenia	9-14%
	Diarrhea	13-21%	Perioral dysesthesia	3-6%
	Altered taste	5-15%	Hyperlipidemia	2-8%
	Anorexia, Vomiting	3-15%	AST/ALT elevation	5-6%
Saquinavir[3] Fortovase, Invirase	Diarrhea	20%	Headache	5%
	Nausea, abd. Pain	11 & 9%	Fatigue	5%
	Dyspepsia, flatulence	8 & 8%	AST/ALT elevation	2-6%
Stavudine[1] Zerit, d4T	Periph. Neuropathy	13-24%	GI upset	4-6%
	AST/ALT elevation	5-10%	Headache	3-5%
Zalcitabine[1] Hivid, ddC	Periph. Neuropathy	10-30%	Stomatitis	2-17%
	Rash	10-20%		
Zidovudine[1] Retrovir, AZT, ZDV	Headache	12-18%	Myopathy/Myalgia	6-18%
	Neutropenia	2-31%	Fatigue, Anemia	2-7%
	Nausea or vomiting	4-26%	Insomnia	4-5%

1 Nucleoside reverse transcriptase inhibitors (NRTIs), 2 Nonnucleoside reverse transcriptase inhibitors (NNRTIs), 3 Protease inhibitors. AST = aspartate aminotransferase, ALT = alanine aminotransferase, CK = creatinine phosphokinase, CNS = central nervous system, WBC = white blood count, Hgb = hemoglobin, GGT = gamma glutamyl transpeptidase, abd. = abdominal, GI = gastrointestinal and periph. = peripheral

Reference: Clin Infect Dis 2000; 30 (Suppl 2): S96.
Reproduced with permission from the Tarascon Adult Emergency Pocketbook, 2nd Ed., Tarascon Publishing.

Typical Cerebrospinal Fluid Parameters

	Normal	Bacteria	Viral	Fungal	TB	Abscess
WBC/ml	0-5	> 1000[1]	< 1000	100-500	100-500	10-1000
%PMN	0-15	> 80[1]	< 50	< 50	< 50	< 50
%lymph	> 50	< 50	> 50	> 80	↑ Monos	varies
Glucose	45-65	< 40	45-65	30-45	30-45	45-60
Ratio[2]	0.6	< 0.4	45-65	< 0.4	< 0.4	0.6
Protein[3]	20-45	> 150	50-100	100-500	100-500	> 50
Pressure[4]	6-20	> 25-30	Variable	> 20	> 20	variable

1 – early meningitis may have lower numbers, 2 – CSF/blood glucose ratio,
3 – mg/dl, 4 - opening pressure in cm H_2O Adapted from EM Reports 1998; 19:94.
Reproduced with permission from the Tarascon Adult Emergency Pocketbook, 2nd Ed., Tarascon Publishing.

Epidemiology of Meningitis

- Majority of cases comprise acute aseptic meningitis ~75,000 cases/year
  - ➢ Most aseptic meningitis in children during summer months of viral etiology
- ~5800 cases of bacterial meningitis annually
- Adult fatality rate for bacterial meningitis 20-25%

Case-fatality rate for different pathogens: *Streptococcus pneumoniae* - 24%, *Listeria monocytogenes* - 40%, *Staphylococcus aureus* - 20%

Microbiology of Meningitis by Age Group

- < 2 months: Group B streptococcus, listeria, E. coli
- 2 months: 50 years - pneumococcus, meningococcus, H. flu
- > 50 years: listeria, gram negative rods, pneumococcus, meningococcus, H. flu
- Hematologic malignancy: listeria, pneumococcus, meningococcus, H. flu

Clinical Presentation of Meningitis

- Most common is subacute presentation that progresses over 3-5 days
- Acute onset of symptoms over the course of a day
- Fulminant course with rapid deterioration over hours to 1 day
- Children with prodromal upper respiratory infection in 75%, fever in 85%, lethargic +/- irritable, nuchal rigidity in 60-80%, 50-60% with nausea/vomiting
  - ➢ 10% of children present comatose*
  - ➢ Seizures in 20-30% (most common with pneumococcus or H. flu)*
  - ➢ Focal neurologic deficits in 7%*
  - ➢ 25% meningococcal meningitis: maculopapular rash, petechiae or purpura
  - ➢ 15% pneumococcal meningitis* presents in shock
- Adults with frontal headache, photophobia, nausea/vomiting, lethargy, malaise, fever in 85%, nuchal rigidity in 90% and seizures in 5-10%

*These data were obtained before routine immunizations given for *Haemophilus influenzae* and pneumococcus and likely are considerably less frequent in immunized children.
H. flu = *Haemophilus influenzae*

References: Infectious Disease Clinics of North America, 1999; 13 (3): 579-94.

Screening for Tuberculosis (Tb)
- Positive PPD (purified protein derivative) test is evidence of prior tuberculosis infection, but not necessarily evidence of active tuberculosis disease.

Whom to Screen:
- Children at 12 months and at preschool age and pregnant patients
- High-risk subgroups: patients > 65 yrs, gastrectomy, gastric bypass, immunosuppressed (HIV-positive, diabetes, renal failure, chronic steroid/immunosuppressive therapy, head/neck or hematologic malignancies), silicosis, organ transplant patients, malabsorptive syndromes, alcoholics, intravenous drug users, close contacts of patients with active pulmonary tuberculosis, immigrants from endemic areas, medically underserved, low socioeconomic class, and residents/employees of long-term care facilities, jails and hospitals
  > High-risk patients should be screened annually
- Chronic cough, hemoptysis, unexplained weight loss/fevers/sweats

PPD Test Positive if (measure induration in transverse axis only)
- ≥ 5 mm: close contacts with active Tb, HIV-positive or chest x-ray findings consistent with old tuberculosis
- ≥10 mm: all high-risk patients as above (excluding those in 5 mm category)
- ≥15 mm: all other patients
- Interpret irrespective of prior bCG (bacillus Calmette-Guerin) vaccine

Management of Positive PPD
- Check chest x-ray for evidence of active or old infection.
- Abnormal chest x-ray → 3 morning sputa for acid-fast bacilli smear and culture.
- Treat for latent Tb infection if PPD + and acid-fast bacilli smear negative x 3
- If acid-fast bacilli smear or culture positive, treat as active tuberculosis

Latent Tuberculosis infection
- isoniazid (INH) 5 mg/kg/d up to 300 mg qd
- pyridoxine 1-2 mg/kg/d to 50 mg qd: minimizes INH-induced neuropathy
- Duration 6 months (adults), 9 months (children) and 9-12 months HIV+

Active Pulmonary Tuberculosis
- Symptoms: cough, fever, sweats, weight loss, anorexia and malaise
- Generally start 4 drug therapy x 2 months then continue 2 drugs (based on acid-fast bacilli sensitivities) x 4 months
  > For isoniazid-containing regimens, add pyridoxine to minimize neuropathy.
- Monitor for adverse med reactions and monthly sputum samples
- Patients **not** infectious if: adequate meds x 2-3 weeks, good clinical response and sputum acid-fast bacilli smear negative x 3

Medication	Monitoring	Adverse reactions
isoniazid	Liver panel	Hepatitis, neuropathy
rifampin	Liver panel	Orange urine, GI upset, hepatitis, rash
pyrazinamide	Liver panel, uric acid	GI upset, hepatitis, gout, arthralgias
ethambutol	Visual acuity	Optic neuritis
streptomycin	Hearing, renal panel	Nephrotoxicity, ototoxicity

Reference: Am Fam Physician, 2000; 61: 2667-82.

Definitions:
- Acute renal failure: The rapid decline in the glomerular filtration rate with the consequent retention of nitrogenous waste products.
- Oliguria: urine output < 400 cc/day
- Anuria: urine output < 100 cc/day

Classification and Causes of Acute Renal Failure (ARF):
- **Causes of Prerenal Azotemia**
  - Hypovolemia
  - Distributive shock (sepsis, anaphylaxis or neurogenic)
  - Decreased effective circulating volume (chronic CHF, nephrotic syndrome, decompensated cirrhosis or "third spacing" of fluids)
  - Decreased cardiac output (cardiogenic shock or pericardial tamponade)
- **Causes of Postrenal Azotemia**
  - Bilateral ureteral obstruction
  - Bladder outlet obstruction (benign prostatic hypertrophy, bladder stone or cancer of the cervix, bladder or prostate)
  - Neurogenic bladder
  - Urethral stricture
- **Causes of Acute Glomerulonephritis (AGN)**
  - Systemic illnesses: systemic lupus erythematosus, Wegener's granulomatosis, Goodpasture's disease and polyarteritis nodosa
  - Immunoglobulin A (IgA) nephropathy
  - Alport's syndrome
  - Henoch Schonlein purpura
  - Infectious: hepatitis B virus, hepatitis C virus, sepsis, endocarditis, HIV and post-streptococcal
  - Malignancy
  - Mixed cryoglobulinemia (often hepatitis C virus-related)
- **Causes of Acute Tubular Necrosis (ATN)**
  - Post-ischemic
  - Medications/toxins: aminoglycosides, cisplatinum, cyclosporin A, amphotericin B, methotrexate, foscarnet, pentamidine, tetracycline, arsenic, chromium, contrast dyes
  - Hypercalcemia
  - Pigment-related: severe hemolysis or rhabdomyolysis
  - Myeloma kidney
- **Acute Interstitial Nephritis (AIN)**
  - Malignancies: lymphoma or leukemia
  - Medications (90% of AIN): penicillins, cephalosporins, sulfas, NSAIDS, ciprofloxacin, thiazide diuretics, furosemide, phenytoin, phenobarbital, carbamazepine, ranitidine, cimetidine, allopurinol, rifampin, ethambutol, erythromycin, acyclovir, tetracycline, vancomycin and azathioprine

Clinical Presentation of ARF
- Asymptomatic
- Fatigue/lethargy/generalized weakness
- Palpitations or arrhythmia-related syncope
- Congestive heart failure or anasarca
- Uremia: somnolence, pericarditis, asterixis, nausea, anorexia or pruritus

Urinary Studies in ARF

Subtype	Urinary sediment	UNa (mmol/L)	Protein (mg/dL)	FENa (%)	FEurea* (%)
Prerenal	Bland	< 20	0	< 1	< 35
Postrenal	Bland	Usually >20	0	> 1	> 35
AGN	RBC casts	< 20	M/H	< 1	< 35
ATN	Gran. casts	> 20	S/M	> 1	> 35
AIN	WBC casts	> 20	S/M	> 1	> 35

U = urine, S = serum, crt = creatinine, BUN = blood urea nitrogen, Na = sodium, RBC = red blood cells,
WBC = white blood cells, Gran. = granular, M = moderate (100-300), H = high (> 300), S = small (< 100)
FENa = fractional excretion of sodium = (UNa x Scrt)/(Ucrt x SNa) x 100
FEurea = fractional excretion of urea = (Uurea x Scrt)/(Ucrt x BUN) x 100
* more useful measure when patient receiving diuretics

Work-up of ARF
- Thorough investigation of medication list
- Calculate FENa or FEurea using equations above and check urinary sediment
- Place a foley catheter and measure the postvoid residual
- 24 hour urine for protein and creatinine clearance
- Renal ultrasound (for size and to check for hydronephrosis/hydroureter)
- Labs to consider depending on classification of ARF and likely causes: urine eosinophils (present in 30% of AIN), complete blood count, electrolytes, renal panel, calcium, phosphate, hepatitis B and C virus serologies, HIV test, anti-streptolysin O titer, anti-glomerular basement membrane antibody, antineutrophil cytoplasmic antibody, antinuclear antibody, complement studies, serum cryoglobulins, blood cultures, serum and urine protein electrophoreses
- When to perform a renal biopsy
  ➤ There is no unanimous consensus about this issue.
  ➤ Reasonable approach is to biopsy patients with an active urinary sediment or who have an unexplained intrarenal process (AGN, ATN or AIN)

Indication for Acute Dialysis (mnemonic AEIOU)
- A – **A**cidosis: persistent arterial pH < 7.2
- E – **E**lectrolytes: hyperkalemia
- I – **I**ntoxications or overdoses
- O – fluid **O**verload
- U – **U**remia

References: NEJM, 1996; 334 (22): 1448-60. NEJM, 1997; 336 (12): 870-1. J. Amer. Soc. Neph., 1999; 10 (8): 1833-9. J. Amer. Soc. Neph., 1998; 9 (4): 710-8 and J. Amer. Soc. Neph., 1998; 9 (3): 506-15.

Select Etiologies (diabetes and hypertension account for 66% of all cases)

• Diabetes mellitus	• Hypertension	• Polycystic kidney disease
• Glomerulonephritis	• Alport's syndrome	• Medullary sponge kidney
• Reflux nephropathy	• Myeloma kidney	• Analgesic nephropathy
• Sarcoidosis	• Amyloidosis	• Chronic obstructive uropathy
• Lupus nephritis	• IgA nephropathy	• Hypercalcemic nephropathy

Work-up of Chronic Renal Failure (CRF)

- History of any systemic diseases or medication usage that may cause CRF?
- Renal ultrasound to assess size and cortical appearance of kidneys
  - ➤ Kidneys tend to be small and cortex exhibits increased echogenicity
- 24 hour urine for creatinine clearance (CrCl)
- Labs: complete blood count, full chemistry panel, HIV and hepatitis B and C virus serologies, intact parathyroid hormone level (iPTH), lipid panel & other labs based on clinical evaluation.

Clinical Presentation

- Asymptomatic
- Uremia: anorexia, nausea, lassitude, pruritus, confusion and lethargy
- Pericarditis (uremic)
- Pulmonary edema +/- anasarca

Typical Lab Findings

• Normocytic anemia	• Hyperkalemia	• Anion gap acidosis
• High blood urea nitrogen (BUN) and creatinine	• Hypocalcemia
• Mild hyponatremia	• Hypermagnesemia	• Hyperphosphatemia

Management

- Blood pressure: keep BP < 130/80 or < 125/75 for overt proteinuria
  - ➤ Best agents are ACEIs or ARBs following potassium, BUN + creatinine.
  - ➤ Use extreme caution starting ACEI or ARB if serum creatinine > 2.5 mg/dL
- Erythropoietin 40-60 units/kg subcutaneous qweek – 3x/week to maintain hemoglobin 11-12 mg/dL.
- Refer patient to nephrologist when CrCl < 25 cc/min.
- Refer patient to surgeon for dialysis access when CrCl < 20 cc/min.
  - ➤ Protect non-dominant arm from venipunctures, IVs or BP checks
- Maintain serum bicarbonate > 18 mmol/L with sodium citrate 30 cc bid or Shohl's solution
  - ➤ Avoid if patient already fluid overloaded
- Dietician consult for low sodium/potassium/phosphate/protein diet
- Initiate multivitamin 1 tablet PO qd and folate 1 mg PO qd
- Calcium acetate 667 mg 2 tablets PO tid with meals
- Calcitriol titrated to iPTH level at upper limit of normal
- Renally dose all medications
- Consider GI prophylaxis with famotidine 20 mg PO qd
- Avoid: phenytoin, meperidine, fleets enemas, milk of magnesia, magnesium citrate, magnesium-aluminum antacids, nitrofurantoin and caution with digoxin and antiarrhythmics
- Lifestyle changes: smoking cessation, weight loss and lipid control
- Vaccinations: hepatitis B, influenza and pneumovax
- Indications for dialysis: refractory acidosis (pH<7.2), severe hyperkalemia, calcium/phosphate product ≥ 70, fluid overload and uremia

References: Mayo Clin. Proc., 1999; 74: 269-73. NEJM, 1998; 339: 1054-62 and 1448-56.

Folstein Mini-Mental Status Exam

Score	Orientation, Registration, Attention, Recall, Language/praxis
5	What is the year, season, date, day, month?
5	Where are we (city, state, country, hospital, floor)?
3	Name 3 objects: one second to say each. Ask patient for all 3 after you have said them. 1 point for each correct answer.
5	Serial 7s backward from 100 (stop after 5X) or spell WORLD backwards
3	Ask 3 objects above to be repeated. 1 point for each correct answer
2	Show pencil & watch and ask subject to name them
1	Ask patient to repeat "no ifs, ands, or buts."
3	Obey:"Take this paper in your right hand, fold in ½, put it on floor"
1	Read & obey written command: "Close your eyes"
1	Write any sentence with a noun, verb (sentence must be sensible)
1	Copy design below: Copy must contain all angles and 2 must intersect

A score ≤ 23 is abnormal (organic brain syndrome)   *J Psychiat Res* 1975; 12: 189.

Differentiating Between Delirium, Dementia, and Acute Psychosis

Feature	Delirium	Dementia	Psychosis
Age of onset	Any	Usually older	13-40 years
Psychiatric history	Usually absent	Usually absent	Present
Emotion	Labile	Normal or labile	Flat affect
Vital signs	Abnormal	Normal	Normal
Onset	Sudden	Gradual	Sudden
24h course	Fluctuates	Stable	Stable
Consciousness	Altered ↓	Clear	Clear
Attention	Disordered	OK unless severe	Can be disordered
Cognition	Disordered	Impaired	Selective
Hallucinations	Visual or sensory	Rare	Auditory
Delusions	Fleeting	Rare	Sustained, grand
Orientation	Impaired	Often Impaired	May be impaired
Psychomotor	↑ or ↓ or Shifting	Normal	Variable
Speech	Incoherent	Perseveration, difficult finding words	Normal, slow or rapid
Involuntary move	Asterixis or tremor	Often absent	Usually absent
Physical illness or drug toxicity	Drug toxicity	Either (esp. Alzheimer's)	Neither

Emerg Med Clin North Am 2000; 18: 243.

The Diagnosis of Delirium Requires the Following 3 Conditions:
- Disturbance of consciousness: decreased awareness of environment, poor attention span leading to poor information recall
- Cognitive change: confusion, disorientation or language impairment
- Sudden onset, fluctuating severity and transient in nature

Commonly Seen Associated Findings
- Alterations in sleep-wake cycle
- Mood lability
- Hallucinations or visual misperceptions

Risk Factors for Delirium
- Advanced age, dementia, comorbid medical disorder, psychiatric disorder, polypharmacy, depression, social isolation, history of substance abuse

Diagnosis
- Patients must meet above-mentioned clinical characteristics
- Confusion Assessment Method reliable tool to detect delirium (Annals Internal Med. 1990; 113: 941.)

Categories	Specific Etiologies (mnemonic = AEIOUMITS)
Alcohol (or illicit drugs)	Alcohol or illicit drug intoxication or withdrawal
Endocrine/Electrolytes/ Environmental	Electrolytes: ↑/↓ sodium, hypercalcemia ↑/↓ thyroid, ↑/↓ cortisol, hyperthermia or hypothermia
Infection/Infarct	Myocardial infarction, hypertensive encephalopathy, hyperviscosity, any infection
Oxygen (gases)	Hypoxia, hypercarbia or carbon monoxide poisoning
Uremia	Usually blood urea nitrogen > 100 mg/dL
Metabolic/Mental (Psychiatric) or Meds (see below)	B_{12} deficiency, Wilson's disease, Wernicke's and/or Korsakoff's syndrome, hepatic encephalopathy or psychiatric (diagnosis of exclusion)
Insulin	Severe hypoglycemia or hyperglycemia
Trauma/Toxins/TTP	Head trauma, toxins (organophosphates, etc.) or Thrombotic thrombocytopenic purpura
Seizures, Space-occupying lesion, Stroke	Stroke, intracranial bleed, brain tumor, hydrocephalus or seizure
Common Implicated Meds	Anticholinergics, histamine receptor$_2$ blockers, phenothiazines, GI antispasmodics, neuroleptics, antiparkinsonian meds, narcotics, aspirin, Nonsteroidal anti-inflammatory, steroids, antihistamines, sedatives, digoxin, quinidine, amiodarone, propranolol, methyldopa

Treatment of Delirium
- Discontinue all nonessential medications.
- Detailed history, exam and lab evaluation for above conditions
- Low-dose haloperidol (2.5 - 5 mg IM) for agitation/psychotic symptoms
- Quiet room with familiar objects, family/friends to calm and reorient patient

References: Emer. Med. Clin. N. Amer., 2000; 18 (2): 243-52. Amer. Fam. Physician. 1997; 55 (5): 1773-80.

Definition of Dementia: Acquired cognitive impairment and behavioral changes severe enough to interfere with daily functioning and affect quality of life
- Folstein Mini-Mental Status Exam (MMSE) < 24/30 indicative of dementia
- Must rule out delirium and depression (see corresponding sections)

Functional Assessment Staging (FAST) Scale to Stage Alzheimer's Disease
- Developed for Alzheimer's but principles applicable to all types of dementia

FAST	Timing*	MMSE	Characteristics and Abilities
Stage 1	N/A	28-30	No problems. Normal adult
Stage 2	N/A	26-28	Forgetful of names and location of objects
Stage 3	0-7 yrs	24-26	↓ job function, concentration deficit
Stage 4	7-11 yrs	14-23	↓ ability to travel, handle finances, plan activities or perform complex task. Withdrawal + denial common
Stage 5	11-13	5-13	Difficulty choosing proper clothing, no recall of some names or numbers important to patient
Stage 6	13-15	0-5	Needs assistance putting on clothes, bathing, toileting. May forget spouse's name. Disoriented. +/- delusions, obsessions, anxiety or loss of will.
Stage 7	15-17	0	Verbal abilities lost→ unable to sit→ unable to smile→ unable to lift head up→ unable to swallow

* timing is the number of years into the disease when most patients will be in the various stages.
Stage 4 = mild dementia, Stage 5 = moderate dementia, Stage 6 = severe dementia, Stage 7 = end-stage

Alzheimer's Dementia (AD: 60-70% of dementias)
- Gradually progressive deterioration following FAST stages as above
- Personality changes (extreme passivity→ severe hostility)
- Psychotic symptoms: 50% with delusions/25% with hallucinations
- Mood disorders: 40% depressed or anxious
- Parkinsonism: 30% can develop Parkinsonian features

Vascular Dementia (10-20% of dementias)
- Stepwise progression of cognitive decline that usually follows a stroke
- Urinary incontinence and gait disturbance common

Parkinson's (Lewy Body) Dementia (~5% of dementias)
- Parkinson's features (see corresponding section)
- Graphic, recurrent hallucinations and delusions common

Frontal Lobe Dementia (1-3%, e.g. Pick's disease)
- Impaired initiation, goal setting and planning more than memory loss
- Apathy, disinhibited behavior and neglect of hygiene and grooming
- Language impairments (logorrhea, echolalia and palilalia)

Reversible Dementias (10-13% of dementias)
- Normal pressure hydrocephalus (ataxia, dementia, incontinence)
- Hypothyroidism
- Vitamin B_{12} deficiency
- Neurosyphilis or HIV dementia

Treatment of Dementia
- Driving restriction if clinical dementia rating ≥ 1 (www.alz.org)
  - ➤ ID bracelets: Alzheimers association's "safe return" program for lost pts
- Cholinesterase inhibitors + Vit E 1000 IU bid→ ↑ cognition in mild-mod. AD
- Low-dose olanzapine or quetiapine for psychotic symptoms
- Selective serotonin reuptake inhibitors for concomitant depression
- Trazodone, carbamazepine or valproic acid for aggressive behavior

References: NEJM, 1996; 335: 330-6 and JAMA, 2000; 284: 47.

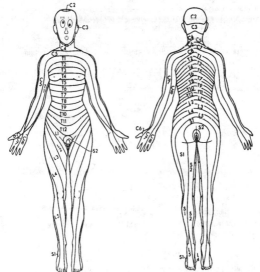

Motor level	Motor function
C1-2	neck flexion
C3	side neck flexion
C4	spontaneous breathing
C5	shoulder abduction/deltoid
C6	biceps (elbow flexion), wrist extension
C7	triceps, wrist flexion
C8	thumb ext, ulnar deviation
C8/T1	finger flexion
T1-T12	intercostal and abdominal muscles

Motor level	Motor function
T7-L1	abdominal muscles
T12	cremasteric reflex
L1/L2	hip flexion, psoas
L2/3/4	hip adduction, quads
L4	foot dorsiflexion, foot inversion
L5	great toe dorsiflexion
S1	foot plantar flexion foot eversion
S2-S4	rectal tone

Causes in Primary Care Setting: Peripheral vestibular disorder 40%, central vertigo 10%, basilar migraine 1%, psychogenic 15%, presyncope 5%, dysequilibrium 2%, multifactorial 15% and idiopathic 12%

Assessment of Vertigo		
Characteristics	Central Vertigo	Peripheral Vertigo
• Onset	• Subacute/insidious	• Abrupt
• Timing	• More continuous	• Paroxysmal
• Positional worsening	• No	• Yes
• Nystagmus	• Often reverses direction	• Always unidirectional
• Type	• Any direction possible	• Horizontal and/or rotational
• Visual fixation	• No effect	• Suppresses
• Other neuro deficits*	• Usually present	• Absent
• Postural instability	• Severe	• Mild-moderate
• Ear findings	• Absent	• Can be present
• Headache	• May be present	• Absent

*Neuro deficits: ataxia, nausea, diplopia, dysarthria, weakness/numbness of face or extremities

Causes of Central Vertigo
• Posterior fossa stroke, vertebrobasilar insufficiency, cerebellopontine angle tumor or multiple sclerosis
• Work-up: magnetic resonance imaging/angiogram of posterior fossa

Benign Paroxysmal Positional Vertigo (BPV)
• Clinical presentation: Symptom duration < 1 min., head movement provokes and symptoms are fatiguable
• Diagnosis: Dix-Hallpike or Nylen Barany maneuver
• Treatment: meclizine, scopolamine, dimenhydrinate or diphenhydramine
• Exercises: Epley's maneuver (see www.charite.de/ch/neuro/englishL.htm)

Labyrinthitis or Vestibular neuronitis
• Clinical presentation: prolonged episode of peripheral vertigo
• Treat with vestibular suppressants
  ➤ diazepam 5-10 mg PO q6h prn or meclizine 25 mg PO q6h prn

Meniere's disease
• Clinical features: unilateral tinnitus, hearing loss, vertigo & aural fullness
• Treatment same as for labyrinthitis +/- sodium restriction or diuretics.

Psychogenic
• Clinical features: Associated with mood or somatization disorders
  ➤ Hyperventilation can replicate symptoms

Presyncope
• Clinical presentation: near fainting and work-up same as syncope

Dysequilibrium
• Sense of imbalance while walking, common in elderly, usually multifactorial
• Risk factors: peripheral neuropathy, visual impairment, arthritis, cervical spondylosis, Parkinson's disease, mood disorder, ischemic heart disease, polypharmacy (especially anticholinergic meds) and hearing impairment

References: South Med J 2000; 93: 160. Am J Med 1999; 107: 468 and Ann Int Med 1992; 117: 898.

Most Common Final Cause of Falls in Elderly Patients			
Accident/Environmental	37%	Syncope	1%
Weak balance or gait	12%	CNS lesion	1%
Drop attack	11%	Unknown	8%
Dizziness/Vertigo	8%	Other (medical illness, eyesight	
Postural/Orthostasis	5%	drugs, confusion)	18%

Emerg Med Clin North Am 1990; 8: 309.

Evaluation of Elderly Patients Presenting After a Fall		
Functional History Concerning a Fall		*Key Physical Exam Findings*
C	Caregiver and housing adequate	**I** Inflammation joints (or immobility)
A	Alcohol (and withdrawal)	**H** Hypotension or orthostasis
T	Treatment (meds, compliance)	**A** Auditory or visual abnormalities
A	Affect (depression)	**T** Tremor
S	Syncope	**E** Equilibrium
T	Teetering (dizziness or vertigo)	**F** Foot problems
R	Recent medical or surgical illness	**A** Arrhythmia, heart block or valve
O	Ocular problems	**L** Leg-length discrepancy
P	Pain or problems with mobility	**L** Lack of conditioning
H	Hearing	**I** Illness – general/medical
E	Environmental hazards (e.g. stairs)	**N** Nutrition (weight loss?)
		G Gait disturbance

Am Fam Phys 2000; 61: 2159.

Probability of Falling in Patients ≥ 75 years Old

Specific Risk Factor	*Total Number of Risk Factors*	*Probability of Falling per Year*
Sedative use		
Cognitive impairment	No risk factors	8%
Lower extremity disability	1 risk factor	19%
Palmomental reflex	2 risk factors	32%
Abnormal balance/gait	3 risk factors	60%
Foot problems	≥4 risk factors	78%

N Engl J Med 1988; 1701.

Headache Syndromes	Location	Characteristics	Duration	Associated Symptoms	Exacerbating factors	Relieving factors
Tension	global bilateral	pressure tightness	variable min.-hours	mood disorders common	stress	relaxation biofeedback
Cluster	retroorbital periorbital unilateral	abrupt onset deep and stabbing People are restless	5-180 min. Headache clusters	ipsilateral lacrimation rhinorrhea, eye redness & sweating	alcohol use and supine position	rest darkness quiet
Migraines	70% unilateral	gradual onset pulsating quality ♀ > ♂ + family history migraine triggers	4 – 72 hours	nausea, vomiting, photophobia phonophobia and/or aura (classical)	activity bright light loud noise valsalva	rest darkness quiet
Temporal Arteritis	temporal frontal	tender temporal artery (33%) & age>55	fluctuating severity	myalgias, fatigue, ipsilateral blindness, ↑ erythrocyte sedimentation rate, sweats, & polymyalgia rheumatica	none
Trigeminal Neuralgia	trigeminal nerve area	shock like paroxysms of pain in cheeks/jaw	seconds – < 2 minute	usually > 50 years	brushing teeth touching face wind on face	none
Subarachnoid Hemorrhage	global	sudden onset of "worst headache of my life"	constant	+/- loss of consciousness vomiting, meningismus and photophobia	darkness	bright light
Medication Rebound	global	chronic, daily analgesic overuse	hours	analgesic abuse mood disorders	not applicable	not applicable

Treatment Options for Tension Headaches
- Abortive therapy typically with acetaminophen or NSAIDS
- nortriptyline or amitriptyline 10-50 mg PO qhs can be used prophylactically

Treatment Options for Cluster Headaches
- Have patient breathe 100% oxygen at 8-10 L/min. by mask for 15-20 minutes
- Abortive agents: dihydroergotamine 1 mg IM or sumatriptan 6 mg SQ
- Prophylactic agents: verapamil 60-160 mg PO tid, lithium 300 mg PO bid, valproic acid 250-1000 mg PO bid or topiramate 50-125 mg PO qd
  > Start prednisone 60 mg PO qd x 5 d then taper off over 10-14 days

Treatment Options for Migraine Headaches
- **Abortive agents**
  > Mild headaches: aspirin 800-1000 mg PO +/- metoclopramide 10 mg PO
  > Moderate headaches: triptans, cafergot 2 tabs PO at onset then 1 tab PO q30 min. prn (max 6 tabs/day), dihydroergotamine 1 mg IM or SQ q1hr prn (max 3 mg/day), isometheptene + dichloralphenazone +acetaminophen 2 caps PO at onset then 1 tab PO q1h prn (max 5 caps/day)
  > Severe headaches: **triptans**

triptans	daily maximum dose
almotriptan 6.25-12.5 mg PO q2hr prn migraine	25 mg
eletriptan 20-40 mg PO q2hr prn migraine	80 mg
frovatriptan 2.5 mg PO q2hr prn migraine	7.5 mg
naratriptan 1-2.5 mg PO q4hr prn migraine	5 mg
rizatriptan 5-10 mg PO q2hr prn migraine	30 mg
sumatriptan 25-100 mg PO q2hr prn migraine	200 mg
6 mg SQ q1hr prn migraine	12 mg
5-20 mg intranasally q2hr prn migraine	40 mg
zolmitriptan 1.25-2.5 mg PO q2hr prn migraine	10 mg

- **Prophylactic agents**
  > propranolol 40-120 mg PO bid, metoprolol 100-200 mg PO daily, amitriptyline 10-75 mg PO qhs, valproic acid 400-600 mg PO bid, gabapentin 300-600 mg PO tid or topiramate 50-200 mg PO bid

Treatment Options for Temporal Arteritis
- prednisone 40-60 mg PO qd x 2-4 weeks and decrease dose 10% q1-2 weeks to minimum effective dose (duration may be as long as 1-2 yrs)
  > Follow clinical symptoms & erythrocyte sedimentation rate at least monthly
  > methylprednisolone 1 gram IV qd x 3 days for impending visual loss

Treatment Options for Trigeminal Neuralgia
- carbamazepine 300-600 mg PO bid is the most effective medication.
- phenytoin 300 mg PO qhs, valproic acid 400-600 mg PO bid, gabapentin 300-1200 mg PO tid, baclofen 10-20 mg PO tid or lamotrigine 100-400 mg PO qd

Treatment of Analgesic Rebound Headaches
- Completely eliminate analgesics

Headache Danger Signs/Symptoms
- Sudden onset, "worst headache of my life", exacerbation by coughing, exertion or valsalva, early AM headaches, altered mental status, nuchal rigidity, fever, papilledema, focal neuro exam or new headache > 50 yrs or in young children
- Work-up of Worrisome Headaches
  > Head CT scan without contrast: ? subarachnoid hemorrhage or brain mass
  > If head CT normal, consider a lumbar puncture to rule out early subarachnoid hemorrhage, meningitis or pseudotumor cerebri

References: Neurology, 2000; 54: 1553. Neurology, 2000; 55: 754 and NEJM, 2002; 347(4): 261-71.

Root	Muscles	Weakness	Reflex loss
C3-4	Trapezius	Shoulder shrugging	
C5	Deltoid	Should abduction	Biceps
	Biceps	Elbow flexion	
C6-7	Triceps	Elbow extension	Triceps
	Brachioradialis	Elbow flexion in half- supination	Brachio-radialis
	Radial nerve injuries produce similar findings except brachioradialis function is normal		
C6	Extensor carpi radialis	"Radial" wrist extension	
C7	Extensor digitorum	Finger extension	
C8-T1	Flexor digitorum	Long flexors of fingers	
	Interossei	Intrinsics of hand (finger abduction, palmar abduction of thumb)	
	Ulnar nerve injuries similar but also weaken thumb adductor		
T10		Beevor's sign (sit-up → umbilicus pulled upwards)	
L1-L2	Iliopsoas	Hip flexion	Cremasteric
L3	Adductors	Thigh adduction	
L3-L4	Quadriceps	Knee extension	Knee jerk
	Femoral nerve injury limited to knee extension; associated hip flexion and adduction weakness localizes to **plexus**		
L4	Tibialis anterior	Ankle dorsiflexion	
L5	Extensor hallux/digiti	Extension of toes	
	Peroneus long/brevis	Foot eversion	
	Glutei	Hip abduction	
	Deep peroneal nerve weakness limited to ankle/toe extensors; **posterior tibial nerve** lesions weaken foot inversion		
L5-S1	Hamstrings	Knee flexion	
S1	Gastroc/soleus	Ankle flexion	Ankle jerk
	Flexor digiti brevis	Toe flexion	
S2	Interossei	Cupping and fanning of toes	
Below S2		Impaired vesicle, anal and sexual function	Anal wink, Bulbo-cavernosus

Epidemiology: 1% of population over 50, but 10% of cases < 50 years of age

Causes of Parkinsonism: Parkinson's disease, viral encephalitis lethargica, carbon monoxide, cyanide or MPTP-induced, dementia pugilistica or medications (neuroleptics, amiodarone, methyldopa or lithium)

Clinical Features	Exam Findings
"Pill-rolling" tremor	Coarse, asymmetric, stress ↑ and intention ↓ tremor
Rigidity	Cogwheeling
Bradykinesia	Decreased automatic movements, micrographia, masked facies and flat affect
Gait/postural instability	Festinating gait, flexed posture, decreased postural reflexes and en bloc turning
Autonomic abnormalities	Hyperhidrosis, constipation, incontinence, drooling, and diminished sense of smell
Dermatologic	Seborrhea
Neuropsychiatric	Dementia (20%), psychosis and depression (50%)

Treatment
- Initiate symptomatic treatment once symptoms are functionally disabling
  ➤ Unified Parkinson's Disease Rating Scale (www.wemove.org)
- **carbidopa-levodopa** is most effective therapy for 1st 4 features above
  ➤ Complications: dyskinesia, dystonia, psychosis and motor fluctuations
- **Dopamine agonists**
  ➤ bromocriptine, pergolide, pramipexole, ropinirole and cabergoline
  ➤ Complications: psychosis, erythromelalgia, orthostasis and sedation
- **Monoamine oxidase inhibitor type B** (e.g., selegiline)
  ➤ May exert mild neuroprotective effect
  ➤ Complications: anticholinergic side effects
- **Amantadine**
  ➤ Effective for early, mild disease
  ➤ Complications: anticholinergic, edema and insomnia
- **Catechol-O-methyltransferase (COMT) inhibitors** (e.g., entacapone)
  ➤ Decreases "off" time and enhances motor response to levo-dopamine
  ➤ Complications: dyskinesias and urine discoloration
- **Anticholinergics** (e.g., benztropine mesylate and trihexyphenidyl)
  ➤ Helps tremor and sialorrhea

Managing Complications of Parkinson's Disease or Therapy
- **Motor fluctuations or "on/off" phenomenon**
  ➤ Add dopamine agonist or COMT inhibitor
  ➤ Dietary protein restriction
  ➤ Surgery (thalamotomy, pallidotomy or deep brain stimulation)
- **Dykinesias or dystonias**
  ➤ Change to controlled release Sinemet + stop selegiline
  ➤ Decrease Sinemet and add dopamine agonist
- **Cognitive impairment**: minimize anticholinergics and dopamine agonists
- **Delirium/Psychosis**: minimize doses of carbidopa levodopa, anticholinergics, selegiline and/or dopamine agonists
  ➤ Trial of low-dose quetiapine or clozapine
- **Incontinence**: Trial of oxybutynin, hyoscyamine or tolterodine

MPTP = methyl-4-phenyl-1,2,3,6-tetrahydropyridine

References: NEJM, 1998; 339: 15 & 16 (two parts) and Neurology, 2001; 56 (11)

- **Definition:** Involuntary activity, perception or behavior as a result of abnormal neuronal discharges in the cerebral cortex

Classification of Seizures

Seizure Type	Conscious-ness impaired	Tongue biting or Incontinence	Aura (*)	Hyper-ventilation triggers	Automatisms (**)	Postictal Duration
Simple Partial Seizure	No	No	Yes	No	No	Seconds
Complex Partial Seizure	Yes	No	Yes 1st	No	Yes (after aura)	Minutes-Hours
Secondary Generalized Partial Seizure	Yes	Yes	Yes 1st	No	Possibly	Minutes-Hours
Absence Seizure	Yes	No	No	Yes	No	Seconds
Grand mal seizure	Yes	Yes	No	No	No	Minutes-Hours

* jerking movements, epigastric discomfort, fear, bad smell, focal sensory or psychic symptoms

** facial grimacing, gesturing, chewing, lip smacking, snapping fingers, walking, undressing, etc.

- **Differential Diagnosis:** migraines, syncope, transient ischemic attack, pseudoseizures, Meniere's disease and movement disorder
- **Etiologies:** post-traumatic, severe hyponatremia, hypomagnesemia, hypoglycemia or hypocalcemia, congenital brain malformations, hyper- or hypothyroidism, dialysis dysequilibrium syndrome, acute intermittent porphyria, severe hypoxia, carbon monoxide poisoning, meningitis, stroke, alcohol or benzodiazepine withdrawal states, medication side effect or idiopathic
- **Seizure Triggers:** strong emotions, intense exercise, flashing lights, fever, menses, lack of sleep and stress
- **History:** positive family history, history of head trauma, febrile seizures, birth complications, substance abuse, prior seizure or cancer, concomitant sinusitis or otitis media or HIV-positive
- **Work-up:** chemistry panel; drug screen; electroencephalogram; thyroid stimulating hormone; lumbar puncture for meningismus (or possible meningitis)
- **Imaging:** Noncontrast head CT scan for head trauma, new severe headache and anticoagulated patients. MRI preferred for focal neuro deficits, persistently altered mental status, history of cancer, and possible AIDS
- **Risk Factors for Recurrent Seizures:** history of closed head injury, structural brain lesion, focal neuro exam, cognitive impairment, partial seizures, abnormal electroencephalogram or positive family history
- **Chronic Medications:** Start after 1st seizure + 2 risk factors or after 2nd seizure.
  - ➢ Absence seizures: ethosuximide or valproic acid
  - ➢ Partial seizure: carbamazepine, valproic acid, oxcarbazepine or phenytoin
  - ➢ Generalized seizures: valproic acid, lamictal or topiramate
- **Miscellaneous:** Check state requirements for mandatory Department of Motor Vehicles reporting (see www.efa.org)
- **Discontinuation of Therapy:** can be attempted once seizure-free x 2 years

References: Epilepsia 2001; 42: 1255. Epilepsia 2001; 42: 1387 and NEJM 2001; 344 (15): 1145.

Classification of Cerebrovascular Accidents
- Hemorrhagic 15% (subarachnoid or intraparenchymal)
- Ischemic 85% (Thrombotic 20%, Lacunar 25%, Cardioembolic 20%, Cryptogenic 30% or Other 5%)
  - ➢ Cryptogenic is most likely embolic in nature
  - ➢ Other: hypercoagulable states, dissection, vasculitis, endocarditis, complicated migraine, stimulant drugs, neurosyphilis, patent foramen ovale
  - ➢ Embolic: patients generally experience a sudden onset of maximal deficit
  - ➢ Thrombotic: patients generally have a stuttering or stepwise progression

Clinical Presentation of Various Strokes	Vascular Area
face = arms > legs aphasia, hemiparesis, hemianesthesia, contralateral homonymous hemianopsia & ipsilateral gaze deviation	MCA (dominant)
Face = arms > legs, neglect, hemiparesis, hemianesthesia, contralateral homonymous hemianopsia & ipsilateral gaze deviation	MCA (nondominant)
Legs = arms = face, hemiparesis, hemianesthesia, incontinence, personality change and grasp/suck reflexes	ACA
Homonymous visual field deficit	PCA
Ipsilateral cranial nerve palsies and contralateral hemiparesis	Brainstem
Headache, vertigo, nausea, ataxia, dysarthria and nystagmus	Cerebellum
Hemiparesis (leg = arm = face) is a pure motor lacunar stroke	Internal capsule
Hemianesthesia (leg = arm = face) is a pure sensory lacunar stroke	Thalamus
Ipsilateral weakness + limb ataxia =ataxia hemiparesis lacunar stroke	Midbrain
Clumsy hand-dysarthria lacunar stroke	Basis pontis
Hemiparesis + hemianesthesia (leg = arm = face) represents a sensorimotor lacunar stroke	Internal capsule or thalamus

MCA (Middle Cerebral Artery), ACA (Ant. Cerebral Artery), PCA (Post. Cerebral Artery)

Risk Factors: hypertension, ischemic heart disease, atrial fibrillation, diabetes, carotid artery stenosis, smoking, hyperlipidemia, obesity, age > 65 & alcohol abuse

Work-up
- Cardiac echocardiogram for thrombus in cardioembolic strokes
- Carotid duplex ultrasound for MCA or ACA strokes
- Noncontrast head CT: rule out an intracranial bleed or mass effect
- Magnetic resonance imaging/magnetic resonance angiogram or transcranial doppler study for suspected posterior fossa strokes
- Electrocardiogram
- Complete blood count, chemistry panel and coagulation studies
- Holter monitor for history of palpitations: rule out atrial fibrillation/flutter
- Patients < 50 years with few vascular risk factors: drug screen, blood cultures, syphilis testing, cardiac echocardiogram with bubble study, lupus anticoagulant, anticardiolipin antibody, Factor V Leiden and Prothrombin gene mutation

Prevention of Ischemic Stroke
- Keep tight glycemic control, BP< 135/85, LDL<100 mg/dL, HDL>35 mg/dL
- Smoking cessation
- Aspirin 81-325 PO qd (clopidogrel 75 mg PO qd for ischemic events on aspirin)
- Indications for anticoagulation: atrial fibrillation, hypercoagulable state, paradoxical embolus, vertebral dissection +/- vertebrobasilar stenosis

BP = blood pressure, LDL = low-density lipoprotein, HDL = high-density lipoprotein

References: Chest 1998: 114: 6835-85. and Circulation 1994; 90 (3): 1588-1600

Causes of Generalized Weakness

- Electrolytes: ↓ potassium/phosphate/magnesium or sodium or ↑ sodium/calcium
  - ➢ Periodic paralysis (look for hypokalemia or hyperthyroidism)
  - ➢ Depression
  - ➢ Medical problems: anemia, chronic ischemic or congestive cardiomyopathy, chronic obstructive pulmonary disease, adrenal insufficiency, thyroid disorders or cachexia of malignancy or AIDS

Patterns of Weakness

- Upper motor neuron (UMN): ↑tone, ↑DTRs, + Babinski sign and spastic
- Lower motor neuron (LMN): ↓ tone, ↓ DTRs, - Babinski sign, severe atrophy, fasciculations, fibrillations and flaccid paralysis
- Myopathic: mild atrophy, proximal weakness, normal DTRs, and - Babinski's

Weakness Syndromes

Location of Defect	Clinical Features	Diagnosis
Cortex	Contralateral hemiparesis/hemianesthesia and upper motor neuron pattern present	CT/MRI
Internal capsule	"pure motor" lacunar syndrome and + UMN	CT/MRI
Brainstem	Ipsilateral cranial nerve palsies, contralateral hemiparesis and + UMN	MRI
Spinal cord lesion	Sensory level, bilateral weakness & + UMN	Spinal MRI
Brown-Sequard syndrome	Hemiparesis, ipsilateral ↓ proprioception and contralateral ↓ pain/temp.	Spinal MRI
Radiculopathy	Back & dermatomal pain/weakness, ↓DTR	Spinal MRI
Anterior Horn cells (polio)	Asymmetric monoparesis, lower motor neuron pattern present & normal sensation	Clinical
Amyotrophic Lateral Sclerosis	Asymmetric combined LMN limb weakness + UMN bulbar palsies, progressive, familial	Clinical
Peripheral nerves	Nerve distribution, lower motor neuron pattern present	EMG/nerve conduction studies
NMJ (MG, Botulism (B) or Eaton-Lambert syndrome)	Fatiguability, bulbar palsies (diplopia, ptosis, dysarthria, dysphagia), descending paralysis	positive edrophonium test (MG) + Botulinum toxin (B)*
Guillain-Barre	Ascending symmetric weakness, absent/↓ DTRs, post-upper respiratory infection	Clinical
Myopathies	Proximal muscle weakness	EMG/Biopsy
PMR	Pain + stiff hip/shoulder girdles,↑ESR > 50	Clinical
Rhabdomyolysis	↑ CPK, sore muscles	↑ CPK

NMJ = neuromuscular junction, MG = Myasthenia Gravis, EMG = electromyogram, DTR = deep tendon reflexes, ESR = erythrocyte sedimentation rate, CPK = creatinine phosphokinase, PMR = polymyalgia rheumatica, MRI = magnetic resonance imaging and CT = computed tomography. * botulinum toxin from serum if food-borne and from tissue if wound botulism

Causes of Peripheral Neuropathies (mnemonic = MOVESTUPID)

Metabolic	B_{12}, thiamine, pyridoxine or folate deficiencies
Other	Rare familial disorders, Amyloidosis
Vasculitis	Systemic lupus erythematosus, Sjogren's, cryoglobulinemia, or polyarteritis nodosa
Endocrine	Diabetes, hypothyroidism
Syphilis	or Sarcoidosis
Tumor-related	Paraneoplastic
Uremia	Blood Urea Nitrogen usually > 100 mg/dL
Paraproteinemia	or porphyria or polycythemia vera
Infectious/idiopathic	Lyme disease, leprosy, mononucleosis, AIDS or chronic inflammatory demyelinating polyneuropathy
Drugs/Toxins	alcohol, arsenic, lead, mercury, phenytoin, isoniazid, hydralazine, dapsone, amiodarone, metronidazole, nitrofurantoin, vincristine, cisplatinum, chloroquine, zalcitabine, didanosine and stavudine

Causes of Myopathies: postviral, polymyositis, dermatomyositis, meds (statins, colchicine, steroids), alcohol, thyrotoxicosis or hyperparathyroidism

Work-up of Weakness
- Is the weakness generalized or fit one of the weakness syndromes above?
- **Evaluation of Generalized Weakness**
  - ➢ Assess for depression or chronic cardiopulmonary disease
  - ➢ Labs: chemistry 7 panel, magnesium, phosphate, calcium, thyroid stimulating hormone (TSH) level and complete blood count
  - ➢ Cosyntropin stimulation test for any suspicion of adrenal insufficiency
  - ➢ Consider a chest x-ray for adult smokers or those with a chronic cough

- **Evaluation of Weakness Syndromes**
  - ➢ Start with the diagnostic test of choice as outlined in the table above
  - ➢ For myopathies or myositis, an open muscle biopsy of the affected muscle indicated for both routine pathology and electron microscopy.
  - ➢ For Guillain-Barre, a lumbar puncture will have few cells and a high protein

- **Evaluation of Peripheral Neuropathies**
  - ➢ Examine for any medication culprits
  - ➢ Routine labs: chemistry 7 panel, TSH, B_{12} and folate levels and a venereal disease research laboratory (VDRL) test
  - ➢ Additional labs if the history and exam are suggestive: antinuclear antibody, anti-SSA and anti-SSB (Sjogren's syndrome A and B) antibodies, serum cryoglobulins, angiotensin converting enzyme level and HIV test

Reference: Emerg. Med. Clin. North America, 1999; 17 (1): 265-78.

Visual Acuity Screen

96

20/800

873

20/400

2843   OXX 20/200

6 3 8 5 2   X O O   20/100

8 7 4 5 9   O X O   20/70

6 3 9 2 5   X O X   20/50

4 2 8 3 6 5   o x o   20/40

3 7 4 2 5 8   X X o   20/30

9 3 7 8 2 6   x o o   20/25

Hold card in good light 14 inches from eye. Record vision for each eye separately with and without glasses. Presbyopic patients should read through bifocal glasses. Myopic patients should wear glasses only.

Pupil Diameter (mm)

.2 3 4 5 6 7 8 9

Rosenbaum pocket vision screen

The Red Eye with No Pain
- Subconjunctival hemorrhage
  - ➢ Exam: sharply-circumscribed red area on sclera & patient has normal vision

The Red Eye with Deep Eye Pain
- **Corneal Ulcer**
  - ➢ Fluorescein staining with white spot on cornea
  - ➢ Remove contacts and treat ulcer with antibiotic ointment and eye patching only after ophthalmologic consultation.
- **Scleritis**
  - ➢ Exam with tender eye and/or decreased visual acuity
  - ➢ Referral to ophthalmologist
- **Uveitis or Iritis**
  - ➢ Exam with mild decreased vision, circumcorneal conjunctival injection, miotic pupil, photophobia and slit lamp exam reveals hypopyon (iritis) or leukocytes in vitreous humor (posterior uveitis)
  - ➢ Consider initiating cycloplegic drops and topical steroids after ophthalmologic consultation and with follow-up appointment within 24 hours.
- **Periorbital or Orbital Cellulitis**
  - ➢ Exam with fever, lid swelling and erythema +/- proptosis and restricted eye movement (if orbit involved)
  - ➢ Treat with intravenous antibiotics (e.g., cefuroxime 1.5 gram IV q8h, cefoxitin 2 grams IV q8h or ampicillin-sulbactam 1.5 grams IV q6h)
  - ➢ Consider CT scan of orbit for proptosis or restricted eye movement to rule out an orbital abscess.
- **Acute Angle-Closure Glaucoma**
  - ➢ Exam: markedly decreased vision, severe brow pain, nausea/vomiting, diffuse conjunctival injection, mid-dilated pupil, hazy cornea, "halos" around lights and increased intraocular pressure
  - ➢ Treatment options include: beta-blocker drops (e.g., timolol or betaxolol), acetazolamide 500 mg x 1 then 250 mg q6h (IV, IM or PO), apraclonidine, 2 drops q8h, mannitol 1 – 1.5 mg/kg intravenously x 1 and 2% pilocarpine 1 drop q15 minutes x 2 hours and immediate ophthalmology referral

The Red Eye with Foreign Body Sensation or Irritation
- **Conjunctivitis**
  - ➢ Presence of clear discharge suggests viral conjunctivitis.
  - ➢ Presence of purulent discharge suggests bacterial conjunctivitis.
    - o Treat with antibiotic eye drops or ointment x 7 days.
  - ➢ No discharge consistent with allergic conjunctivitis
    - o Treat with antihistamine eye drops (e.g., naphazoline/pheniramine, levocabastine or azelastine eye drops)
  - ➢ Dendrites on fluorescein staining suggests herpes simplex conjunctivitis.
    - o Treat with trifluridine drops, cycloplegic drops & ophthalmology referral
- **Corneal Laceration/Abrasion or Foreign Body**
  - ➢ History of trauma or exposure to foreign body. Pupil often constricted.
  - ➢ Foreign body can usually be removed with a sterile Q-tip.
  - ➢ Treat a laceration or abrasion with antibiotic ointment and eye patching.
- **Keratitis**
  - ➢ Exam: slightly decreased visual acuity, circumcorneal conjunctival injection, corneal opacification and positive fluorescein staining
  - ➢ Consider initiating topical steroids and refer to an ophthalmologist
- **Episcleritis**
  - ➢ Exam: Engorged, episcleral vessels and nodule adjacent to limbus, vision unaffected, dull achiness and tenderness on palpation
  - ➢ Often associated with an autoimmune disorder and is self-limited.

Reference: Amer. Family Physician, 1996; 53 (2): 565-74 and NEJM, 2000; 343: 345.

Mechanisms of Visual Impairment

Subtypes	Refractive Error	Media Opacity	Retina or Optic Nerve Disease	Neurological Insult
Mechanism	Image poorly focused	Opacity of eye tissue	Damaged retina or nerve	Abnormal brain tissue
Examples	• Myopia • Hyperopia • Astigmatism • Presbyopia • Hyperglycemia-induced lens swelling	• Cataract • Corneal ulcer or scar • Hyphema • Vitreous hemorrhage	• Retinal detachment • Retinal vein occlusion • Glaucoma • Optic neuritis • Optic nerve trauma • Macular degeneration • Ischemic optic neuropathy*	• Pituitary tumor¥ • CNS infarct • Brain tumor • Head trauma
Exam	Pinhole normalizes vision	No red reflex with ophthalmoscope	Relative afferent papillary defect	Visual field cuts on confrontation

* caused by temporal arteritis or retinal artery occlusion, ¥ - presents as bitemporal hemianopsia

Onset of Visual Loss
- **Sudden Visual Loss**: trauma, acute glaucoma, stroke, hyphema, ischemic optic neuropathy, optic neuritis, vitreous hemorrhage or retinal detachment
- **Transient Visual Loss**: migraine headaches or amaurosis fugax
- **Gradual Visual Loss**: refractive error, cataracts, chronic glaucoma or expanding pituitary tumor

Treatment of Visual Impairment by Cause
- **Refractive Error**
  - ➢ Corrective lenses
- **Media Opacity**
  - ➢ Ophthalmology referral for definitive therapy
- **Retinal or Optic Nerve Disease**
  - ➢ Ophthalmology referral for retinal detachment, retinal vein occlusion, glaucoma or optic nerve injury or globe trauma
  - ➢ Prednisone 1 mg/kg PO qd x 11 days then taper for optic neuritis
- **Neurological Insult**
  - ➢ **Pituitary Tumor**
    - o Bromocriptine or cabergoline for microprolactinomas
    - o Consider transsphenoidal excision of pituitary tumors or macroprolactinomas
  - ➢ **Brain Tumor or Head Trauma**
    - o Neurosurgical consult for possible excision or evacuation of clot.

Epistaxis
Anterior Nosebleeds
- 80% occur within Kiesselbach's plexus
- **Risk Factors:** arid places, rhinitis, nosepicking, foreign body, facial trauma, anticoagulation, blood dyscrasias, Osler-Weber-Rendu disease, Wegener's granulomatosis and angiofibromas (young boys)
- **Work-up:** complete blood count, coagulation studies and bleeding time
- **Management:** compression of nasal alae x 5 min→ cautery with silver nitrate stick→ control hypertension→ apply cotton pledgets soaked with 10 cc 4% cocaine or neosynephrine/lidocaine→ Replace pledgets with nasal tampon x 24 - 48 hours
- Consider antibiotic prophylaxis with trimethoprim-sulfamethoxazole DS or amoxicillin-clavulanate until nasal packing removed.

Posterior Nosebleeds
- **Risk Factors:** nasopharyngeal tumors, hypertension, coagulopathies or patients over 60 years.
- **Work-up as above**
- **Management:** admission→ control of hypertension→ tamponade posterior structures with 14 French foley catheter secured on nasal end with a clamp or with an Epistat catheter→ Pack anterior nose→ antibiotics as above and remove pack and catheter in 48 – 72 hrs

Acute Hoarseness (< 2 weeks)
- **Etiologies:** Acute laryngitis, vocal strain, peritonsillar abscess or post-operative from anterior neck surgery
- **Therapy:** Treat peritonsillar infection if present, hydration, humidification and voice rest
- **Natural history:** Voice returns to normal within 1 week

Chronic Hoarseness (> 2 weeks)
- **History:** Duration, onset abrupt or insidious, smoking history, alcohol use, prior neck surgery or radiation therapy and occupation
- **Associated symptoms:** dyspnea, stridor, cough, hemoptysis, ear/throat pain, dysphagia, odynophagia or weight loss
- **Etiologies:** inhaled toxins, chronic gastroesophageal reflux, chronic sinusitis with postnasal drip, chronic vocal strain, vocal cord polyps, spasmodic dysphonia, vocal cord paralysis, laryngeal conversion disorder (psychogenic), laryngeal cancer or lung cancer
- **Work-up:** Direct laryngoscopy indicated
- **Treatments:** cigarette/alcohol cessation, voice rest and other treatments based on underlying disorder

Reference: Postgraduate Med 1996; 99: 83.

ENT COMBINATIONS (selected)	Decon-gestant	Antihis-tamine	Anti-tussive	Typical Adult Doses
OTC				
Actifed Cold & Allergy	PS	TR	-	1 tab or 10 ml q4-6h
Allerfrim, Aprodine	PS	TR	-	1 tab or 10 ml q4-6h
Dimetapp Cold & Allergy	PS	DBR		1 tab q12h
Robitussin CF	PS	-	GU, DM	10 ml q4h*
Robitussin DM, Mytussin DM	-	-	GU, DM	10 ml q4h*
Robitussin PE, Guaituss PE	PS	-	GU	10 ml q4h*
Drixoral Cold & Allergy	PS			1 tab q12h
Triaminic Cold & Allergy	PS	CH		20 ml q4-6h‡
Triaminic Cough	PS	-	DM	20 ml q4h‡
Rx Only				
Allegra-D	PS	FE	-	1 tab q12h
Bromfenex	PS	BR	-	1 cap q12h
Claritin-D 12 hour	PS	LO	-	1 tab q12h
Claritin-D 24 hour	PS	LO	-	1 tab qd
Deconamine	PS	CH	-	1 tab or 10 ml tid-qid
Deconamine SR, Chlordrine SR	PS	CH	-	1 tab q12h
Deconsal II	PS	-	GU	1-2 tabs q12h
Dimetane-DX	PS	BR	DM	10 ml PO q4h
Duratuss	PS	-	GU	1 tab q12h
Duratuss HD	PS	-	GU, HY	10ml q4-6h
Entex PSE, Guaifenex PSE 120	PS	-	GU	1tab q12h
Histussin D ©III	PS	-	HY	5 ml qid
Histussin HC ©III	PE	CH	HY	10 ml q4h
Humibid DM	-	-	GU, DM	1-2 tabs q12h
Hycotuss	-	-	GU, HY	5ml pc & qhs
Phenergan/Dextromethorphn	-	PR	DM	5 ml q4h
Phenergan VC	PE	PR	-	5 ml q4-6h
Phenergan VC w/codeine©V	PE	PR	CO	5 ml q4-6h
Polyhistine	-	PT/PY/PH		10ml q4h*
Robitussin AC ©V	-	-	GU, CO	10 ml q4h*
Robitussin DAC ©V	PS	-	GU, CO	10 ml q4h*
Rondec syrup	PS	CX	-	5 ml qid*
Rondec DM syrup	PS	CX	DM	5 ml qid*
Rondec Infant Drops	PS	CX	-	0.25 to 1 ml qid†
Rondec DM Infant drops	PS	CX	DM	0.25 to 1 ml qid†
Rynatan	PE	CH	-	1-2 tabs q12h
Rynatan-P Pediatric	PE	CH, PY		2.5-5ml q12h†
Semprex-D	PS	AC	-	1cap q4-6h
Tanafed	PS	CH	-	10-20ml q12h*
Triacin-C, Actifed w/codeine©V	PS	TR	CO	10 ml q4-6h
Tussionex	-	CH	HY	5 ml q12h

AC=acrivastine	CX=carbinoxamine	HY=hydrocodone	PS=pseudoephedrine
AZ=azatadine	DM=dextromethorphan	LO=loratadine	PT=phenyltoloxamine
BR=brompheniramine	DBR=dexbrompheniramine	PE=phenylephrine	PY=pyrilamine
CH=chlorpheniramine	FE=fexofenadine	PH=pheniramine	TR=triprolidine
CO=codeine	GU=guaifenesin	PR=promethazine	

*5 ml/dose if 6-11 yo. 2.5 ml if 2-5yo. †1 ml/dose if 10-18 mo. ¾ ml if 7-9 mo. ½ ml if 4-6 mo. ¼ ml if 1-3 months old. ‡10 ml/dose if 6-11 yo. 5 ml if 2-5 yo. 2.5 ml if 13-23 mo. 1.25 ml if 4-12 mo.

History

- Onset and progression of hearing loss
- Auralgia or ear discharge
- History of trauma including barotraumas?
- Associated tinnitus, vertigo or dysequilibrium
- History of loud noise exposure?
- Family history of hearing loss and at what age?
- Ototoxic medication exposure (e.g., aminoglycosides, erythromycin, vancomycin, tetracycline, 5-fluorouracil, bleomycin, cisplatin, aspirin, furosemide, quinine and chloroquine)

Examination

- Weber test: lateralizes to good ear in sensorineural hearing loss and to bad ear in conductive hearing loss
- Rinne test: negative test (bone ≥ air) consistent with conductive hearing loss
- External auditory canal: blockage or stenosis
- Tympanic membrane: color, mobility or any fluid in the middle ear

Audiologic testing

- Assesses hearing at frequencies between 250 Hz – 8000 Hz
- Hearing impairment if > 20 dB (mild 20-40, mod. 40-60, severe > 60 dB)

Tympanometry

- Measures acoustic impedance of middle ear with change in air pressure
- Decreased mobility: suggests fluid in middle ear
- Negative pressure: corresponds to retracted tympanic membrane
- Subtype AS: very stiff middle ear (e.g., otosclerosis, myringosclerosis)
- Subtype AD: highly compliant tympanic membrane (e.g., ossicular chain discontinuity)

Imaging considerations

- Sensorineural hearing loss should be evaluated with an MRI in adults and a CT scan with bone algorithms in children.
  - ➤ Causes in adults: acoustic neuroma, meningiomas, abnormal labyrinth, multiple sclerosis or neuronitis
  - ➤ Causes in children: inner ear dysplasias
- Conductive hearing loss: CT scan with bone algorithms in adults and children
  - ➤ Causes: external canal atresia, myringosclerosis, middle ear anomalies, effusions, cholesteatomas, exostosis, TM perforation and neoplasms
- Mixed hearing loss: CT scan with bone and soft tissue algorithms
  - ➤ Causes: otosclerosis, osteogenesis imperfecta and Paget's disease

Treatment/Prevention

- Consideration of hearing aids
- Surgical excision of cholesteatomas, exostoses or tumors
- Meniere's disease (episodic vertigo, aural fullness, tinnitus and low frequency sensorineural hearing loss)
  - ➤ Low sodium diet, avoid caffeine/alcohol and a trial of thiazide diuretics
- Ear plugs or hearing protection should be worn with any noise blasts or with chronic noise exposure > 85 dB time-weighted average

Hz = Hertz, dB = decibels, MRI = magnetic resonance imaging and CT = computed tomography imaging
References: Radiology 1996; 199: 593-611 and Medical Clinics North America, 1999; 83 (1): 139-49.

Rhinitis Definition: Rhinorrhea, nasal itching, sneezing, congestion and pressure
Allergic Rhinitis: affects up to 20% of the U.S. population

- Associated conditions: postnasal drip, eczema, asthma, sinusitis, eustachian tube dysfunction and conjunctivitis
- Common allergens:
  - ➢ Tree, grass or weed pollens and fungi (seasonal)
  - ➢ Dust mites, cockroaches, animal dander & fungi (perennial). Patients are symptomatic for at least 9months of the year.
- Risk Factors: family history of atopy, ♂>♀, early introduction of formula, smoke exposure in infancy, birth during pollen season, history of asthma (25 - 50% concomitant) or eczema (30% association)
- Clinical Features: nose rubbing, "allergic salute", transverse nasal crease, "allergic shiners" or Denie-Morgan lines under eyes, itchy palate, nasal polyps, edematous nasal mucosa with faint bluish hue or pallor, irritability, fatigue, mouth breathing and snoring
- Diagnosis: Clinical and/or confirmed presence of allergen-specific IgE by hypersensitivity skin testing
  - ➢ Skin test panel: tree and grass pollens, mold, dust mites & animal dander
- Treatment: Allergen avoidance strategies (see www.aaaai.org)
  - ➢ Nasal corticosteroids - mainstay of therapy (fluticasone and mometasone have the least systemic absorption)
  - ➢ Newer antihistamines additive for combined allergic rhinitis/conjunctivitis
  - ➢ Limit vasoconstrictor nasal sprays to 3 days of therapy
  - ➢ Allergen immunotherapy for refractory cases

Non-Allergic Rhinitis Syndromes

- All distinguished from allergic rhinitis by negative skin testing

Vasomotor Rhinitis

- Exacerbated by rapid changes in temperature, humidity, strong odors or alcohol
- Exam: Nasal turbinates of nonallergic rhinitis erythematous and boggy

Infectious Rhinitis: symptoms of the common cold – (viral or bacterial)

Non-Allergic Rhinitis with Nasal Eosinophilia Syndrome (NARES)

- Perennial symptoms, 50% with sinusitis, 33% with nasal polyps and 15% with asthma. Poor response to antihistamines

Hormonal: pregnancy, hypothyroidism and oral contraceptive pills
Rhinitis Medicamentosa: abuse of cocaine or vasoconstrictor nasal sprays
Gustatory Rhinitis: IgE-mediated condition exacerbated by taste
Atrophic Rhinitis: elderly, *Klebsiella ozaenae* colonization, smells a foul odor
Mechanical: foreign body, nasal polyps or deviated nasal septum
Granulomatous: Wegener's granulomatosis (c-antineutrophil cytoplasmic antibody or biopsy +) or sarcoidosis (high angiotensin converting enzyme level or biopsy +)
Treatment: steroid nasal sprays can benefit all types of non-allergic rhinitis

- Ipratropium bromide nasal spray as adjunct therapy for profuse rhinorrhea
- Treat underlying condition for mechanical & granulomatous rhinitis

Ann Allergy Asthma Immunology 1998; 81: 478. Allergy 2000; 55: 116 and Immunology and Allergy Clinics of North America 2000; 20: 383.

History: duration, prior ear disease, noise exposure, hearing status, medications, history of prior neck injury, quality of tinnitus, exacerbating/relieving factors, associated mood disorder or insomnia

The Different Causes of Tinnitus with Suggested Evaluation and Treatment

Hearing impairment: Noise-induced, presbycusis or congenital
- **Work-up:** audiogram and tympanometry
- **Treatment:** hearing aids or cochlear implants for refractory cases

Otosclerosis: often conductive hearing loss
- **Treatment:** surgery to correct conductive defect

Vascular
- Pulsating/humming quality. Head position or exertion changes pitch or intensity
- **Etiologies:** Arteriovenous (AV) fistulas, glomus tumors, arterial bruits or venous hum (can occur with systemic hypertension or pseudotumor cerebri)
- **Work-up**
  - ➤ Auscultate for bruits
  - ➤ Compression of ipsilateral internal jugular vein can suppress venous hum
  - ➤ MRI/MRA to rule out a dural AV fistula or skull-based glomus tumor
- **Treatment:** Selective embolization or excision/ligation depending on etiology

Middle Ear Spasmodic Activity
- Clicking quality
- **Etiologies:** middle ear disease or multiple sclerosis
- **Work-up:** tympanometry and otoscopy
- **Treatment:** Middle ear surgery or botulinum injections

Eustachian Tube Dysfunction
- Ocean wave quality. Occurs because eustachian tube has impaired patency.
- Frequently occurs after marked weight loss or radiation treatment to nasopharynx
- **Treatment:** Topical nasal steroids or antihistamines

Ototoxic Medications
- Aminoglycosides, angiotensin converting enzyme inhibitors, chloroquine, hydroxychloroquine, benzodiazepines, calcium channel blockers, carbamazepine, cisplatin, clarithromycin, cyclooxygenase-2 inhibitors, cyclobenzaprine, dapsone, α_1-blockers, doxepin, fluoroquinolones, isotretinoin, local anesthetics, loop diuretics, proton pump inhibitors, quinidine, aspirin, NSAIDs, sertraline, tricyclic antidepressants and valproic acid

Temporomandibular Joint Dysfunction
- **Treatment:** stop chewing gum/bruxism and use of custom-fitted oral devices

Whiplash/craniocervical Injury
- **Treatment:** physical therapy and soft cervical collar

Acoustic Neuroma and Cerebellopontine Angle Tumors
- Hearing loss and intermittent vertigo
- **Work-up:** MRI of posterior fossa and auditory canal
- **Treatment:** Surgical resection

Barotrauma to Ear
- **Infections:** neurosyphilis, Lyme disease, meningitis or chronic otitis media
- **Meniere's disease:** low-pitched tinnitus, hearing loss, aural fullness + vertigo

Other therapies: Tinnitus retraining therapy, biofeedback, masking devices and antidepressants if associated mood disorder present.

Reference: NEJM, 2002; 347: 904-10.

Diagnosis of Asthma in Patients over 5 Years of Age
History/Exam
- Episodic wheezing, chest tightness, dyspnea or cough
- Symptoms worsened by certain allergens, exercise or infection
- Symptoms may worsen at night
- History of allergic rhinitis or eczema
- Family history of asthma, allergic rhinitis, eczema or recurrent sinusitis
- Exam with hyperexpansion of chest, wheezing, prolonged expiratory phase

Reversible Airflow Obstruction on Spirometry
- FEV_1 < 80% predicted or FEV_1/FVC < 65%
- FEV_1 increases ≥ 12% with inhaled β_2-agonist
  FEV_1 = forced expiratory volume in 1 second, FVC = forced vital capacity

Exclude Alternative Diagnoses
- Vocal cord dysfunction, vascular rings, foreign bodies, chronic obstructive pulmonary disease, congestive heart failure
- Same criteria used for children under 5 although spirometry not possible

Classification of Asthma Severity (excludes periods of exacerbation)

Class	Days with sxs	Nights with sxs	*PEF or FEV_1	PEF variability
Mild intermittent	≤ 2/week	≤ 2/month	≥ 80%	< 20%
Mild persistent	3-6/week	3-4/month	≥ 80%	20-30%
Mod. persistent	Daily	≥ 5/month	> 60%-< 80%	> 30%
Severe persistent	Daily	Most	≤ 60%	> 30%

sxs = symptoms, PEF = Peak expiratory flow, Mod. = moderate
* percent of personal best for PEF or FEV_1 (or predicted PEF if personal best unknown)
Adapted from 2002 NIH Practical Guide for the Diagnosis and Management of Asthma

Predicted PEF (liters/min) for Nonsmoking Patients Am Rev Resp Dis, 1963; 88: 644

Age (yrs)	Women (height in inches)					Men (height in inches)						Child (height in inches)	
	55	60	65	70	75	60	65	70	75	80			
20	390	423	460	496	529	554	602	649	693	740	44	160
30	380	413	448	483	516	532	577	622	664	710	48	214
40	370	402	436	470	502	509	552	596	636	680	52	267
50	360	391	424	457	488	486	527	569	607	649	56	320
60	350	380	412	445	475	463	502	542	578	618	60	373
70	340	369	400	432	461	440	477	515	550	587	64	427

Risk Factors for Death in Asthmatics

Sudden severe attacks	Prior intubation	Prior ICU admission
≥ 2 ER/hospitalizations/yr	>2 albuterol canisters/mo.	Heart/psychiatric disorder

2002 NIH asthma guidelines at www.nhlbi.nih.gov/guidelines/asthma/index.htm

Pulmonology:

Trigger Avoidance/Con...

- Possible triggers: smok...
- Exercise-induced starts ...
- Allergic rhinitis: control w...
- Gastroesophageal reflux: r...

Stepwise Approach to Asthma ...

- Gain control early with oral stero...
- Step down therapy every 1-2 mor...
- Can add theophylline for severe as...
- Never use salmeterol alone without ...

Class	Short-acting β2-agonist	Long-acting β2-agonist		
Mild intermittent	prn	-		
Mild persistent	prn	-	lo...	+/- >12 y.o.
Mod. persistent	prn	+	me...	+/- >12 y.o.
Sev. persistent	prn	+	high ...	

* steroid equiv. to beclomethasone 200-400 mcg/day (lo...), 400-800 (med), >800 (high)
Advair diskus is combination inhaler (fluticasone + salmeterol) for moderate-severe asthma

Stepwise Approach to Asthma Management in Patients Under 5 Years

Class	Short-acting β2-agonist	Inhaled Steroid	Inhaled antihistamine	Theophylline*
Mild intermittent	prn	-	-	-
Mild persistent	prn	+/- low dose	+	-
Mod. persistent	prn	low-med dose	+	+
Sev. persistent	prn	high dose	-	+

* aim for theophylline level 5-15 mcg/mL

Asthma Action Plan for Patients Older than 5 Years

- Green zone (doing well): PEF ≥ 80%
- Yellow zone (worsening asthma): PEF ≥ 50% - < 79%
  Albuterol 2-4 puffs q2-4hrs, double dose of inhaled steroids x 7-10 days
  Oral prednisone 1 mg/kg/day up to 60 mg/day x 5-7 days
- Red zone (medical emergency that needs evaluation): PEF < 50%
  albuterol 2-4 puffs or nebulizer q20 minutes x 3 then q1-2 hours
  Oral prednisone 1 mg/kg/day up to 60 mg/day x 5-7 days

Asthma Action Plan if Younger than 5 Years (add points for each 4 categories)

Score	Cough past 5 min.	Wheezing	Retractions	Tachypnea
0	None	None	None	None
1	< 1/minute	End-expiratory	Barely	RR ↑ < 50%
2	1-4/minute	--	--	RR ↑ < 100%
3	> 4/minute	Entire Expir.	Obvious	RR ↑ > 100%
5	--	Inspir + Expir.	Severe	--

RR=respiratory rate, ↑= increased, Inspir.= inspiratory, Expir.= expiratory
Green Zone = 0-1 points, High Yellow Zone = 2-3, Low Yellow 4-6, Red Zone > 6 points
Reference: National Asthma Education Program in J. Allergy & Clin. Immunology 2002; 110(5): S141-210.

...eeks duration

...ugh

...aused by either postnasal drip, cough variant asthma or
...geal reflux.

...mmon causes of chronic cough include: chronic bronchitis,
...nchiectasis, postviral bronchospasm, angiotensin converting enzyme
inhibitor (ACEI)-induced cough, lung cancer, interstitial lung disease, occult
CHF ("cardiac asthma"), foreign body, pulmonary embolus, pulmonary infection
(typical or atypical bacteria, tuberculosis, coccidiomycosis, histoplasmosis or
aspergillosis) or psychogenic cough

Evaluation and Treatment of The Common Causes of Chronic Cough

- **Postnasal drip:** symptoms of rhinitis, itchy throat or palate and exam may
  reveal edematous nasal turbinates and a glistening, "cobblestone" appearance
  to the pharyngeal mucosa
  ➢ Empiric trial of an oral antihistamine-decongestant pill, nasal corticosteroids
    or ipratropium nasal spray
- **Cough variant asthma:** atopic history or family history of eczema, allergies or
  asthma. Often discover cough triggers (e.g., exercise, cold exposure,
  environmental allergens, animal dander or fragrances)
  ➢ Test with routine spirometry and if normal consider methacholine challenge
  ➢ Consider an empiric trial of inhaled bronchodilators
  ➢ Trigger avoidance
- **Gastroesophageal reflux (GERD):** history of heartburn, dyspepsia or sour
  taste in the mouth exacerbated by meals and the supine position. Up to 35% of
  patients with GERD-induced cough are asymptomatic.
  ➢ Avoid fatty foods, chocolate and excess alcohol
  ➢ Smoking cessation
  ➢ Avoid bedtime snacks
  ➢ Elevate head of the bed 6 inches
  ➢ Empiric trial of Histamine$_2$-blocker or proton pump inhibitor
  ➢ Definitive diagnosis may require esophageal pH probe testing

Evaluation of Less Common Causes of Chronic Cough

- **Initial studies and interventions to consider**
  ➢ Chest x-ray, place a PPD test, check for offending meds (e.g., ACEI)
  ➢ Investigate for toxic occupational exposures
  ➢ Smoking cessation counseling
  ➢ Pulmonary function tests if chronic bronchitis a consideration
- **Second-tier studies if cause remains unclear**
  ➢ Bronchoscopy to rule out lung cancer, foreign body or occult infection
  ➢ High-resolution CT scan if chest x-ray equivocal for interstitial lung disease

References: Archives Internal Medicine, 1996; 158: 1222 and NEJM, 2000; 343: 1715.

Diagnosis of Chronic Obstructive Lung Disease (COPD)

- **History**
  - ➤ Exertional dyspnea that is persistent and usually progressive
  - ➤ Chronic cough worse in the morning is typical
  - ➤ Chronic sputum production (>3 months/year x 2 years=chronic bronchitis)
  - ➤ History of smoking (most patients have ≥ 20 pack-year tobacco history)
  - ➤ History of occupational dust or chemical exposure
  - ➤ Patients usually are ≥ 50 years of age
- **Exam**
  - ➤ Auscultation may reveal expiratory wheezing, prolonged expiratory phase and/or diminished air movement
  - ➤ Anteroposterior dimension of thorax often enlarged ("barrel chest")
  - ➤ Ruddy face may be a sign of secondary polycythemia
  - ➤ Breathing through pursed lips in severe emphysema
  - ➤ Lower extremity edema may represent Cor pulmonale
- **Spirometry**
  - ➤ FEV_1/FVC ratio < 70% predicted and postbronchodilator FEV_1 < 80%
  - ➤ Increase in the postbronchodilator FEV_1 of 200 mL or ≥ 15% after inhaled glucocorticoid therapy for 6-12 weeks predicts long-term steroid benefit
  - ➤ FEV_1 = forced expiratory volume in 1 second, FVC = forced vital capacity

Therapy at Various Stages of Stable COPD

Stage	Spirometry	Therapy
All	Smoking cessation, influenza and pneumococcal vaccines, exercise	
0 (at risk)	Normal	chronic cough +/- sputum & smoker
1 (mild)	FEV_1/FVC ratio<70% FEV_1 >80% predicted	ipratropium +/- albuterol meter-dosed inhaler prn
2A (mod.)	50%≤ FEV_1 < 80%	albuterol + atrovent +/- inhaled
2B (mod.)	30%≤ FEV_1 < 50%	glucocorticoids and pulmonary rehab*
3 (severe)	FEV_1 < 30% or respiratory failure or Cor pulmonale	as for Stage 2A/2B but may also need home oxygen

* includes aerobic exercise, nutritional support and education

Management of Acute COPD Exacerbations

- **3 diagnostic criteria:** ↑ in dyspnea, sputum volume and sputum purulence
- **Mild exacerbation** if 1 criterion present + one of the following: URI in past 5 d, fever of unclear source, ↑ wheezing, ↑ cough, 20% ↑ heart or resp. rate
  - ➤ Check a chest x-ray and intensify bronchodilator therapy
- **Moderate exacerbation** if 2 criteria present
  - ➤ Check a chest x-ray, bronchodilators, systemic corticosteroids[1], oxygen therapy or non-invasive positive pressure ventilation as needed
- **Severe exacerbation** if 3 criteria present
  - ➤ As for moderate exacerbation but add antibiotics[2] +/- invasive ventilation

1. SCCOPDE trial used methylprednisolone 125 mg IV q6h x 3d → prednisone 60 mg/d x 4d → 40 mg/d x 4d → 20 mg/d x 4d then off. Lower doses of methylprednisolone may be as effective
2. standard antibiotics used are amoxicillin, trimethoprim-sulfamethoxazole or tetracycline
References: Ann Int Med, 2001; 134 (7): 595-9. Chest, 2001; 119: 1185-9. NIH publication 2701, 4/01.

Test	Transudate	Exudate‡
Specific gravity	< 1.016	≥ 1.016
PF protein (gm/dL)	< 3.0	≥ 3.0
PF protein/serum protein	< 0.5	≥ 0.5
PF LDH (IU)	< 200	≥ 200 or > 2/3 upper limit of labs normal range
PF LDH/serum LDH	< 0.6	≥ 0.6
PF glucose (mg%)	> 60	≤ 60*

PF = pleural fluid, LDH = lactate dehydrogenase, IU = international units
* glucose < 60 suggests cancer, tuberculosis, empyema or effusion from rheumatoid lung
‡ only one test needs to be abnormal to classify effusion as an exudate

Causes of Transudative Effusions

- Constrictive pericarditis
- Hepatic hydrothorax
- Nephrotic syndrome
- Severe ↓ albumin
- Urinothorax
- Heart Failure
- Peritoneal dialysis
- Superior vena cava syndrome

Evaluation of Exudative Effusions

Diagnosis	PF appearance	Diagnostic Pleural Fluid Testing
Empyema	Purulent	Pleural fluid pH<7.2*, ↑ WBC‡, + culture
Malignant	+/- Bloody	Positive pleural fluid cytology
Chylothorax	Milky	Triglycerides > 110 mg/dL
Pancreatitis	-	High amylase
Uremia	-	Very high BUN (usually > 100 mg/dL)
Sarcoidosis	-	High angiotensin converting enzyme level
Lupus pleuritis	-	Positive pleural fluid ANA
Rheumatoid lung	Yellow-green	Characteristic cytology, glucose< 30 mg%
Ovarian hyper-stimulation syn.	-	Fertility medication use
Meig's syndrome	-	+ Ascites and ovarian fibroma
Amebic abscess	Anchovy paste	+ Amebic titers and + liver abscess
Pulmonary embolus	Bloody	+ Ventilation/perfusion scan
Tuberculosis	Bloody	+ Acid fast bacilli on pleural biopsy and < 5% mesothelial cells in pleural fluid

* fluid for pleural fluid pH should be collected in an arterial blood gas tube and kept on ice
‡ ↑ WBC = elevated pleural fluid white blood count. Cell count should be collected in a purple top tube.

Contraindications to Diagnostic Thoracentesis

- International normalized ratio > 2.0 or partial thromboplastin time > twice normal
- Platelets < 25,000 cells/mL
- Caution if creatinine > 6 mg/dL
- Small volume of pleural fluid: <1 cm between pleural fluid line & chest wall on decubitus chest radiograph.

References: Chest, 1997; 111: 970. Semin. Respir. Crit. Care Med., 1995; 16: 269.

Definitions
- Apnea is the cessation of airflow for at least 10 seconds
- Apnea index is number of apneas per hour of sleep
- Hypopnea is reduction in airflow > 50% + oxygen saturation decreases > 4%
- Respiratory disturbance index = apneas + hypopneas per hr. of sleep
- Obesity-Hypoventilation syndrome is a subset of obstructive sleep apnea patients who have chronic daytime hypoxemia and hypercapnia.

Risk Factors for Obstructive Sleep Apnea
- Central obesity (body mass index > 29), age > 40, male, postmenopausal women, alcoholics, hypothyroidism, sedative/narcotic use, micrognathia, retrognathia, macroglossia, tonsillar hypertrophy and nasal congestion

Clinical Features of Obstructive Sleep Apnea
- **Symptoms**: Restless and nonrestorative sleep, daytime hypersomnolence, morning headaches, cognitive impairment, mood disorders and irritability, decreased libido, impotence, hearing impairment, night sweats, morning dry mouth and sore throat and nocturnal drooling
- **Signs**: Loud snoring, obesity, short and thick neck, excessive pharyngeal tissue, large uvula, sleepiness and hypertension
- Cor pulmonale can lead to congestive hepatopathy and leg edema
- Left ventricular dysfunction can cause symptoms of left heart failure
  - ➢ 30% of patients with severe obstructive sleep apnea have this complication.

Diagnosis of Obstructive Sleep Apnea
- Nocturnal polysomnography in a sleep lab is the gold standard for diagnosis.
  - ➢ Study will simultaneously measure the patients electroencephalogram, electrocardiogram, chin electromyogram, electrooculogram and monitor oral airflow, oxygen saturation and thoracic cage excursion
- Apnea index > 5 with persistent ventilatory effort & oxygen desaturation < 90%

Classification of Obstructive Sleep Apnea
- Mild obstructive sleep apnea has a respiratory disturbance index of 5-19 and minimum oxygen saturation > 79%.
- Moderate obstructive sleep apnea has a respiratory disturbance index of 20- 49 and minimum oxygen saturation > 69%.
- Severe obstructive sleep apnea has a respiratory disturbance index of > 49 and minimum oxygen saturation < 70%

Treatment Options for Obstructive Sleep Apnea
- Weight reduction
- Nasal continuous positive airway pressure (CPAP) for patients with only obstructive sleep apnea to keep the upper airway open at night.
  - ➢ Compliance major issue: only 25% of patients used mask for ≥ 3 hrs/night
  - ➢ Bidirectional machine positive airway pressure (BiPAP) more appropriate for obesity-hypoventilation syndrome by providing pressure support ventilation
- Uvulopalatopharyngoplasty gave significant improvement in ~ 50% of patients.
- Tracheostomy
- Tongue-retaining devices or mandibular-advancing devices
- protriptyline 10-20 mg PO qhs increases upper airway muscle tone (appropriate for mild obstructive sleep apnea).
- Sleep on side
- Minimize alcohol, narcotics and sedatives

References: Chest, 1999; 116 (5): 1426-33 and American Family Physician, 1999; 60 (8): 2279-86.

Spirometry in a healthy individual

Abbreviations
ERV= expiratory reserve vol.
FEF$_{25-75\%}$=forced expiratory flow from 25-75% VC
FEV$_1$= forced expiratory volume in 1 second
FRC= functional residual capacity
FVC= forced vital capacity
IC= inspiratory capacity
RV= residual volume
TLC= total lung capacity
VC= vital capacity

Spirometry Patterns

- **Normal:** FVC, FEV$_1$, PEFR and FEF$_{25-75\%}$ > 80% predicted; FEV$_1$/FVC > 95% predicted ◆ Can be seen with intermittent disease (e.g. asthma); also pulmonary emboli and pulmonary vascular dz.

Flow-Volume Loop

- **Obstructive:** Obstruction to airflow prolongs expiration ◆ FEV$_1$/FVC < 95% predicted and airway resistance ↑ ◆ Differential diagnosis: asthma, COPD, bronchiectasis, cystic fibrosis, bronchiolitis, proximal airway obstruction.

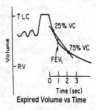

- **Restrictive:** Reduced volumes without changes in airway resistance ◆ VC and TLC ↓, FEV$_1$ and FVC ↓ proportionately (FEV$_1$/FVC ratio >95% pred) ◆ Must confirm lung volumes by helium dilution or plethysmography (reduced FVC on spirometry not specific for restrictive disease, although normal FVC predicts normal TLC) ◆ Differential diagnosis: interstitial disease, CHF, pleural disease, pneumonia, neuromuscular disease, chest wall abnormalities, obesity, lung resection.

Expired Volume vs Time

- **Bronchodilator response:** Positive if FVC or FEV$_1$ increase by 12% (≥ 200 cc).

- **Poor effort:** Most reliably diagnosed by technician performing test rather than spirometric values.

Grading of PFT abnormalities

Obstruction	% Predicted FEV_1
Mild	70 - 100%
Moderate	60 - 69%
Mod-severe	50 - 59%
Severe	35 - 49%
Very Severe	< 35%

Restriction	% Predicted $TLC^\#$	% Predicted FVC
Mild	70% - LLN*	70% - LLN*
Moderate	50 - 69%	60 - 69%
Mod-severe		50 - 59%
Severe	< 50%	35 - 49%
Very Severe		< 35%

\# TLC superior to FVC in assessing restrictive disease
* LLN= lower limits of normal

Diffusion capacity (DL_{CO})

- Expensive, imprecise and generally less helpful than what the textbook says. Measured value needs to be adjusted for alveolar ventilation (VA). Most useful for: (1) evaluating pulmonary vascular disease (2) diagnosing pulmonary hemorrhage (3) assessing change in collagen-vascular or drug-related pulmonary disease
- **Reduced:** emphysema, interstitial lung disease, pulmonary embolism, pulmonary vascular disease, lung resection, severe CHF
- **Increased:** pulmonary hemorrhage, mild CHF
- **Normal:** asthma, chronic bronchitis, chest wall and pleural abnormalities, neuromuscular disease

Mechanical upper airway obstruction

- Most reliably diagnosed by contour of flow-volume loop (see below). If suspected, alert technician to emphasize performance of inspiratory limb of loop.
- **Variable extrathoracic:** bilateral or unilateral vocal cord paralysis ◆ rheumatoid arthritis ◆ post-intubation vocal cord adhesions ◆ obstructive sleep apnea ◆ burns
- **Variable intrathoracic:** non-circumferential tracheal tumors which make walls "floppy" ◆ relapsing polychondritis ◆ tracheomalacia following surgery ◆ mainstem bronchus tumors
- **Fixed upper airway obstruction:** benign stricture after prolonged intubation ◆ tracheal tumor ◆ goiter ◆ small endotracheal or tracheostomy tube ◆ bilateral stenosis of mainstem bronchi (rare)

Risk factors for perioperative pulmonary complications

• Smoking within 8 weeks of surgery	• Chronic obstructive pulmonary
• Poor general health	disease or significant airway
• Inability to exercise, chronic cough, or	obstruction
unexplained dyspnea	• Elevated arterial carbon dioxide
• Abnormal lung exam (wheezing,	pressure ($PaCO_2$)
prolonged expiration, dullness, etc)	• Thoracic or upper abdomen surgery
	• Surgery lasting > 3 hours
	• General anesthesia
	• Long-acting neuromuscular blockade

Note: obesity and advanced age by itself do not appear to increase risk

Pre-operative risk stratification

- Despite high rate of minor pulmonary complications, few patients have an absolute pulmonary contraindication to surgery. *Pearl:* If patient breathes spontaneously prior to surgery, probability is high that they will wean from ventilator post-op (**unless** lung resection is planned).
- No validated indices (i.e. similar to Goldman cardiac index) exist that accurately assess risk of perioperative pulmonary complications
- Pre-operative screening tests (spirometry ± arterial blood gas) have been recommended[1] for the following patient groups:
  - ➢ Undergoing coronary artery bypass graft or upper abdominal surgery **and** history of smoking or dyspnea
  - ➢ Patients with unexplained dyspnea or pulmonary symptoms who are undergoing head and neck, orthopedic or abdominal surgery
  - ➢ Patients undergoing lung resection
- However, given lack of predictive value, testing should not be used as prerequisite to surgery but rather as tool to optimize preoperative lung function

Lung resection candidates[2]

- Best predictors of poor outcome: (1) predicted postoperative forced expiratory volume in 1 second (FEV_1) < 0.8 liters by spirometry combined with quantitative perfusion scanning or (2) predicted postoperative max oxygen ventilation (VO_2) < 10 ml/kg/min by cardiopulmonary exercise testing
- Other preoperative risk factors: ◆ Forced vital capacity (FVC) < 50% predicted ◆ FEV_1/FVC< 50% ◆ FEV_1 < 2 L ◆ MVV < 50% predicted ◆ residual volume/total lung capacity (RV/TLC) >50% ◆ pulmonary hypertension by echocardiography

Interventions to reduce perioperative risk

- Smoking cessation: beneficial if patient quits ≥ 8 weeks prior to surgery (although shorter periods may actually increase risk)
- Optimize pulmonary function in patients with chronic obstructive pulmonary disease or asthma: oral/inhaled steroids, bronchodilators, antibiotics, physical therapy, etc. Brief steroid treatment does not appear to increase rate of infections or other postoperative complications.
- Defer elective surgery for acute exacerbations of pulmonary disease
- Consider shorter procedures (< 3 hrs) and spinal/epidural or regional anesthesia for high-risk patients. Avoid long-acting neuromuscular blockers.
- Deep breathing exercises or incentive spirometry beneficial (requires intense supervision, otherwise patient compliance is generally low)

[1] Zibrak G et al. Indications for Pulmonary Function Testing. *Ann Intern Med* 1990;112:763.
[2] Olsen GN et al. Pulmonary function evaluation of the lung resection candidate: a prospective study. *Am Rev Resp Dis* 1979;111:379; Wyser C et al. Prospective evaluation of an algorithm for the functional assessment of lung resection candidates. *Am J Resp Crit Care Med* 1999;159:1450-56.

Epidemiology
- Condition of elderly men: 40-50% in men age 50-60 yrs and ~ 80% if ≥ 80 yrs

Clinical Presentation
- Asymptomatic
- Irritative symptoms: urinary frequency, nocturia and urinary urgency
- Obstructive symptoms: hesitancy, weak or intermittent stream, straining to void and sensation of incomplete bladder emptying
- Hematuria or dysuria (urinary tract infection)
- Bladder outlet obstruction with postrenal azotemia
- American Urological Association has developed a urinary symptom score that evaluates the frequency of the 7 irritative and obstructive symptoms as above.
  ➢ Each symptom is scored on a scale of 0 to 5 based on symptom frequency: not at all (0), less than 20% of the time (1), less than 50% of the time (2), 50% of the time (3), more than 50% of the time (4) or almost always (5)
  ➢ Score 0 – 7 = mild, 8 – 19 = moderate and ≥ 20 = severe symptoms

Physical Exam
- Typically find a diffusely enlarged, nontender prostate with no discrete nodules
- Rarely, patients have a normal-sized prostate

Lab Evaluation
- Urinalysis to check for blood or evidence of infection
- Serum creatinine +/- prostate specific antigen (PSA) level

Pharmacologic Treatments for Benign Prostatic Hyperplasia (BPH)
- Generally initiated for men with moderate-severe urinary symptom scores
- **Nonselective alpha$_1$ blockers**
  ➢ doxazosin 1-8 mg PO qhs and terazosin 1-10 mg PO qhs
  ➢ 3 head-to-head studies have shown greater efficacy of alphablockers compared with finasteride on urinary symptom score and urine flow rate.
  ➢ Side effects: postural hypotension, dizziness, fatigue and weakness
- **Selective alpha$_{1A}$ blockers**
  ➢ tamsulosin 0.4 mg PO qhs/bid
  ➢ less orthostatic hypotension than nonselective alpha-blockers
- **5-alpha-reductase inhibitors**
  ➢ finasteride 5 mg PO qd and dutasteride 0.5 mg PO qd
  ➢ induce an 80-90% reduction in serum dihydrotestosterone
  ➢ Greater efficacy the larger the initial prostate size
  ➢ Side effects: decreased libido, ejaculatory dysfunction and impotence

Surgical Treatments for Benign Prostatic Hyperplasia
- Consider in all patients who fail medical therapy, have recurrent urinary tract infections, recurrent hematuria, renal failure or severe urinary symptom score.
- Transurethral resection of the Prostate (TURP): most common surgical procedure for BPH
  ➢ Symptom improvement in 90% of patients
  ➢ Complications: retrograde ejaculation (70%), impotence (14%), urethral stricture (4%) and urinary incontinence (6% with partial & 1% with complete)
- Other surgical options: transurethral incision of the prostate, transurethral microwave thermotherapy or laser prostatectomy.

Reference: American Family Physician, 2002; 66: 77-88.

Definition of Hematuria: ≥ 5 red blood cells (RBCs) per high powered field.

Etiologies of Hematuria
- Urinary tract infection
- Nephrolithiasis or ureterolithiasis
- Exercise-induced hematuria
- Glomerular disease: glomerulonephritis, Immunoglobulin A (IgA) nephropathy, hereditary nephritis or thin basement membrane disease
- Cancer of the bladder, kidney or ureters
- Hypercalciuria or hyperuricosuria
- Loin pain-hematuria syndrome

Work-up of Hematuria
- Urine culture to rule out infection
- Repeat urinalysis in 1 week to determine if hematuria transient or persistent.
- Examine urinary sediment for dysmorphic RBCs or RBC casts and check for renal insufficiency and significant proteinuria (>500 mg/24 hrs) all of which suggest a glomerular source of hematuria
  > For suspected glomerular bleeding, renal biopsy indicated
- Intravenous pyelogram can assess for renal cell cancers and stones
- Urine cytology
- Cystoscopy indicated for persistent hematuria if all tests above are negative.
- For unexplained hematuria, consider 24 hr urine for calcium and uric acid

Clinical Presentation of Nephrolithiasis
- Renal stones may be asymptomatic, but most cause flank pain associated with hematuria and often nausea, vomiting and radiation to the groin.

Management of Nephrolithiasis
- Confirm the diagnosis with an intravenous pyelogram or a non-contrast-enhanced CT scan with 3 mm cuts down the urinary tract.
- Hydration and strong analgesics (may need admission for pain control or if the nausea precludes adequate oral hydration and pill consumption)
- Strain urine for stones
- All patients must drink at least 2 liters of water daily to prevent recurrences.
- Thiazide diuretics can minimize calciuria in patients with hypercalciuria.
- Treatment options for patients who do not pass ureroliths spontaneously include shock wave lithotripsy or flexible ureteroscopy by a urologist.
- Percutaneous nephrostolithotomy procedure reserved for large (>2 cm) or complex calculi or those resistant to shock wave lithotripsy.

Work-up of Nephrolithiasis
- Medications that can cause stones: indinavir, sulfadiazine and triamterene.
- Stone analysis
- Labs for calcium stones: serum calcium and bicarbonate +/- intact parathyroid hormone level and at least two 24 hour urine collection for calcium, citrate, oxalate and creatinine.
- Labs for noncalcium stones: serum uric acid and at least two 24 hour urine collection for uric acid or cystine depending on the stone analysis.

References: J Urology, 1989; 141: 350. : J Urology, 1990; 144: 99. NEJM, 1992; 327: 1141.
J Urology, 2002; 167: 1607 and J Urology, 1997; 158: 1915.

Causes of Transient Incontinence (mnemonic is DIAPPERS)
- D – Delirium
- I – Infection of urinary tract
- A – Atrophy of genitourinary tract
- P – Pharmaceuticals (e.g., diuretics, caffeine, alcohol, β-blockers, sedatives)
- P – Psychological conditions
- E – Endocrine disorders (e.g., diabetes mellitus, diabetes insipidus or hyperparathyroidism)
- R – Restricted mobility
- S – Stool impaction

Causes of Established Urinary Incontinence
- **Genuine Stress Urinary Incontinence (GSUI)**
  - ➤ Caused by weakness of the muscles of the urethral sphincter or pelvic floor.
  - ➤ Hallmark is the loss of urine with increased intra-abdominal pressure as occurs with coughing, sneezing, laughing, running or position changes.
  - ➤ Provocative stress test: have patient vigorously cough with full bladder in recumbent and, if needed, upright position → loss of urine indicates GSUI.
  - ➤ Bonney test: perform provocative stress test while elevating bladder neck and it is positive if there is no loss of urine.
  - ➤ Q-tip test: place sterile Q-tip in distal urethra and have patient valsalva. A change of the angle > 30º is positive and suggests urethral hypermobility.
- **Urge Incontinence**
  - ➤ Most common cause of urinary incontinence in patients over 60 years.
  - ➤ Hallmark is sudden onset of urinary urgency followed by loss of urine.
  - ➤ Definitive diagnosis by identifying detrusor instability by cystometrogram.
- **Overflow Incontinence**
  - ➤ Causes include bladder outlet obstruction (BOO) or a neurogenic bladder.
  - ➤ Causes of BOO: prostatism, cervical cancer, urethral stricture or bladder CA
  - ➤ Neurogenic bladder: diabetic neuropathy, sacral cord lesions or medications
  - ➤ Diagnosis by elevated by postvoid residual urine > 150-200 mL
- **Functional Incontinence**
  - ➤ Patients unable to maintain continence because of cognitive, physical or emotional problems.

Treatment of Urinary Incontinence
- **Nonpharmacologic Interventions**
  - ➤ Bladder retraining with timed voids at progressively longer intervals for UI
  - ➤ Avoid caffeine and alcohol
  - ➤ Kegel exercises, pessaries or electrical stimulation devices for GSUI
  - ➤ Absorbent pads or condom catheters can help to ensure dryness.
- **Pharmacologic therapy**
  - ➤ Urge incontinence: oxybutynin 7.5-20 mg PO or tolterodine 2-4 mg PO qd
  - ➤ Imipramine 10-25 mg PO tid for mixed incontinence from GSUI and UI
  - ➤ Genuine stress urinary incontinence: estrogen therapy if atrophic vaginitis or pseudoephedrine 30-60 mg PO tid
  - ➤ Neurogenic bladder: bethanechol 10-50 mg PO tid
  - ➤ Prostatism with bladder outlet obstruction: terazosin 2 - 10 mg PO qhs or tamsulosin 0.4 mg PO qhs or doxazosin 2 – 8 mg PO qhs
  - ➤ Surgery for stress incontinence: retropubic suspension procedures

References: Southern Med J., 2001; 94: 952-7 and Amer Fam. Physician, 2000; 62: 2433-44.

Common Causes of Abnormal Vaginal Bleeding in Premenopausal Women

Premenarchal	Reproductive Years*	Perimenopausal
• Foreign body • Trauma • Precocious puberty • Sexual abuse • Urethral prolapse	• Anovulation • Pregnancy • Cervical or endometrial polyp • Cervical cancer • Adenomyosis • Hypothyroidism • Pituitary disorders • Bleeding diathesis • Fibroids • Cervicitis‡ • Progestin breakthrough bleeding • Copper IUD	• Anovulation • Endometrial cancer • Cervical cancer • Cervical polyp • Endometrial polyp • Adenomyosis • Fibroids • Cirrhosis • Uremia • Cervicitis‡ • Progestin breakthrough bleeding

* In postmenarchal adolescents, the common etiologies are pregnancy, anovulation and bleeding diatheses.
‡ gonorrhea, chlamydia or trichomonal infections.

An Approach to Work-up of Abnormal Vaginal Bleeding
- **Pregnant vs non-pregnant**
- **Ovulatory vs Anovulatory Bleeding**
  - ➤ Favoring ovulatory cycles: regular menses, molimina symptoms, Mittelschmerz, basal body temperature increase mid-cycle, mid-luteal serum progesterone > 5 ng/mL, luteinizing hormone surge noted by ovulation kit
- **Menorrhagia vs Metrorrhagia vs Post-coital bleeding**
  - ➤ Menorrhagia typically from fibroids, adenomyosis, bleeding diathesis or a systemic disorder (e.g., hypothyroidism, chronic liver or renal disease).
  - ➤ Metrorrhagia: cervical/endometrial polyps or cancer, cervicitis or anovulation.
  - ➤ Post-coital bleeding: cervicitis, cervical polyps, prolapsed myomas or cancer.
- **Postmenopausal bleeding** is endometrial or cervical cancer until proven otherwise. Can occur during 1st 6 months of hormone replacement therapy.

Lab Evaluation
- Pregnancy test (if positive consider miscarriage or ectopic pregnancy)
- Complete blood count & thyroid stimulating hormone
- Endometrial biopsy in all anovulatory women and those > 35 years
- Pap smear
- Cervical cultures for gonorrhea, chlamydia & a saline prep for trichomonas
- Pelvic ultrasound, sonohysterography or hysteroscopy if women have persistent abnormal bleeding
- Any suspicious cervical lesion should be biopsied

Treatment Options for Various Conditions
- **Anovulatory bleeding**: correction of underlying cause, cyclic oral progesterone or combined oral contraceptive pills (OCPs)
  - ➤ Clomiphene indicated for anovulatory women desiring pregnancy
- **Endometrial polyps**: hysteroscopic excision or dilatation and curettage
- **Fibroids**: hysterectomy, myomectomy, uterine artery embolization or hysteroscopic resection of submucous fibroids
- **Menorrhagia treatments**: nonsteroidal anti-inflammatory drugs, combined oral contraceptive pills, progesterone-releasing intrauterine device, hysterectomy or endometrial ablation procedure.
- **Severe menometrorrhagia**: trial of the equivalent of one 35 mcg ethinyl estradiol OCP tablet tid x 7 days then 1 active tablet qd x 21 days or admission for either IV conjugated estrogen or a dilatation and curettage.

References: Am J Obstetrics Gynecology, 1996; 175: 787 and Clinics Obstet Gynecology, 1998; 41: 928.

Evaluation of Primary Amenorrhea (absence of menarche by age 16)

- **History**
  - ➤ Any signs of pubertal development: presence of a growth spurt, axillary/pubic hair or breast development
  - ➤ Family history of amenorrhea or delayed puberty
  - ➤ Any symptoms of hyperandrogenism or virilization (e.g., hirsutism, acne, central obesity, male-pattern baldness, clitoromegaly and deepened voice)
  - ➤ Recent stress, weight change, strenuous exercise or dietary changes
  - ➤ Galactorrhea, headache, visual field deficits
  - ➤ Examine medication list for those that cause hyperprolactinemia
- **Exam**
  - ➤ Any secondary sexual characteristics
  - ➤ Any hirsutism, acne or virilization
  - ➤ Pelvic exam to determine the presence or absence of Mullerian structures
  - ➤ Presence of an imperforate hymen or a transverse vaginal septum
  - ➤ Physical features of Turner syndrome?
- **Lab Testing if Pelvic Exam is Normal**
  - ➤ Pregnancy test
  - ➤ Follicle stimulating hormone (FSH): low in hypothalamic amenorrhea
  - ➤ Prolactin: hyperprolactinemia from pituitary adenoma or medications
  - ➤ Thyrotropin (TSH): high in hypothyroidism
  - ➤ Serum testosterone: 80-200 ng/dL→ polycystic ovary syndrome (PCOS)
  - ➤ Dehydroepiandrosterone sulfate (DHEAS): 330-700 mcg/dL→ PCOS.
- **Lab Testing if Uterus is Absent**
  - ➤ Karyotype (46, XY in androgen insensitivity syndrome and vanishing testes syndrome and 45, XO in Turner syndrome)
  - ➤ Serum testosterone (high in androgen insensitivity syndrome and very low in vanishing testes syndrome

Evaluation of Secondary Amenorrhea

- **Definition:** the absence of menses for at least 3 cycles or for 6 months.
- **Step 1:** exclude pregnancy, hypothyroidism or hyperprolactinemia
  - ➤ Pituitary MRI for all unexplained hyperprolactinemia to rule out an adenoma.
- **Step 2:** progestational challenge test using Provera 10 mg PO qd x 5 days.
  - ➤ A withdrawal bleed suggests chronic anovulation. No bleeding→ step 3.
  - ➤ For signs of hyperandrogenism check a serum testosterone and DHEAS to rule out PCOS, adrenal or androgen-secreting ovarian tumor
- **Step 3:** conjugated estrogen 1.25 mg PO qd x 21 days and add medroxyprogesterone acotate 10 mg PO qd on days 16-21.
  - ➤ No withdrawal bleed suggests a disorder of the outflow tract or uterus (e.g., Asherman's syndrome or cervical stenosis).
  - ➤ Check FSH and luteinizing hormone (LH) if a withdrawal bleed occurs.
    - ○ High levels indicate premature ovarian failure
    - ○ Low-normal levels indicate hypothalamic amenorrhea
- **Premature ovarian failure work-up**
  - ➤ A karyotype to rule out Turner syndrome if the patient is ≤ 30 years.
- **Work-up of unexplained hypothalamic amenorrhea**
  - ➤ Cranial MRI to rule out a hypothalamic mass

References: American Journal Obstet. Gynecol., 1986; 155: 531. Amer. Fam. Physician, 1999; 60: 209-24.

Initial Prenatal Visit
- Medical, surgical, social, family and obstetrical history
- Complete physical exam
- Pap smear, cervical cultures for gonorrhea and chlamydia
- Consider a varicella antibody test if pt unsure about prior varicella infection.
- Urinalysis and urine culture
- Order prenatal labs to include a complete blood count, blood type, antibody screen, rubella titer, VDRL, hepatitis B surface antigen and an HIV test.
- An Ob ultrasound for dating in all women presenting after 16 weeks gestational age, unsure last menstrual period, for a size/dates discrepancy on exam or for inability to hear fetal heart tones by 12 gestational weeks.
- Offer genetic testing and counseling to all women who will be > 35 years at delivery and those who have a personal or family history of birth defects.
- Place a tuberculosis skin test for all medium-to-high risk patients.
- Consider a 1 hour 50 gram glucose tolerance test for certain high-risk groups:
  > History of gestational diabetes, macrosomia, unexplained stillbirth or malformed infant, family history of diabetes, body mass index (BMI) > 30, glucosuria $\geq 2+$ and certain high-risk ethnic groups.
- Obtain an operative report in all women who have had a prior cesarean to determine if they are candidates for a vaginal birth after c-section.

Frequency of Visits for Uncomplicated Pregnancies
- Every 4 weeks until the patient is 28 gestational weeks
- Every 2 weeks between 28-36 gestational weeks
- Weekly after 36 gestational weeks

Antepartum lab testing
- Offer alpha-fetoprotein/triple marker screen between 16-20 gestational weeks.
- 1 hour 50 gram glucose tolerance test to assess for gestational diabetes in all women between 24-28 weeks.
- Rho immune globulin 300 mcg IM for all Rh-negative women with negative antibody screens between 26-28 weeks.

Follow-up Visits
- Assess weight, fundal height, blood pressure, urine for glucose and protein, fetal heart tones, edema and ask about any regular uterine contractions, leakage of fluid, vaginal bleeding or decreased fetal movement.

Prenatal Counseling
- Cessation of smoking, drinking alcohol or use of any illicit drugs.
- Avoid cat litter boxes and hot tubs
- Do not initiate any strenuous exercise program
- Proper nutrition and expected weight gain
  > National Academy of Sciences advises weight gain 28-40 pounds (prepregnancy BMI < 20), 25-35 pounds (BMI 20-26), 15-25 pounds (BMI 26-29) and 15-20 pounds (BMI ≥ 30).
- Benefits of breast versus bottle feeding
- Discuss contraceptive options postpartum
- Discuss analgesia and anesthesia options
- Discuss repeat c-section versus vaginal birth after cesarean (if applicable).
- Offer prenatal classes around 24 weeks
- Discuss the option of circumcision if a boy is delivered
- Avoid travel past 36 weeks
- Labor precautions reviewed each visit starting in the third trimester

Adapted from American College of Obstetricians and Gynecology Guidelines for Prenatal Care

Tests for Antepartum Fetal Surveillance
- **Nonstress test (NST)**
  - ➢ Reactivity defined as two accelerations (at least 15 beats per minute above the baseline lasting 15 seconds) in a 20 minute period.
  - ➢ The stillbirth rate within 1 week of a reactive NST is 1.9 per 1,000.
  - ➢ A nonreactive NST warrants further testing with either a CST or BPP.
- **Biophysical Profile (BPP)**
  - ➢ Assigns a score of 0 or 2 for each of 5 parameters: an NST and ultrasound assessments of fetal breathing movements, gross fetal movement, fetal tone and amniotic fluid index (AFI): a score of 8 or 10 is a normal BPP.
  - o Stillbirth rate within 1 week of a normal BPP or MBPP is 0.8 per 1,000.
- **Modified BPP (MBPP):** consists of an NST and an AFI
  - ➢ Normal if there is a reactive NST and an AFI > 5
- **Contraction Stress Test (CST)**
  - ➢ Uterine contractions (UCs) induced with either pitocin or nipple stimulation.
  - ➢ A satisfactory test has at least 3 UCs in a 10 minute period.
  - ➢ A positive CST shows late decelerations after > 50% of UCs.
  - ➢ CST equivocal if late or variable decelerations occur with < 50% of UCs.
  - ➢ A negative CST demonstrates no late or significant variable decelerations.
    - o The stillbirth rate within 1 week of a negative CST is 0.3 per 1,000.
  - ➢ An equivocal CST warrants a repeat CST in 24 hours or a full BPP. Contraindications to a CST: preterm labor, ruptured membranes, history of a classical cesarean section or placenta previa.
- **Timing of Delivery:** consult an Ob/Gyn specialist for the optimal timing of delivery for the conditions below (beyond the scope of this pocketbook)
- **Suggested Guidelines for Antepartum Fetal Surveillance**

Indicator condition(s)	When to initiate testing	Frequency of testing/test
Postdates pregnancy	41 weeks	Twice weekly / MBPP
Decreased fetal movement	When it occurs	Single NST
Chronic hypertension	32 weeks	Twice weekly / MBPP
Preeclampsia	At diagnosis	Twice weekly / MBPP
Class A_1 GDM	40 weeks	Twice weekly / NST
Class A_2 or B GDM	32 weeks	Twice weekly / NST
DM with vascular disease	28-32 weeks*	Twice weekly / MBPP
Fetal growth restriction	At diagnosis	Twice weekly / MBPP‡
History of fetal demise	2 weeks before demise	Twice weekly / NST
Active substance abuse	32-34 weeks	Weekly / NST
Increased serum AFP	32-34 weeks	Weekly / NST
Multiple gestation	32 weeks	Weekly / NST /q3wk UTZ
Collagen vascular disease	28-32 weeks*	Twice weekly / MBPP
Oliguhydramnios	At diagnosis	Twice weekly / MBPP
Thyroid disease	32-34 weeks*	Weekly / NST
Cholestasis of pregnancy	At diagnosis	Twice weekly / MBPP
Polyhydramnios	At diagnosis	Weekly / NST
Chronic renal disease	28-32 weeks*	Twice weekly / NST
Congestive heart failure	28 weeks	Twice weekly / NST
Major congenital anomalies	32 weeks	Twice weekly / NST
Isoimmunization	28 weeks	Twice weekly / NST
Thrombophilias	32 – 34 weeks	Twice weekly / MBPP

GDM=gestational diabetes, * initiate testing earlier if poor disease control, AFP= alpha fetoprotein, ‡ = consider qwk umbilical artery doppler, UTZ = ultrasound. References: ACOG Practice Bulletin No. 9, 1999.

History
- Duration mass has been present
- Painful or asymptomatic?
- Change in size or consistency over time and relationship to menstrual cycle.
- Associated skin changes or nipple discharge

Risk Factors for Breast Cancer (RR = relative risk)[1]
- Family history of breast or ovarian cancer in first-degree relative (RR = 2.6)
- Personal history of breast cancer or atypical hyperplasia (RR = 3-5)
- Female sex (RR = 150)
- Age over 70 (RR = 17 vs age 30-34)
- Nulliparous
- Age at first live birth > 30 (RR 1.9-3.5)
- Age of menarche < 12 (RR = 1.5)
- Age of menopause ≥ 55 (RR = 2 vs menopause < 45)
- Postmenopausal body mass index (BMI) > 30.7 (RR = 1.6 vs BMI < 23)
- Current use of estrogen replacement therapy (RR = 1.2-1.4)
- Positive for Breast Cancer Genes 1 or 2 (BRCA1 or BRCA2) (RR 4-7)

Screening Guidelines for Breast Cancer
- Self-breast exams monthly beginning at age 20-30
- Clinical breast exam (CBE) for all women q3 years beginning age 20-30.
- CBE annually for all women starting at age 40
- Annual screening mammogram beginning at age 40
- Start screening 5-10 years earlier for positive family history of breast cancer.

Genetic Testing for BRCA1 and BRCA2 Genes
- Recommended if ≥ 10% risk of finding a gene mutation or if a first-degree relative has breast cancer & is positive for the BRCA1 or BRCA2 gene.
- Risk can be determined using assessment tool at http://bcra.nci.nih.gov/brc/

Suggested Algorithm for Evaluation of A Breast Mass
- In women < 40, breast ultrasound to determine if mass cystic or solid
- Women ≥ 40 require a diagnostic mammogram +/- breast ultrasound
- Fine needle aspiration (FNA) of cysts with pathologic analysis if fluid is bloody or blood-tinged (non-bloody fluid can be discarded).
  > If fluid benign and mass disappears, repeat breast exam in 4-6 weeks.
  > A residual mass, recurrence of mass, bloody cyst fluid or malignant cytology should be referred for diagnostic mammogram and excisional biopsy.
- Triple test score of solid masses using clinical breast exam, imaging and either FNA cytology or core needle biopsy
  > Women under 40 should be imaged using a breast ultrasound and those 40 or older need a diagnostic mammogram
  > Each test scores mass as benign, suspicious or malignant
  > If all 3 tests suggest benign disease, the chance of cancer is 0.7% and patient can be followed with a clinical breast exam in 3-6 months.
  > If any test is suspicious or suggests malignancy, patient is referred for an excisional biopsy.
  > If all tests suggest malignancy, patient is referred for definitive therapy.
  > Women with a non-palpable suspicious breast mass detected by screening mammogram should undergo a stereotactic needle biopsy.

References: 1. NEJM, 2001; 344: 276. Mayo Clin. Proc., 2001; 76 (6): 641-7, NEJM, 1992; 327: 937-42

Adapted from the 2002 Guidelines of the American Society for Colposcopy and Cervical Pathology
Algorithms for management of cytologic and histologic cervical abnormalities available at www.asccp.org

Management of Cytologic Abnormalities

Options for Atypical Squamous Cells (ASC)

- Atypical Squamous Cells possibly High-grade Squamous Intraepithelial Lesion (ASC – H) evaluated by colposcopic examination.
- Options for Atypical Squamous Cells of Undetermined Significance (ASC – US)
  - Repeat pap smear in 6 months and colposcopy for persistent ASC – US
  - HPV DNA testing‡ (only if positive for high-risk subtypes
    - HPV negative for high-risk subtypes → resume annual pap smears

Low-grade Squamous Intraepithelial Lesions (LSIL)

- Most conservative option is colposcopy with endocervical sampling

Options for High-grade Squamous Intraepithelial Lesions (HSIL)

- Colposcopy with endocervical sampling
- "See and treat" using a diagnostic excisional procedure* if lesion(s) seen.

Options for Atypical Glandular Cells (AGC)

- Endometrial biopsy for atypical endometrial cells or age > 35
- Other subcategories require both colposcopy with endocervical sampling and an endometrial biopsy for age > 35 or abnormal vaginal bleeding.

Management of Histologic Abnormalities

- Desire cytocolpohistologic correlation (i.e., pap smear, cervical biopsy histology and colposcopic exam findings all correlate).
  - Discrepancies require a review of original cytology and histology.
  - For worrisome cytocolpohistologic discrepancies (e.g., HSIL with low-grade histology), consider repeat colposcopy or a diagnostic excisional procedure.
- Diagnostic conization procedure for unsatisfactory colposcopies with at least CIN II histology, if the endocervical curettage (ECC) is positive or if the lesion extends > 5 mm up the endocervical canal.

Options for Cervical Intraepithelial Neoplasia I (CIN I)

- Follow with q4-6 month pap smears for 2 years.
  - Repeat colposcopy for persistently abnormal pap smear at 12 months or for any worsening pap smears.
- Cryotherapy if high-risk (e.g., HIV-positive) patient and satisfactory colposcopy.

Options for Cervical Intraepithelial Neoplasia II (CIN II)

- Diagnostic excisional procedure* can be used for all cases of CIN II
- Ablative therapy if satisfactory colposcopy, small lesion (< 2 quadrants), does not extend up canal > 5 mm and has no deep gland duct involvement.

Options for Cervical Intraepithelial Neoplasia III (CIN III)

- Diagnostic excisional procedure* can be used in all cases of CIN III.
- Ablative therapy acceptable option if satisfactory colposcopy with focal CIN III and no deep gland duct involvement.

Options for Adenocarcinoma in-situ or AGC "favor neoplasia"

- Diagnostic conization procedure (cold-knife conization preferred).

Management of Cervical Intraepithelial Neoplasia in Pregnancy

- Endocervical curettage contraindicated
- Colposcopic examination performed for same indications as above
- Cervical biopsies performed only if high-grade lesion seen

HPV= Human Papilloma Virus, ‡can be performed on same thin prep pap smear, * includes laser conization, cold-knife or loop electrosurgical conization and loop electrosurgical excision procedure (i.e., LEEP).
References: JAMA, 2002; 287 (16): 2120-9. NEJM, 1996; 334 (16): 1030-7, NEJM, 2003; 348: 489-90 and American Journal of Obstetrics and Gynecology, 2003; 189 (1): 295-304.

Constipation/Hemorrhoids
- Increase exercise, 8-10 glasses of water daily and increase fiber intake
- docusate 100 mg PO bid or Milk of Magnesia can be taken if needed.
- Anusol or witch hazel pads can help ease hemorrhoid pain.

Heartburn
- Avoid spicy or greasy foods, eat small frequent meals & avoid bedtime snacks.
- Prop up the head of the bed 6 inches
- Tums, all Histamine$_2$-blockers and the proton pump inhibitors (except for omeprazole) are safe in pregnancy. Antacids are considered safe for use after the first trimester.

Nausea/Vomiting
- Eat a package of soda crackers before rising from bed in the morning.
- Eat frequent, small meals and adding ginger may help
- Eat high protein, high carbohydrate, citrus and salty foods
- Avoid greasy, spicy and fatty foods
- pyridoxine 50 mg PO bid
- Trial of doxylamine (Unisom) 25 mg bid (not FDA-approved).
- metoclopramide 10 mg PO ac and hs
- ondansetron 4 mg PO q4h prn severe nausea/vomiting
- Acupressure wrist bands may be of benefit to some patients.

Varicose veins
- Compression stockings
- Avoid standing or sitting for prolonged periods of time or crossing legs.
- Elevate legs above the level of the heart while at home and while sleeping.

Backache
- Avoid lifting anything over 10 pounds and lift with the legs.
- Frequent light aerobic exercise
- Pelvic tilt exercises
- Heating pads to the affected area
- Sleep on the side with a pillow between the legs and knees bent.

Headache
- Rule out preeclampsia or excessive eye strain
- Stress reduction and massage techniques
- acetaminophen as needed for analgesia

Leg cramps
- Often from too little calcium or potassium in diet
  - ➤ Recommend 1,200-1,500 mg elemental calcium daily
- Stretch out affected muscle
- Stretch leg muscles and keep legs warm at night

Nasal Congestion
- Stay well hydrated
- Use warm mist humidifier and saline nasal sprays

Insomnia
- Avoid stimulants at bedtime
- Take warm, relaxing bath before retiring to bed
- Explore patient's worries or concerns

Method	Advantages	Disadvantages	Failure rate ideal use (typical use)
Combined Oral Contraceptive Pills (OCPs)	• Regular menses • Decreased risk of: ➤ Ovarian CA/cysts ➤ Endometrial CA ➤ Fibrocystic changes of the breast ➤ Dysmenorrhea ➤ ↓ Pelvic inflammatory disease ➤ Ectopic pregnancy • ↓ menstrual flow • ↓ acne • ↓ endometriosis	• Can ↑ migraines • Daily compliance • No STD protection • Can have: ➤ Breakthrough bleeding ➤ Breast tenderness ➤ +/- Weight gain • Drug interactions • Increased risk of VTEs • Possible nausea • Can ↓ breast milk	1 per 1,000 users per year (70 per 1,000 users per year)
Micronor	• No ↓ breast milk • Preferred for smokers	• Irreg. Bleeding • Can ↑ acne and ovarian cysts • Must take pills at same time daily	5 per 1,000 users per year (30 per 1,000 users per year)
Ortho Evra	• Compliance weekly • Cycle regularity • Noncontraceptive benefits as OCPs	• Same OCP disadvantages • Unrecognized detachment	3 per 1,000 users per year (No data for typical use)
NuvaRing (etonogestrel/ethinyl estradiol vaginal ring)	• Less nausea than OCPs • Same noncontraceptive benefits as OCPs • Can remain in place for 3 weeks	• Requires vaginal insertion/removal • No STD protection • Unrecognized ring expulsion • Disadvantages same as OCPs	3 per 1,000 users per year (10-20 per 1,000 users per year)
Condoms	• STD protection • Readily available • No delay in fertility once discontinued	• Less spontaneity • Can break/fall off • Can ↓ sexual sensitivity	40 per 1,000 users per year (180 per 1,000 users per year)
Diaphragm	• No delay in fertility once discontinued • Can remain in place for 4-5 hours	• Requires vaginal insertion • Less spontaneity • Physician visit for fitting	60 per 1,000 users per year (160 per 1,000 users per year)

Method	Advantages	Disadvantages	Failure rate ideal use (typical use)
Natural Family Planning	• Free • No side effects • Self awareness	• Requires motivation • No STD protection • Periodic abstinence	90 (200) per 1,000 per year
Spermicide	• Readily available • Some ↓ STD risk	• Nonoxynol 9 may ↑ HIV transmission • High failure rate • Less spontaneity	150 (290) per 1,000 per year
Intrauterine Device (IUD) Mirena (M) ParaGard (P)	• Prolonged efficacy ➤ 5 yr (M)/10 yr (P) • ↓ Menstrual flow (Mirena) • ↓ Dysmenorrhea (Mirena)	• High initial cost • Office insertion • Expulsion possible • No STD protection • Initial irregular bleeding (M) • ↑ menstrual flow and cramps (P)	ParaGard: 6 (8) per 1,000 users per year Mirena: 1 (1) per 1,000 users per year
Tubal ligation (TL)	• Permanent • ↓ Risk of PID • No compliance needed	• High initial cost • Risks of surgery • No STD protection • Post-TL regret	2 per 1,000 users per year (4-5 per 1,000 users per year)
Vasectomy (V)	• Permanent • Office procedure	• High initial cost • No STD protection • Post-V regret	1 per 1,000 users per year (15 per 1,000 users per year)
Depo-provera (medroxy-progesterone acetate)	• Quarterly injections • ↓ Sickle cell crises • ↓ PID risk • ↓ Endometriosis	• Can ↑ nausea, acne and wt gain • Irreg. bleeding • Possible delayed return to fertility • No STD protection	3 per 1,000 users per year (3 per 1,000 users per year)
Lunelle (medroxy-progesterone acetate/ estradiol cypionate)	• Cycle regularity • Quickly reversible • Monthly injections	• No STD protection • +/- Nausea, acne weight gain • Initial irregular bleeding	0.5 per 1,000 users per year (data not known)

CA= cancer, STD = sexually transmitted disease, VTE = venous thromboembolic event, PID = pelvic inflammatory disease, irreg. = irregular, trans. = transmission and poss. = possible, wt = weight

Screening for Gestational Diabetes (GDM)
- **One Hour Glucose Tolerance Test** with a 50-gram oral glucose load
  - ➤ Perform test in all women between 24-28 gestational weeks.
  - ➤ Perform at the first prenatal visit for any of the following high-risk groups:
    - ○ Marked obesity (body mass index ≥ 30), personal history of GDM or glucose intolerance, macrosomia, unexplained stillbirth, malformed infant, family history of DM, ≥ 2+ glucosuria or certain ethnic groups (Hispanic, Native American, Southeast Asian or African-American).
  - ➤ 3 hour glucose tolerance test (GTT) for 1 hour glucose levels ≥ 140 mg/dL.
- **3 hour Glucose Tolerance Test Abnormals** (100-gram oral glucose load)

	Carpenter-Coustan (C-C) Criteria*	NDDG Criteria*
Fasting	≥ 95 mg/dL	≥ 105
1 hour	≥ 180 mg/dL	≥ 190
2 hours	≥ 155 mg/dL	≥ 165
3 hours	≥ 140 mg/dL	≥ 145

Diagnosis of Gestational Diabetes
- Two or more abnormal values on a 3 hr GTT confirms GDM
- Elevated fasting glucose indicates probable need for insulin (Class A_2 GDM)

White Classification of Diabetes in Pregnancy

Class	Age of onset	Duration	Vascular disease	Insulin needed
A_1	Any	Any	No	No (diet only)
A_2	Any	Any	No	Yes
B	> 20 yrs	< 10 yrs	No	Yes
C	10 -19 yrs	10 -19 yrs	No	Yes
D	< 10 yrs	> 20 yrs	Nonproliferative retinopathy	Yes
F	Any	Any	Nephropathy	Yes
R	Any	Any	Proliferative retinopathy	Yes
H	Any	Any	Heart disease	Yes

Management of Diabetes During Pregnancy
- **Nutrition:** recommend 40-50% carbohydrate, 20% protein and 30-40% fat
  - ➤ 35-40 kcal/kg/day if pregestational weight 10% < ideal body weight
  - ➤ 30 kcal/kg/day if pregestational weight is at ideal body weight
  - ➤ 25 kcal/kg/day if pregestational weight 20-50% above ideal body weight
  - ➤ 20 kcal/kg/day if pregestational weight > 50% above ideal body weight
- **Home Blood Glucose Monitoring:** fasting & 1 hr postprandial chemsticks
  - ➤ Desire fasting chemsticks ≤ 95 and 1 hr postprandial chemsticks ≤ 130 -140
- **Insulin:** typical regimen includes long-acting and short-acting insulins given as multi-dose injections (e.g., NPH/regular or insulin 70/30).
  - ➤ Average insulin requirements for pregestational diabetics are 0.7 units/kg/day in 1st trimester, 0.8 units/kg/day 18-26 weeks, 0.9 units/kg/day 26-36 weeks and 1.0 units/kg/day after 36 weeks.

Antepartum Testing and Management Considerations
- Class A_1 GDM does not need antepartum testing until ≥ 40 weeks
- Class A_2 GDM and pregestational diabetics typically begin antepartum testing with twice weekly nonstress tests beginning at 32-34 weeks.
  - ➤ Consider earlier testing for poor glycemic control or vascular disease.
- Consider induction of labor after confirming fetal lung maturity for all insulin-requiring diabetics between 38-39 gestational weeks.

Postpartum Screening in Women with Class A GDM
- Screen at 6 weeks postpartum with a 75 gm 2 hr glucose tolerance test.

* The two criteria for diagnosing gestational diabetes. ADA and Sweet Success use the C-C criteria. NDDG = National Diabetes Diagnostic Group. References: Diabetes Care, 2003; 26: S103-S108

Adapted from the 2002 recommendations by the Centers for Disease Control and the American College of Obstetricians and Gynecologists for the management of Group B Streptococci in Pregnancy.

Screening of Pregnant Women for Group B Streptococci (GBS)
- Universal screening of all pregnant women for GBS colonization recommended between 35 - 37 gestational weeks.
- This approach has replaced the risk-based strategy for which women should receive intrapartum antibiotic prophylaxis.
- GBS screening cultures should be collected by swabbing the lower vagina and the rectum.

Intrapartum Antibiotic Prophylaxis (IAP)
- Indicated for all pregnant women in labor or with ruptured membranes in the following circumstances:
  - ➢ positive GBS screening cultures
  - ➢ unknown GBS status with intrapartum risk factors (ruptured membranes >18 hours, intrapartum fever, preterm labor or preterm premature rupture of membranes.
  - ➢ History of a previous infant with invasive GBS disease.
  - ➢ History of GBS bacteriuria this pregnancy
- Not indicated for pregnant women with any of the following:
  - ➢ Negative GBS screening cultures
  - ➢ Unknown GBS status with no intrapartum risk factors
  - ➢ Planned cesarean section without labor or rupture of membranes
- Antibiotic treatment to eradicate GBS colonization not indicated.
- Ideal IAP is at least 2 doses of antibiotic prior to delivery.
- Adequate IAP is 1 dose of antibiotic at least 4 hours prior to delivery.
- Inadequate IAP is 1 dose of antibiotic given < 4 hours before delivery.

Antibiotics Used for Intrapartum Antibiotic Prophylaxis
- penicillin G is the drug of choice
  - ➢ 5 million units IV x 1 then 2.5 million units IV q4h until delivery
- ampicillin is an alternative
  - ➢ 2 grams IV x 1 then 1 gram IV q4h until delivery
- cefazolin 2 grams IV x 1 then 1 gram IV q8h until delivery for penicillin-allergic patients with no history of anaphylaxis.
- vancomycin 1 gram IV q12h until delivery for penicillin-allergic patients with a history of anaphylaxis.

Suggested Approach to the Management of Newborns born to Mothers with Suspected or Confirmed GBS Colonization
- Newborn with signs of neonatal sepsis
  - ➢ Full diagnostic evaluation: including a complete blood count, blood culture, chest x-ray, urine culture, lumbar puncture (LP) +/- C-reactive protein (CRP)
  - ➢ Empiric antibiotics with ampicillin and gentamicin (LP-) or cefotaxime (LP+).
- If gestational age < 35 weeks and infant received inadequate IAP
  - ➢ Limited evaluation: complete blood count, blood culture +/- CRP
  - ➢ Observation in house for at least 48 hours
- If gestational age > 35 weeks and infant received inadequate IAP
  - ➢ Observation in house for at least 48 hours (24 hours for reliable, intelligent parents able to comply with home observation & with close clinic follow-up).

References: MMWR, 2002; 51(RR11): 1-22.

Summary based on recommendations by the U.S. Preventive Services Task Force, the American College of Obstetricians and Gynecologists and the North American Menopause Society.

Overview of Hormone Replacement Therapy (HRT)

- Estrogen is the most effective treatment of menopausal vasomotor symptoms and urogenital atrophy.
- Based on the results of the Women's Health Initiative (WHI) and the Heart and Estrogen/Progestin Replacement Studies (HERS/HERS II), there is no reason to prescribe HRT for the primary or secondary prevention of cardiovascular disease.

Women's Health Initiative[1]

- One arm was a randomized, controlled trial of Prempro (0.625/2.5 mg) daily versus placebo in over 16,000 women.
- The study was prematurely terminated after 5.2 years of follow-up because of a significantly increased risk in the treatment arm of cardiovascular events, breast cancer, stroke and venous thromboembolic events (VTE).
  - ➢ The absolute risk of an adverse event was 19 additional events per 10,000 person years using Prempro versus placebo.
- Cardiovascular events (nonfatal MI, coronary heart disease deaths, need for revascularization procedures): number of events in the HRT group versus placebo group was 37 versus 30 per 10,000 person years or a hazard ratio (HR=1.29).
- Stroke: incidence of stroke in the HRT group versus placebo group was 29 versus 21 per 10,000 person years or a HR = 1.41.
- Venous Thromboembolism: incidence of VTE in the HRT group versus placebo group was 34 versus 16 per 10,000 person years or a HR 2.11.
- Breast Cancer: incidence of breast cancer in the HRT group versus placebo group was 38 versus 30 per 10,000 person years or a HR = 1.26.
- Osteoporotic fractures: the incidence of osteoporotic fractures in the HRT group versus placebo group was 5 fewer fractures per 10,000 person years.
- Colorectal cancer: the incidence of colorectal cancer in the HRT group versus placebo group was 6 fewer cases per 10,000 person years.
- A second arm of the WHI involving unopposed estrogen versus placebo in menopausal women who have had a hysterectomy is still in progress.

Heart and Estrogen/Progestin Replacement Studies[2]

- A randomized, controlled trial investigating 2,703 women with known coronary artery disease using continuous estrogen-progestin therapy versus placebo with 6.8 years average follow-up.
- No decrease in the risk of cardiovascular events with the use of HRT.

References: 1. JAMA 2002; 288: 321. 2. JAMA, 2002; 288: 49 and Obstet Gynecol., 1994; 83: 5.

Adapted from the 2002 American College of Obstetricians and Gynecologists Guidelines

Definitions
- Pregnancy-induced hypertension: Blood pressure ≥ 140/90 mmHg developing during pregnancy in the absence of pathologic edema or proteinuria.
- Chronic hypertension: Hypertension preceding pregnancy or developing prior to 20 gestational weeks.
- Preeclampsia: Blood pressure ≥ 140/90 mmHg measured on 2 separate occasions at least 6 hours apart developing after 20 gestational weeks and associated with proteinuria (≥ 300 mg protein in a 24 hour urine collection).

Risk Factors for Preeclampsia
- Nulliparity
- Family history of preeclampsia
- History of preeclampsia in a previous pregnancy
- Obesity (body mass index > 29 kg/m²)
- Chronic hypertension
- Chronic renal insufficiency
- Diabetes mellitus
- Multiple gestations
- Low socioeconomic class
- Cigarette smoking

Labs for Preeclampsia
- 24 hour urine for total protein and creatinine clearance
- Complete blood count, creatinine, uric acid and liver panel
- Modified or full biophysical profile to assess fetal well-being
- Obstetric ultrasound to rule out fetal growth restriction or oligohydramnios

Criteria for Severe Preeclampsia
- Systolic blood pressure (SBP) ≥ 160 or diastolic blood pressure (DBP) ≥ 110
- Proteinuria ≥ 5 grams/24 hours
- Presence of headache, visual disturbances, upper abdominal pain, oliguria
- HELLP syndrome (hemolysis, elevated liver enzymes and low platelets)
  ➤ Liver transaminitis alone sufficient to diagnose severe preeclampsia
- Eclampsia: new grand mal seizure in association with preeclampsia
- Pulmonary edema

Management of Preeclampsia
- Treatment is delivery and one must justify any decision not to do so.
- Mild preeclampsia remote from term may be managed expectantly with at least weekly modified biophysical profiles and labs as outlined above.
  ➤ Serial ultrasounds every 3 weeks to rule out fetal growth restriction
- Severe preeclampsia remote from term should be referred.
- Magnesium sulfate 4 grams IV load then 2 grams/hour drip initiated during labor (or immediately if preeclampsia severe) and continued for 24 hours postpartum to minimize the chance of an eclamptic seizure.

Management of Chronic Hypertension in Pregnancy
- Increased risk of preeclampsia, stroke, myocardial infarction, fetal growth restriction, oligohydramnios, preterm delivery or placental abruption.
- Antihypertensives recommended for DBP > 100 or SBP > 160
  ➤ Methyldopa, hydralazine, labetalol or calcium channel blockers.
- Antepartum testing with modified biophysical profiles twice weekly starting at 32-34 gestational weeks.

References: ACOG Practice Bulletin No. 33 in Obstet. Gynecol., 1/02; and NEJM, 1996; 335 (4): 257-64.

Definition: inability to conceive after 12 months of unprotected intercourse.

Etiologies of Infertility

- Male factor, anovulation, tubal disease, endometriosis, uterine factor, cervical factor or unexplained infertility

History of Infertile Couples

- Obstetric history including prior uterine surgery or ectopic pregnancy
- History of sexually transmitted diseases, endometritis, pelvic surgery, dysmenorrhea, deep dyspareunia or chronic pelvic pain (endometriosis)?
- Menstrual and contraception history
- Any symptoms of ovulation? (regular menses, premenstrual molimina or Mittelschmerz)
- History of oily skin, acne, hirsutism, oligomenorrhea, acanthosis nigricans or central obesity? (polycystic ovary syndrome)
- Tobacco, alcohol or illicit drug use
- Prescribed medication use
- Has the man ever fathered any children?
- History of galactorrhea or amenorrhea? (hyperprolactinemia)
- Maternal age (work-up may be initiated earlier for advanced maternal age)

Initial Evaluation of Infertility

- Labs: thyrotropin, prolactin and day 3 follicle stimulating hormone (FSH) if anovulatory, oligomenorrheic or amenorrheic
  - ➢ Day 3 FSH > 10 international units/L is abnormal.
- Serum testosterone and dehydroepiandrosterone sulfate if any clinical evidence of hyperandrogenism.
- Various tests of ovulation
  - ➢ Ovulation predictor kits testing for salivary changes or urine LH surge
  - ➢ Serum progesterone on days 18-25 ≥ 6 ng/mL
  - ➢ Basal body temperature charting
- Semen analysis (normal values):
  - ➢ Semen volume ≥ 2 mL, sperm concentration ≥ 20 million/mL, ≥ 50% with progressive motility and ≥ 30% with normal morphology
- Postcoital test to assess for any cervical factor **of little clinical utility.**
- Hysterosalpingogram to assess for uterine abnormalities (septum, submucous fibroids or synechia) or tubal obstruction.
- For unexplained infertility
  - ➢ Consider laparoscopy to rule out endometriosis or tubal adhesions
  - ➢ Endometrial biopsy on days 25-26 (after a negative pregnancy test) to assess for a luteal phase defect **of little clinical utility.**

Treatment Options for Women by Primary Care Physicians

- Hyperprolactinemia can be treated with dopamine agonists.
- Hypothyroidism can be treated with levothyroxine.
- Empiric trial of clomiphene citrate 50 mg PO qd on days 5-9 of menstrual cycle for anovulation (attempt no more than 3 ovulatory cycles)
  - ➢ May increase in increments of 50 mg daily after each cycle to 150 mg qd.
- Referral to an infertility specialist indicated for persistent infertility despite above measures.

References: NEJM, 2001; 345: 1388 and American College of Ob/Gyn Practice Bulletin #34, Feb., 2002.

132 Obstetrics: Oligohydramnios and Polyhydramnios

Diagnosis of Oligohydramnios
- Amniotic fluid index ≤ 5 cm on ultrasound examination

Etiologies of Oligohydramnios
- Uteroplacental insufficiency
  - preeclampsia, chronic hypertension, collagen vascular diseases, chronic renal insufficiency or Type I Diabetes with vascular disease.
- Placental abruption
- Twin-to-twin transfusion syndrome
- Chromosomal anomalies
- Congenital urinary tract anomalies
- Fetal demise
- Postdates pregnancy (at least 42 gestational weeks)
- Ruptured membranes

Management of Oligohydramnios
- Sterile speculum examination to rule out ruptured membranes
- High resolution ultrasound examination to evaluate for fetal anomalies
- Consider amniocentesis for karyotype analysis (if feasible).
- Consider induction of labor if patient is at term or postterm.
- Patients remote from term with intact membranes can be managed expectantly with a modified biophysical profile twice weekly until delivery.

Diagnosis of Polyhydramnios
- Amniotic fluid index ≥ 25 cm on ultrasound examination

Etiologies of Polyhydramnios
- Congenital anomalies of the intestinal tract or nervous system
- Fetal hydrops
- Maternal diabetes mellitus
- Multiple gestation pregnancy
- Maternal syphilis
- Chromosomal anomalies (e.g., Trisomy 18 or Trisomy 21)
- Idiopathic

Management of Polyhydramnios
- High resolution ultrasound examination to evaluate for fetal anomalies
- Reinvestigate for maternal diabetes or syphilis
- Consider amniocentesis for karyotype analysis
- Can choose to expectantly manage patients with weekly nonstress tests.
- Consider referral for serial amnioreduction if hydramnios is severe and patient having respiratory compromise.
- Consider referral for trial of indomethacin 25 mg PO qid x 48 hours
  - Indomethacin may cause life threatening constriction of the fetal ductus arteriosus.

References: J. of Perinatology, 1990; 10: 347, Obstet. Gynecol., 2002; 100: 134, Obstet. Gynecol. Survey, 1991; 46: 325 and Am J. of Obstet. Gynecol, 1994; 170: 1672.

- The causes of a pelvic mass are myriad and include GI sources (e.g., colon cancer, fecal impaction, diverticular or appendiceal abscesses), genitourinary sources (e.g., pelvic kidney or a distended bladder) or gynecologic sources.
  - ➤ The colon can be evaluated by lower endoscopy and/or barium enema.
  - ➤ If a distended bladder is suspected, urinary catheterization will resolve the mass and further investigation of the underlying cause can be undertaken.
  - ➤ Pelvic ultrasound can identify gynecologic abnormalities or a pelvic kidney.

Gynecologic Causes of a Pelvic Mass by Age Group
Premenarchal girls
- Newborns and infants with adnexal masses almost always from follicular cysts that will spontaneously regress within 6 months.
- Prepubertal children age 2-15 years with adnexal masses have an 80% risk of a malignant ovarian neoplasm (85% of these are germ cell tumors).

Adolescence
- An imperforate hymen causes hematocolpos and a vaginal septum can cause hematometrium.
- Virtually all ovarian cysts are physiologic cysts and tend to be unilocular, thin-walled simple cysts < 10 cm in diameter.
- Other causes of a pelvic mass: benign teratomas, paratubal cysts, hydrosalpinx, uterine fibroids or pregnancy.

Premenopausal women
- Pregnancy
- Physiologic ovarian cysts
- Polycystic ovary syndrome: patient classically obese, hirsute, infertile from anovulation, has multicystic ovaries on ultrasound and usually has elevated serum testosterone and dihydroepiandrosterone sulfate levels.
- Uterine fibroids (~25% of reproductive aged women with this condition).
- Endometrioma: patients may have dysmenorrhea, dyspareunia or pelvic pain.
- Benign teratomas: most commonly identified between 20-40 years of age.
- Tubal masses: hydrosalpinx, pyosalpinx or tuboovarian abscesses.

Postmenopausal Women
- Malignant ovarian neoplasm: 40-60% of all ovarian masses are malignant.
- Metastatic carcinoma: breast and gastric cancers are the most common.
- GI or genitourinary sources of pelvic masses must be ruled out in this group.
- Endometrial hyperplasia or cancer: presents as postmenopausal bleeding.

ACOG Guidelines for Management of Adnexal Masses in Premenopausal Pts.
- Size < 10 cm, unilateral, mobile simple cyst with no ascites
  - ➤ Recheck bimanual exam and ultrasound in 4-6 weeks.
  - ➤ Suppression of ovarian cysts using birth control pills does not work.
  - ➤ Surgical exploration for unchanged or enlarging mass, for all solid masses, complex cysts, cysts > 10 cm, bilateral masses and if ascites present.

Management of Adnexal Masses in Postmenopausal Women
- Perform a pelvic ultrasound, serum tumor marker CA-125 and bimanual exam.
- Surgical exploration for all symptomatic masses, solid or complex cystic masses, cystic masses > 3 cm, elevated serum CA-125 > 200 U/mL or on unchanged or increasing size during observation.
- Asymptomatic masses with a normal exam, normal pap smear, normal CA-125 level and simple, unilateral cyst ≤ 3 cm on ultrasound can be followed with serial ultrasound exams every few months.

References: Obstet. Gynecol., 2002; 100: 1413, Cancer, 1994; 74: 1398 & Obstet. Gynecol., 1988; 71: 319.

Postpartum Blues/Depression

- "Postpartum blues" occurs in up to 80% of all women
  - Symptoms begin in the first week and may include sadness, fatigue, insomnia, anxiety, headaches, irritability, poor appetite and confusion.
  - Usually resolves spontaneously during the first month
- Postpartum depression occurs in up to 10% of all women
  - Onset anytime within the first 6 months postpartum
  - Symptoms may include anhedonia, poor concentration, fatigue, guilt, anorexia, agitation, anxiety, psychomotor retardation, sleep disturbance, tearfulness and feelings of hopelessness, helplessness or worthlessness.
  - Mothers often find it difficult to function and to take care of their infant.
  - Selective serotonin reuptake inhibitors are the antidepressants of choice

Exercise

- Post-cesarean section, women should avoid lifting >10 pounds for 6+ weeks
  - Avoid sit-ups, jumping jacks or high-impact aerobics for at least 6 weeks
  - Recommend against driving for at least 2 weeks.
- Following a vaginal delivery women may resume light exercise immediately
  - Gradually increase to prepregnancy level of exercise over the first month

Constipation/Hemorrhoids

- Drink 8-10 glasses of water daily and eat high fiber foods
- May benefit from a stool softener such as docusate sodium 100 mg PO bid.
- Anusol cream or witch hazel pads can help soothe hemorrhoid discomfort.

Episiotomy Care

- Sitz baths 3-4x/day for perineal discomfort
- Avoid intercourse until the perineal discomfort has completely resolved

Breast Engorgement

- If breastfeeding, women can either pump the engorged breast(s) or increase the frequency of nursing.
- If bottle feeding, mothers should use a tight-fitting bra or bind breasts with an ace wrap, avoid any nipple stimulation or hot water on the breasts.
  - Ice packs to the affected breast(s) 3x/day

Inadequate Milk Supply

- Increase hydration by drinking 8-10 glasses of water daily
- Can pump breasts between sessions of nursing
- Apply warm compresses to breast to help encourage let down
- metoclopramide 10 mg PO q6 hours can help stimulate milk production
- Avoid combined oral contraceptive pills or patches for at least 6 weeks.

Late Endometritis

- Generally presents with low-grade fever, pelvic pain and foul-smelling lochia
- Onset is between 2-6 weeks postpartum
- Treat with doxycyline 100 mg PO bid or clindamycin 300 mg PO qid x 14 days.

Mastitis

- Presents with fever, breast pain, warmth, redness +/- flu-like symptoms
- Breastfeeding women should continue to nurse
- Treat with warm compresses to affected area 3-4x/day
- dicloxacillin or cephalexin 250-500 mg PO qid x 10 days.
- Exclude possibility of a breast abscess and hospitalize if pt appears toxic.

Progestin	OCP's that Contain Progestin	Anorogenicity*	Progestational‡ activity	Notes
desogestrel (0.15 mg)	Desogen, Ortho Cept, Mircette	Low	High	2-fold increased risk of venous thromboembolic events compared with levonorgestrel
drospernnone (3 mg)	Yasmin	Antiandrogenic	Very high	Antimineralocorticoid, can cause ↑ potassium, ↓ libido + ↓ sexual sensitivity. Contraindicated with renal, hepatic or adrenal insufficiency
ethynodiol (1mg)	Demulen 1/35	Low	High	
etonogestrel (0.12 mg)	NuvaRing	Intermediate	High	
levonorgestrel (.1 mg/.15 mg)	Alesse/Triphasil (.1) Levlen/Nordette .(.15)	Intermediate(.1) High (.15)	Low (.1) Intermediate(.15)	
norelgestromin (0.15 mg)	Ortho Evra patches	Very low	Low	
norethindrone (1 mg)	Loestrin, Ovcon, Ortho Novum	Intermediate	Intermediate	
norgestimate (.15 mg/.21 mg)	Ortho-Cyclen (.15) Ortho-Tricyclen (21)	Very Low	Low	
norgestrel (.3 mg)	Lo-Ovral	High	Intermediate	

OCP = oral ocntraceptive pill. * features include hirsutism, acne, weight gain, oily skin, hyperglycemia and hyperlipidemia
‡ ovulation suppression, cycle control and increased endometrial stability

Vaginitis

- Microscopy of saline (NS) + potassium hydroxide (KOH) preps of discharge

Categories	Yeast Vaginitis	Bacterial Vaginosis	Trichomoniasis
Microscopy	Hyphae on KOH	Clue cells on NS	Trichomonads on NS
Discharge	Thick + white	Watery, positive "sniff test*"	Frothy + malodorous
Vaginal pH	< 5	5 - 7	5 - 7
Symptoms	Itching and burning	Foul discharge	Itching and burning
DNA hybridization‡	Sensitivity – 80% Specificity – 98%	Sensitivity – 94% Specificity – 81%	Sensitivity – 90% Specificity – 100%
Preferred treatment	• Antifungal vaginal suppositories qhs x 3d • Fluconazole 150 mg PO x 1	• metronidazole 500 mg PO bid x 7d • metronidazole 0.75% gel 1 applicator qhs x 5 d	• metronidazole 2 gm PO x 1 • metronidazole 500 mg PO bid x 5 d

* "fishy" odor with application of potassium hydroxide solution
‡ office assays like Affirm VIP III can test for all three types of infection

Infectious Diseases of the Vulva

- **Herpes Simplex Virus**
  - ➢ Presents as intermittent painful vesicles or ulcerations
  - ➢ Treatment of first episode: acyclovir 400 mg PO tid, famciclovir 250 mg PO tid or valacyclovir 1000 mg PO bid x 7-10 days
  - ➢ Treatment of recurrent episodes: acyclovir 400 mg PO tid, famciclovir 125 mg PO bid or valacyclovir 500 mg PO bid x 5 days
  - ➢ Prophylaxis for frequent genital herpes: acyclovir 400 mg PO bid, famciclovir 250 mg PO bid or valacyclovir 500 mg PO qd
- **Condyloma acuminata (genital warts)**
  - ➢ Treat with physician-applied weekly treatments of podophyllin, cryotherapy or trichloroacetic acid or patient-applied 0.5% podofilox gel bid for 3 consecutive days per week or 5% imiquimod cream applied 3 times weekly
  - ➢ Extensive disease may require electrocautery or laser excision
- **Molluscum contagiosum**
  - ➢ Presents as clustered umbilicated flesh-colored papules
  - ➢ Treat with dermal curettage, liquid nitrogen or serial podophyllin applications
- **Pubic lice**
  - ➢ Presents as pruritic papules on vulva with nits on pubic hair
  - ➢ Treat with either 1% permethrin rinse or pyrethrins/piperonyl butoxide shampoo applied for 10 minutes then rinse off. Use a fine comb for nits.
- **Tinea cruris**
  - ➢ Presents as a pruritic, erythematous plaque with scaling and raised borders
  - ➢ Topical antifungal bid-tid prn rash
- **Erythrasma** (caused by *Corynebacterium minutissimum*)
  - ➢ Reddish brown rash that illuminates coral red under Wood's lamp.
  - ➢ Treat with erythromycin 250 mg PO qid x 14 days

Vulvovaginal Masses

- **Bartholin's cyst:** cyst of inner aspect of lower vaginal vestibule
  - ➢ Symptomatic or infected cyst can be treated with Word catheter placement.

- **Sebaceous cyst**: cyst on the anterior half of the labia majora
  - ➤ Infected cysts generally treated with incision and drainage.
- **Benign tumors of the vulva**
  - ➤ Fibromas: firm mass of labia majora usually 1-10 cm in diameter.
  - ➤ Lipomas: mass of labia majora with rubbery consistency
  - ➤ Hidradenoma: < 2 cm sessile, pinkish-gray nodules on vulva.
  - ➤ Syringoma: < 5 mm flesh-colored/yellow, subcutaneous papules on vulva
- **Pelvic relaxation**: cystocele, rectocele, enterocele or uterine prolapse
  - ➤ If symptomatic, surgical correction usually necessary
- **Vulvar hematoma**: tender, purplish vulvar mass that occur following vaginal delivery, straddle injuries or blunt trauma
  - ➤ Non-expanding hematomas < 10 cm treated conservatively with ice packs
  - ➤ Large or expanding or very symptomatic hematomas require evacuation.

Noninfectious Causes of Vulvar Discomfort

- **Contact/irritant dermatitis**
  - ➤ Eliminate allergen. Apply low-potency steroid cream bid until rash resolves
- **Lichen planus**: 5 P's (purple, polygonal, planar, pruritic papules)
  - ➤ Very high-potency steroid ointment qd x 3 - 6 weeks then 2x/week maintenance or prednisone 40 mg PO qd tapered over 4 weeks or griseofulvin 250 mg PO bid x 4 - 6 months.
- **Acanthosis nigricans**: thickened, brown, velvety plaques in inguinal folds.
  - ➤ May be a cutaneous sign of diabetes mellitus or glucose intolerance
- **Lichen sclerosis et atrophicus**: white, atrophic plaque with a wrinkled surface
  - ➤ Very high-potency topical steroids qd x 6-12 weeks then 1-3x/week as maintenance.
  - ➤ Intralesional steroids can be beneficial in refractory cases
- **Hyperplastic dystrophy**: lichenified, white or red plaque with overlying scale
  - ➤ Commonly the result of neurodermatitis with chronic scratching
  - ➤ Low-medium potency topical steroids, antihistamines and behavioral modification
- **Hyperplastic dystrophy with atypia**: 5% will progress to vulvar carcinoma
  - ➤ Treat with topical 5-fluorouracil
- **Endometriosis**: blue, red or purple subcutaneous lesions usually in sites of healed obstetrical lacerations.
- **Bowenoid papulosis of vulva**: multiple brown or violaceous vulvar papules that are histologically identical to vulvar carcinoma-in-situ
  - ➤ Treat with local excision or laser ablation
- **Vulvar carcinoma**
  - ➤ Refer to Gyn oncologist for a radical vulvectomy and inguinal lymphadenectomy
- **Paget's disease of vulva**: well-demarcated, hypopigmented scaling plaque
  - ➤ Treat with wide local excision and investigate for anogenital adenocarcinoma.
- **Psoriasis**: well-demarcated, erythematous plaques with silvery scale
  - ➤ Initial therapy with low-potency topical steroids and calcipotriene ointment
  - ➤ Tazarotene gel qhs can be used for refractory cases

Note: all vulvar lesions of unclear etiology must be biopsied (punch biopsy sufficient)
References: Dermatology Clinics, 1992; 10: 297. Amer. Family Physician, 2000; 62(5): 1095-1104.

Etiologies of Back Pain

Condition	History	Exam Findings
Mechanical Low Back Pain (MLBP)	• No "alarm" symptoms • No radiation down legs • Precipitating event common	• Normal neuro exam • Paraspinous muscle tenderness • Negative SLR test
Vertebral compression fracture	• Often worse with sitting • Acute onset • H/O osteoporosis	• Focal bony tenderness • Dorsal kyphosis • Loss of height
Spondylolysis or spondylolisthesis	• Subacute/chronic LBP • Some have sciatica	• Typical findings are same as in MLBP
Degenerative joint disease of the spine	• Chronic LBP • Often osteoarthritis of other joints	• Typical findings are same as in MLBP • Limited spine ROM
Herniated intervertebral disc	• Radicular back pain • Sudden onset • Usually follows a precipitating event • Worse with spine flexion, coughing, straining	• Positive SLR test • May have positive crossed SLR test • See nerve root syndromes below
Spinal stenosis "neurogenic claudication"	• Crampy pain radiating down both legs • Worse with spine extension	• Good peripheral pulses • May have focal neurologic deficits if stenosis severe
Pelvic causes • Endometriosis • Fibroids	• Dysmenorrhea • Dyspareunia • Menorrhagia	• Enlarged uterus • Uterosacral ligament nodularity
Abdominal aortic aneurysm	• Abdominal pain • Age > 50 • Multiple risk factors for vascular disease	• Pulsatile abdominal mass • Abdominal bruit • Decreased foot pulses
Osteomyelitis	• Intravenous drug use • Fever, malaise • H/O tuberculosis • Unremitting night pain	• Focal spine tenderness • Neurologic deficits if an epidural abscess
Metastatic cancer or myeloma	• Weight loss • Fever and chronic LBP • Age > 50 years • Unremitting night pain	• Focal spine tenderness • Neurologic deficits or incontinence suggests cord compression
Ankylosing Spondylitis	• Male < 20 years • Morning back stiffness • Activity improves pain	• ↓ Chest excursion • ↓ Spine flexion
Cauda equina syndrome	• Bowel/bladder incontinence • Bilateral leg weakness	• Saddle anesthesia • ↓ Anal sphincter tone • Neuro deficits in legs

SLR = straight leg raise, LBP=low back pain, ROM=range of motion, h/o=history of

Alarm Symptoms and Red Flags for Low Back Pain
- Unremitting back pain not relieved in supine position or at night
- Fever
- Unexplained weight loss
- Associated bilateral lower extremity weakness, numbness or paresthesias
- Bowel/bladder incontinence
- New back pain occurring in person > 50 years
- Known history of cancer
- Chronic immunosuppression
- Active intravenous drug use

Lumbosacral Radiculopathies

Nerve Root	Symptoms	Signs
L4	• Pain/numbness of anteromedial thigh/knee	• Weak quadriceps/iliopsoas • Decreased patellar reflex
L5	• Pain/numbness of posterolateral thigh/calf & dorsomedial foot	• Weak extensor hallucis longus and ankle dorsiflexion • Normal reflexes
S1	• Pain/numbness of posterolateral thigh/calf & lateral foot	• Weakness of toe flexors and ankle plantar flexion • Decreased ankle reflex

Work-up of Acute Back Pain
- For nonradicular pain and no alarm signs/symptoms, no specific lab or radiographic testing needed
- Plain spine x-rays indicated for possible vertebral fracture, spondylolysis, spondylolisthesis, ankylosing spondylitis ("bamboo spine" and sacroiliitis) or suspicion of metastatic cancer or osteomyelitis.
- Bone scan indicated to rule out occult spine fracture, metastatic cancer or osteomyelitis.
- Magnetic resonance imaging study of spine to assess for epidural abscess, cauda equina syndrome, spinal stenosis or herniated intervertebral disc.
- Labs (if malignancy or infection possible): complete blood count, blood cultures, erythrocyte sedimentation rate, alkaline phosphatase +/- prostate specific antigen and serum and urine protein electrophoresis testing.
- HLA-B27 testing helpful if ankylosing spondylitis is a strong possibility.

Medical Treatment of Acute Back Pain
- Ice affected area for the first 24 hours then warm compresses thereafter.
- Avoid any heavy lifting > 10 pounds, prolonged sitting for > 20-30 minutes at a time and limited twisting/bending until symptoms essentially resolved.
- McKenzie physical therapy exercises initiated as soon as patient capable
- Scheduled nonsteroidal anti-inflammatory drugs or COX-2 inhibitors for the first week then taken as needed thereafter.
- Muscle relaxants such as diazepam or cyclobenzaprine helpful if component of muscle spasm for the first 1-2 weeks.
- Tricyclic antidepressants (e.g., amitriptyline, desipramine or nortriptyline) or gabapentin are helpful for any neuropathic component of pain.
- Decompressive surgeries needed for spinal stenosis, metastatic cancer with cord compression, epidural abscesses and cauda equina syndrome and may be needed for herniated discs refractory to conservative management.

References: AHCPR Clinical Practice guideline No. 14; 1994 and Current Opin. Rheum., 1999; 11: 151.

Clinical Presentations of Gout
- **Acute gouty arthritis**
  - ➤ 80% of cases are attacks of monoarticular arthritis
  - ➤ Most common joints affected are knees and 1st metatarsophalangeal joints.
  - ➤ Elderly patients with gout more likely to present with polyarticular arthritis
  - ➤ Typically, swelling, redness & tenderness of the joint, fever & leukocytosis
- **Interval gout**
  - ➤ The period between acute gouty attacks usually completely asymptomatic
- **Chronic tophaceous gout**
  - ➤ Clinically or radiographically identifiable collections of urate crystals (tophi) in periarticular connective tissue
  - ➤ The most common locations are in the hand or feet joints, the helix of the ear, the Achilles tendon and the olecranon bursa.
- **Asymptomatic hyperuricemia**
  - ➤ Serum uric acid level > 7 mg/dL
  - ➤ No indication for standard gout therapy in asymptomatic individuals

Diagnosis of Gout
- Polarizing microscopy of joint fluid shows negatively birefringent urate crystals
- Presumptive diagnosis by history of: acute attacks of monoarticular arthritis followed by asymptomatic periods; rapid resolution of inflammation with colchicine therapy; involvement of the 1st metatarsophalangeal joint (podagra); +/- hyperuricemia (although gouty attacks occur with normal uric acid levels); and sterile joint fluid from an affected joint
- Histologic exam of tissues with gouty tophi showing urate crystals

Precipitating Factors of Acute Gout
- Trauma, surgery, starvation, alcohol intake, protein overindulgence
- Myeloproliferative or lymphoproliferative disorders with marked leukocytosis
- Medications: chemotherapy, nicotinic acid, warfarin, loop and thiazide diuretics, cyclosporine, ethambutol, pyrazinamide, baby aspirin, didanosine and levodopa
- Chronic renal insufficiency
- Endocrine: hypothyroidism, hyperparathyroidism and obesity
- Miscellaneous: hypertriglyceridemia or psoriasis

Complications of Gout
- **Urate renal stones:** occur in 20% of untreated patients with gout
- **Chronic urate nephropathy**
  - ➤ Uric acid deposition in the renal medulary interstitium leading to fibrosis
  - ➤ Typically causes mild proteinuria and isosthenuria

Pretreatment Labs in Gout
- Complete blood count, uric acid, glucose, renal panel, liver panel and 24 hour urine for uric acid and creatinine.

Acute Treatment of Gout
- Nonsteroidal anti-inflammatory drugs (NSAIDs)
  - ➤ Treatment of choice for young patients with no comorbid conditions
  - ➤ Classically, use indomethacin 50 mg PO tid until patient is pain-free for 24 hours then rapidly taper over 2-3 days.

> Use with caution in elderly patients, those with a history of gastritis/peptic ulcer disease, renal insufficiency, blood dyscrasia, congestive heart failure or significant hepatic impairment
- colchicine 0.6 mg PO q1hr until inflammation resolved, diarrhea, nausea or vomiting occur or a total dose of 6 mg is reached.
  > Avoid with renal or hepatic insufficiency
- Oral, intramuscular or intra-articular steroids
  > Effective for patients with renal failure, hepatic failure or if neither NSAIDs nor colchicine can be used.
  > Typical regimen is 0.5 mg/kg/day (to 60 mg) PO prednisone x 5 - 7 days.
  > Intra-articular triamcinolone acetonide or methylprednisolone 20-40 mg (large joints) or 5-20 mg (small joints)
  > 0.6 mg/kg intramuscular dexamethasone
  > Extreme caution with diabetes, immunosuppression or systemic infection

Chronic Prophylaxis of Recurrent Gout or Treatment of Tophaceous Gout
- Inhibitors of uric acid synthesis
  > allopurinol initiated at 100 mg PO qd at least 2 weeks after an attack of acute gout and ↑ 100 mg every 2-3 weeks until maximum dose achieved.
  > Indicated when uric acid >10 mg/dL, 24 hour urine uric acid > 800 mg, presence of tophi, nephrolithiasis or serum creatinine > 2.0 mg/dL.
  > Use concomitant colchicine 0.6 mg PO qd/bid or low-dose NSAIDs and continue for 3-6 months after serum uric acid level normal (< 6.0 mg/dL)
  > Maximum allopurinol PO dose depends on renal function: 300 mg qd (creatinine clearance ≥100 mL/min.), 200 mg qd (≥ 60 mL/min.), 100 mg qd (≥ 30 mL/min.) and 100 mg qod (≤ 10 mL/min.)
- Uricosuric medications
  > Indicated when 24 hour urine uric acid < 800 mg
  > Contraindicated with renal insufficiency, history of nephrolithiasis or need for low-dose aspirin therapy
  > probenecid started at 250 mg PO bid and titrated up to maximum 3 gm qd
  > sulfinpyrazone 50 mg PO tid and titrated up to maximum 400 mg PO bid

Presentation of Pseudogout (calcium pyrophosphate crystal disease)
- Self-limited attacks of acute monoarticular arthritis
  > Same joints involved as in gout, but greater propensity to affect the knee.
  > Commonly affects individuals over the age of 65.
- Asymptomatic chondrocalcinosis (calcium pyrophosphate crystal deposition)
- Polyarticular arthritis that may mimic osteoarthritis or rheumatoid arthritis

Diagnosis of Pseudogout
- Synovial fluid with positively birefringent calcium pyrophosphate crystals
- Identifying calcium pyrophosphate crystals by histologic exam of tissues.
- Chondrocalcinosis identified on x-ray provides a probable diagnosis.

Treatment of Pseudogout
- Can use NSAIDs, steroids or colchicines as in acute gout
- No role for hypouricemic or uricosuric medications

References: J. Rheumatology, 1992; 19: 8, Curr Opin. Rheumatology, 2000, 12: 213. American Family Physician, 1999; 59 (4): 925-36 and NEJM, 1996; 334 (7): 445-51.

American College of Rheumatology 1990 Diagnostic Criteria for Fibromyalgia
Must have all of the following
- Diffuse, chronic musculoskeletal pain
- Absence of myositis or inflammatory arthritis
- Excessive tenderness at ≥ 11 of 18 predefined anatomic sites (see below)

Associated Findings that Support the Diagnosis of Fibromyalgia
- Chronic fatigue ≥ 6 months resulting in ≥ 50% reduction in normal activities
- Unexplained generalized muscle weakness
- Insomnia and nonrestorative sleep
- Cognitive impairment and/or mood disorder
- Headache (either tension-type or migraine-type)
- Abdominal pain relieved by a bowel movement +/- altered bowel habits
- Musculoskeletal pain ↓ by heat or massage & ↑ by sitting or standing
- Female patient between 20-55 years old
- All laboratory tests normal

Nine Trigger or Tender Point Areas in Fibromyalgia
- Base of the sternocleidomastoid muscle
- The second costochondral junction
- 2 cm distal to the lateral epicondyles
- The greater trochanter
- The medial fat pad of the knee
- Insertion of the suboccipital muscle
- Mid-portion of the trapezius muscle along the side of the neck
- Origin of the supraspinatous muscle
- Upper outer quadrant of the buttock

Differential Diagnosis
- There is considerable overlap between fibromyalgia (FM), chronic fatigue syndrome (CFS), temporomandibular joint disorder (TMJ) or mood disorders with multiple psychosomatic complaints.
- CFS patients tend to have a persistent low-grade fever, chills and sore throat that FM patients lack.
- TMJ patients complain of pain in the jaw +/- inner ear that FM patients lack.
- Patients with a mood disorder and multiple psychosomatic complaints usually do not meet the strict tender point criteria needed to diagnose FM.

Treatment of Fibromyalgia
- Educate patients that FM is a chronic illness, but it is not progressive, contagious, infectious or life-threatening.
- Nonpharmacologic interventions
  ➤ Physical therapy, massage, good sleep hygiene & regular aerobic exercise
  ➤ Counseling helpful for superimposed mood disorders
- Medications
  ➤ Low-dose tricyclic antidepressants (e.g. amitriptyline 25-50 mg PO qhs)
  ➤ Muscle relaxants (e.g. cyclobenzaprine 10 mg PO qhs-tid)
  ➤ Consider adding a selective serotonin reuptake inhibitor in AM
  ➤ Serial trigger point injections at most symptomatic areas

References: Arch. Int. Med., 1999; 159: 777. Arthritis and Rheum, 1990; 33: 160 and Arch. Int. Med., 2000; 160: 221.

Plantar Fasciitis
- **Clinical Presentation**
  - ➢ Heel pain worst the first few steps after resting and improves with walking.
- **Exam**
  - ➢ Focal tenderness in areas along the plantar fascia or at the calcaneal origin
  - ➢ Often tight heel cord
- **Treatment**
  - ➢ Calf and Achilles tendon stretching and toe curl exercises
  - ➢ Heel pads (silicone heel inserts tend to be the most effective)
  - ➢ Avoid wearing thin sandals, walking barefoot, jumping or running exercises
  - ➢ Wear well-padded athletic shoes with good arch support
  - ➢ Steroid/local anesthetic injections at areas of point tenderness
  - ➢ Surgery for refractory cases

Metatarsalgia
- **Clinical Presentation**
  - ➢ Pain under metatarsal head(s) made worse by walking, standing or jumping.
- **Exam**
  - ➢ Tenderness with plantar palpation of affected metatarsal head
  - ➢ For equivocal cases, a diagnostic injection of local anesthetic into the dorsal aspect of the affected metatarsophalangeal (MTP) joint relieves the pain.
- **Treatment**
  - ➢ Wear well-padded shoes and may need custom orthotics
  - ➢ Taping techniques to keep affected toes in plantar flexed position

Morton's Neuroma
- **Clinical Presentation**
  - ➢ Pain in the ball of the foot that radiates to the 3rd and 4th toes.
  - ➢ Patients feel like there is a fixed small pebble in their shoe.
- **Exam**
  - ➢ Tenderness with any compression of the 3rd intermetatarsal interspace
- **Treatment**
  - ➢ Silicone shoe inserts or custom orthotics
  - ➢ Cortisone injections directly into the 3rd intermetatarsal space
  - ➢ Surgical excision

Bunions (Hallux valgus)
- **Clinical Presentation**
  - ➢ Pain and skin redness along the medial aspect of the 1st MTP joint.
- **Exam**
  - ➢ Lateral deviation of great toe and red, calloused skin along medial 1st MTP
- **Treatment**
  - ➢ Wide-toed shoes, felt or foam pads to protect bunion and devices to separate the 1st and 2nd toes at night
  - ➢ Surgical correction of Hallux valgus

Hammer Toes
- **Clinical Presentation**
  - ➢ Often foot pain occurs at the affected MTP joints
- **Exam**
  - ➢ Claw-like deformity of toes usually with a corn on the top of the toe.
- **Treatment**
  - ➢ Mild cases can be treated with foot manipulation and splinting
  - ➢ Severe deformities usually require surgical correction

Condition	History	Exam Findings	Diagnostic tests
Osteoarthritis of the hip	• Insidious onset • Groin/anterior thigh pain • Activity ↑ pain • Stiffness after inactivity	• Restricted IR/ER • Pain with IR/ER • Anterior hip tenderness • Trendelenberg or antalgic gait	• Pelvis or hip x-rays
Trochanteric bursitis	• Lateral hip pain • Activity ↑ pain • ↑ pain lying on affected side	• Tenderness over greater trochanter • Normal hip ROM	• Clinical diagnosis • No imaging studies needed
Hip osteonecrosis	• Atraumatic • Groin/anterior thigh pain • Activity ↑ pain • 2/3 have rest pain • risk factors* exist	• Restricted IR/ER • Pain with IR/ER • Antalgic limp • Anterior hip tenderness	• Pelvis x-rays • MRI to stage osteonecrosis • Bone scan if x-rays normal and no MRI
Septic arthritis	• Atraumatic • Anterior thigh pain • Pain at night	• Same as for osteonecrosis • Fever	• Arthrocentesis • ESR, blood cultures
Femoral neck fracture	• Fall or trauma • Elderly • Osteoporosis • Groin/anterior thigh pain • Activity ↑ pain	• Leg may be shortened + ER • Inability to walk or antalgic gait • Pain with IR/ER	• Pelvis x-rays • MRI or bone scan if x-rays normal looking for occult fracture
Metastatic disease to hips	• Known cancer • Elderly patient • Night pain • Activity ↑ pain	• Antalgic gait • Anterior hip tenderness • Normal hip ROM	• Pelvis x-rays • Bone scan • Bone biopsy if ? diagnosis
Meralgia paresthetica	• Numbness or dysesthesias of anterolateral thigh	• Normal hip ROM • No tenderness • Negative SLR	• Clinical diagnosis
Aortoiliac disease	• Buttock/thigh claudication • Impotence	• Arterial bruits • Diminished peripheral pulses	• Duplex ultrasound • Arteriogram
L4 radiculopathy	• Back pain radiating to thigh • Dermatomal	• Positive SLR • Weak quadriceps • ↓ patellar reflex	• MRI of lumbar spine

IR=internal rotation, ER=external rotation, ROM=range of motion, ESR=erythrocyte sedimentation rate, SLR = straight leg raise, *alcoholics, oral steroid use, sickle cell disease, divers, pelvic radiation + post-traumatic

History
- Any prior knee problems?
- Any history of trauma or precipitating event that may have injured knee?
- What is patient's occupation and what activities/sports does he/she play?
- Does knee ever buckle under, lock or click?
- Does the patient have morning stiffness or stiffness after prolonged sitting?

Etiologies of Anterior Knee Pain
- **Patellofemoral pain syndromes**
  - ➢ Generally occurs in patients under the age of 45 (women more than men)
  - ➢ Pain exacerbated by repetitive knee flexion
  - ➢ Sunrise x-ray view of knee is the best view to examine for patellar disease
  - ➢ **Chondromalacia patellae:** retropatellar crepitus+patellar compression pain
  - ➢ **Patellar subluxation** (laterally)
  - ➢ **Patella alta** (high-lying patella)
- **Prepatellar bursitis** (or "nursemaid's knee")
  - ➢ Frequently occurs in occupations requiring prolonged kneeling
- **Patellar tendonitis** (or "jumper's knee")
  - ➢ Pain localized to the inferior edge of the patella
- **Osgood-Schlatter disease**
  - ➢ Tibial tubercle epiphysitis seen in adolescents
- **Anterior cruciate ligament injury**
  - ➢ Generally occurs after traumatic accident with immediate hemarthrosis
  - ➢ Laxity noted with Lachman or anterior drawer sign

Etiologies of Medial Knee Pain
- **Osteoarthritis** (of medial knee compartment)
  - ➢ Typical findings are morning stiffness < 30 minutes, knee crepitus, bony enlargement, absence of warmth or effusion in a patient over 50 years
- **Anserine bursitis**
  - ➢ Medial pain located 3-5 cm below the joint line
  - ➢ Pain occurs with motion and at rest (particularly at night)
- **Medial collateral ligament strain**
  - ➢ Pain increased during valgus stress maneuver
- **Medial meniscal tear**
  - ➢ Exam: Knee may lock, often an effusion and medial joint line tenderness

Etiologies of Lateral Knee Pain
- **Osteoarthritis** (of the lateral knee compartment)
- **Lateral collateral ligament strain**
  - ➢ Pain increased during varus stress maneuver
- **Lateral meniscal tear**
- **Iliotibial band syndrome**
  - ➢ Focal aching or burning pain at the lateral femoral condyle

Indications for Knee in Patients with Knee Trauma (Ottawa Rules)
- Knee effusion developing within 24 hours of injury
- Tenderness of the fibular head or patella
- Inability to fully bear weight on leg
- Inability to fully flex the knee

Imaging to Assess for Internal Derangement of the Knee
- MRI is the best imaging study to evaluate for damage to the menisci and ligaments of the knee.
- Plain x-rays are not helpful if an internal derangement of the knee suspected.

Epidemiology
- Prevalence of 1 case per 133 persons over age 50 years in U.S.
- Polymyalgia rheumatica occurs in 50% of patients who have temporal arteritis.
- 15% of patients with polymyalgia rheumatica develop temporal arteritis.

Clinical Manifestations
- Chronic aching and stiffness in the shoulders and hip girdles
- Pain worsens with movement of the affected area
- Malaise, fatigue, anorexia, weight loss & low-grade fevers in 1/3 of patients.
- Synovitis may occur in the knees, wrists and the metacarpophalangeal joints in up to 50% of patients.

Exam
- Decreased active range of motion of shoulders, hips and neck due to pain
- Normal muscle strength
- May detect synovial thickening in affected knees, wrists or metacarpophalangeal joints

Diagnosis of Polymyalgia Rheumatica
- Onset after the age of 50 years
- Bilateral aching and morning stiffness of at least 2 of the following 3 areas for at least 1 month: neck, shoulders, proximal arms, hips or proximal thighs
- Erythrocyte sedimentation rate ≥ 40 mm/hour
- Exclusion of other diagnoses that can cause similar symptoms

Laboratory Findings in Polymyalgia Rheumatica
- Elevated erythrocyte sedimentation rate
  - ➢ Normal erythrocyte sedimentation rate can be seen in 7-20% of patients
  - ➢ Elevated C-reactive protein or interleukin-6 levels may be more sensitive tests for both diagnosis and for monitoring of disease flares
- Normocytic anemia may be present
- Imaging studies play no role in the diagnosis or monitoring of this condition
  - ➢ For atypical cases, an MRI or ultrasound of the shoulder can identify subacromial or subdeltoid bursitis and help confirm the diagnosis.

Treatment of Polymyalgia Rheumatica
- prednisone 10-20 mg PO qd and continued for 2-4 weeks after the pain and stiffness have resolved
  - ➢ Classically, clinical response to steroids is rapid with symptom resolution after a few days of therapy.
- Decrease prednisone dose approximately 10% every 2 weeks until a minimum effective dose has been reached
  - ➢ Once prednisone dose has been weaned to less than 10 mg PO daily, reduce the dose no faster than 1 mg every month.
- Calcium and Vitamin D supplementation while patient on steroids
- Typically, polymyalgia rheumatica is a self-limited disease that eventually resolves after 1-3 years.

Reference: NEJM, 2002; 347 (4): 261-71.

American Rheumatism Association Criteria for Rheumatoid Arthritis:
Must have at least four of the following seven criteria present for ≥ 6 weeks
- Morning stiffness ≥ 1 hour
- Inflammatory arthritis of ≥ 3 joints with soft tissue swelling or effusion:
  - ➢ Typical joints are proximal interphalangeal, metacarpophalangeal, wrist, elbow, knee, ankle and metatarsophalangeal joints
- Arthritis of hand joints
- Symmetric arthritis
- Rheumatoid nodules: over bony prominences or extensor surfaces
- Positive rheumatoid factor (RF) in 80% of rheumatoid arthritis patients
- Joint space narrowing, juxtaarticular osteopenia and bony erosions by x-ray

Other Clinical Features of Rheumatoid Arthritis (RA)
- Labs: Anemia of chronic disease, leukocytosis and/or thrombocytosis
- Autoantibodies: + Antinuclear antibody (ANA) in 30-40%
  - ➢ Positive anti-citrulline antibody highly specific for rheumatoid arthritis
- Symptoms: fatigue, tactile fevers, weight loss and depression are common
- Late exam findings: ulnar deviation, "swan neck" finger deformities, volar subluxation and radial drift of the carpal bones. Olecranon or retrocalcaneal bursitis both can occur.
- Subluxation of C1 on C2→ spinal cord compression or radicular pain
- Cricoarytenoid joint arthritis in up to 30%→ hoarseness or stridor
- Erythrocyte sedimentation rate or C-reactive protein levels may help to assess disease activity.

Treatment Options for Rheumatoid Arthritis
- Nonpharmacologic: range-of-motion exercises, regular aerobic exercise, physical therapy and splinting of fingers/wrists to prevent deformities
- Nonsteroidal anti-inflammatory drugs: do not alter disease progression
- Disease-modifying antirheumatic and anti-tumor necrosis factor-alpha drugs

Medication	Dosing	Side effects	Labs to follow
methotrexate	7.5–20 mg PO qweek	Folate ↓, hepatitis, marrow ↓, diarrhea	LFTs, CBC, renal panel
hydroxy-chloroquine	200–400 mg PO qd	Retinopathy, headache, marrow ↓, nausea and vomiting	Retinal check twice yearly, CBC
leflunomide	10-20 mg PO qd	Hepatitis, anemia	LFTs, CBC
sulfasalazine	0.5-1 gm PO qd-bid	Hepatitis, marrow ↓, infertility, headache, nausea and vomiting	CBC, renal panel and LFTs
azathioprine	1-2.5 mg/kg/day PO	Nausea and vomiting, marrow ↓,	CBC + differential
infliximab	3 mg/kg IV q8wks	Reactivation Tb, headache, nausea, vomiting + dyspnea	PPD or any active infection
etanercept	25 mg SQ 2x/wk	Reactivation Tb, injection site reaction	PPD or any active infection

LFTs = liver function tests, CBC = complete blood count, Tb = tuberculosis, PPD = purified protein derivative

References: Arthritis Rheum, 1988; 31: 315 and NEJM, 2000; 343: 1586-93.

Disease	Test	Specificity	Sensitivity	Positive Predictive Value	Diagnosis
Systemic Lupus Erythematosus (SLE)	Antinuclear antibodies (ANA)	No	99%	Moderate	Yes
	anti-double-stranded DNA	95%	70%	95%	Yes
	anti-cardiolipin/Lupus anticoagulant	Yes	No	Low	No
	anti-Smith antibodies	High	25-30%	97%	Yes
Drug-induced Lupus	anti-histone antibodies*	High	95%	High	Yes
Rheumatoid Arthritis	Rheumatoid factor	No	75-80%	Moderate	Yes
	anti-citrulline antibodies	High	No	High	No
Scleroderma (CREST)	Antinuclear antibodies (ANA)	No	97%	High	Yes
	anti-centromere	High	25-30%	High	Yes
	anti-Scl70	High	15-30%	High	Yes
Mixed Connective Tissue Disease	Antinuclear antibodies (ANA)	No	93%	High	Yes
	anti-U$_1$-RNP (ribonucleoprotein)*	High	Moderate	High	Yes
Polymyositis Dermatomyositis	Creatinine phosphokinase (CPK)	No	High	Low	No
	anti-Jo-1 antibodies	Yes	30-50%	High	Yes
	muscle biopsy	Yes	Moderate	High	Yes
Sjogren's syndrome	Antinuclear antibodies (ANA)	No	90%	Moderate	Yes
	anti-SSA/Ro (Sjogren's syndrome A)‡	87%	8-70%	~40%	Yes
	anti-SSB/La (Sjogren's syndrome B)	94%	14-60%	~40%	Yes
Wegener's granulomatosis	anti-proteinase 3 antibody	Yes	Moderate	High	Yes
	c-antineutrophil cytoplasmic antibodies	Yes	95%	High	Yes

Adapted with permission from Robert Gonzalez, M.D. & Cheryl Lambing, M.D., Rheumatology division at the Ventura County Medical Center. CREST = calcinosis, Raynaud's phenomenon, esophageal dysmotility, sclerodactyly and telangiectasias. * false positives from SLE. ‡ false positive from cutaneous lupus erythematosus

Disease	Test	Disease Activity	Tests for End-Organ Damage and Additional Notes
Systemic Lupus Erythematosus (SLE)	Antinuclear antibodies (ANA)	No	Positive anti-SSA (Sjogren's syndrome A) in cutaneous
	anti-double-stranded DNA	Yes	Lupus erythematosus. Follow serial renal panel, urinalysis
	anti-cardiolipin/Lupus anticoagulant	Yes	with micro and complete blood count with differential
	anti-Smith antibodies	No	
Drug-induced LE	anti-histone antibodies	No	Usual meds procainamide, hydralazine or isoniazid
Rheumatoid Arthritis	Rheumatoid factor	No	X-rays of affected joints, baseline PPD and pulmonary
	anti-circline antibodies		function tests. Follow complete blood count with differential
			and liver panel with most therapies
Scleroderma (CREST)	Antinuclear antibodies (ANA)	No	anti-centromere specific for CREST syndrome. Chest x-ray,
	anti-centromere	No	screening pulmonary function tests, blood pressure checks,
	anti-Scl70	No	renal panel, urinalysis with micro, baseline barium swallow
			and esophagogastroduodenoscopy for dysphagia
Mixed Connective	Antinuclear antibodies (ANA)	No	Renal panel, complete blood count with differential, creatinine
	anti-U₁-RNP (ribonucleoprotein)	No	phosphokinase, urinalysis with micro and BP checks
Polymyositis Dermatomyositis	Creatinine phosphokinase (CPK)	Yes	Note: electromyogram can help to diagnose myositis
	anti-Jo-1 antibodies	No	Consider search for malignancy in adult dermatomyositis.
	muscle biopsy	No	Follow creatinine phosphokinase in response to therapy
Sjogren's syndrome	Antinuclear antibodies (ANA)	No	Schirmer test for ↓ tear production. Saxon test for ↓
	anti-SSA/Ro (Sjogren's syndrome A)	No	saliva production. Needs dental care and eye exams.
	anti-SSB/La (Sjogren's syndrome B)	No	
Wegener's granulomatosus	anti-proteinase 3 antibody	Yes	Diagnosis secured with biopsy of nasopharyngeal lesion.
	c-antineutrophil cytoplasmic antibodies	Yes	Ear/Nose/Throat exam, chest x-ray, renal panel & urinalysis
			+/- pulmonary function tests

American College of Rheumatology Criteria for Systemic Lupus Erythematosus Classification

4 or more of the following 11 criteria serially or simultaneously for diagnosis:

- **Malar rash** – erythematous rash over malar eminences.
- **Discoid rash** – erythematous plaques with adherent scale, atrophy, scarring and follicular plugging.
- **Photosensitivity**
- **Oral ulcers** – usually painless
- **Arthritis** – oligoarticular with swelling and tenderness of affected joints
- **Serositis**
  - ➢ Pleuritis – pleuritic pain, pleural rub or unexplained pleural effusion
  - ➢ Pericarditis
- **Nephritis**
  - ➢ Overt proteinuria > 500 mg/day or ≥ 3+ protein on dipstick
  - ➢ Active urinary sediment
- **Neuropsychiatric disorder**
  - ➢ Seizures or encephalopathy
  - ➢ Psychosis
- **Hematologic**
  - ➢ Hemolysis
  - ➢ Leukopenia (white blood cells < 4,000/mm^3)
  - ➢ Lymphopenia (lymphocytes < 1,500/ mm^3)
  - ➢ Thrombocytopenia (platelets < 100K/ mm^3)
- **Immunologic**
  - ➢ anti-double-stranded DNA antibodies
  - ➢ anti-Sm (Smith) antibodies
  - ➢ Antiphospholipid antibodies (positive lupus anticoagulant or anticardiolipin antibodies or false-positive venereal disease research laboratory test)
- **Antinuclear Antibody (ANA) – positive**

Treatment Guidelines for SLE

- **Options for Cutaneous Lupus Erythematosus**
  - ➢ Hydroxychloroquine 200-400 mg PO qd
  - ➢ Chloroquine phosphate 250 -500 mg PO qd
  - ➢ Dapsone 25-200 mg PO qd
  - ➢ Oral auranofin 3 mg PO bid
  - ➢ Tretinoin cream or oral isotretinoin
  - ➢ Sunscreen
  - ➢ Topical corticosteroids (may need fluorinated steroids for thick facial plaques x 2 weeks then change to hydrocortisone cream)
- **Options for Lupus nephritis**
  - ➢ Prednisone 0.5-1 mg/kg PO daily for mild-moderate disease
  - ➢ Cyclophosphamide 0.75-1.0 gm/m^2 body surface area IV qmonth

References: Arthritis Rheum, 1982; 25: 1271-77 and Arthritis Rheum, 1997; 40: 1725.
Clinical Nephrology, 2002; 57: 95 and Dermatology clinics, 2000; 18 (1): 139-46.

Name	Sedation	Anticholinergic	Agitation	Gastrointestinal upset	Sexual Dysfunction
Selective Serotonin Reuptake Inhibitors					
citalopram	Low	Very low	Moderate	High	Moderate
escitalopram	Very low	Very low	Low	Moderate	Low/Mod.
fluoxetine	None	None	Very high	Very high	Very high
fluvoxamine	Moderate	Very low	None	Very high	High
paroxetine	Moderate	Low	Low	High	High
sertraline	Low	Very low	High	High	High
Mixed Noradrenergic/Serotonergic Agonist Antidepressants					
bupropion	None	Very low	High	Moderate	Low
mirtazepine	High	Very low	None	Very low	Very low
nefazodone	High	Low	Low	Moderate	Low
venlafaxine	Low	Low	Moderate	High	High
Tricyclic antidepressants	High	High	Very Low	Low	Low

Name	Other Uses	Comments
Selective Serotonin Reuptake Inhibitors		
citalopram	panic attack and neuropathic pain	Selective serotonin reuptake inhibitor side effects:
escitalopram	panic attack	• headache, diarrhea, constipation, tremor, nausea and sweating
fluoxetine	obsessive compulsive or premenstrual dysphoric disorder and bulimia	• Serotonin syndrome from drug interactions consists of following triad:
fluvoxamine	obsessive compulsive disorder and panic attack	➤ delirium
paroxetine	obsessive compulsive, post-traumatic stress, premenstrual dysphoric and generalized anxiety disorders, panic attack and social phobia	➤ autonomic instability ➤ neuromuscular dysfunction
sertraline	obsessive compulsive disorder, panic attack, post-traumatic stress disorder and premenstrual dysphoric disorder	
Mixed Noradrenergic/Serotonergic Agonist Antidepressants		
bupropion	smoking cessation and bipolar disorder	Avoid if seizures/eating disorder
mirtazepine	generalized anxiety disorder and somatization disorder	Weight gain, tremor
nefazodone	generalized anxiety disorder and insomnia	Hepatotoxicity, orthostasis
venlafaxine	generalized anxiety disorder, bipolar disorder and panic attack	Nausea, headache, hypertension
Tricyclic antidepressants	neuropathic pain, chronic pain and migraine prophylaxis	Severe overdose → cardiac & neuro toxicity, orthostasis, caution in elderly

Name	EPS effects	Sedation	Anticholinergic	Orthostasis	Comments/potential side effects
chlorpromazine	Low/moderate	High	Moderate	High	Photosensitivity, rare cytopenias
clozapine	Very low	High	High	High	Agranulocytosis, seizures, weight gain
fluphenazine	Very high	Low	Low	Low	GI upset, headache, edema, leukopenia
haloperidol	Very high	Very low	Very low	Very low	Akathisia, anxiety and lethargy
olanzapine	Very low	Moderate	Low	Low	Agitation, headache, rhinitis, weight gain
perphenazine	High	Low	Low	Low	Anorexia, rare cytopenias, hepatotoxicity
quetiapine	Very low	Moderate	Low	Low/moderate	Agitation, headache and insomnia
risperidone	Low/Moderate*	Very low	Very low	Moderate	Rhinitis, headache and QT prolongation
thioridazine	Low	High	High	High	Decreased libido, retrograde ejaculation
thiothixene	High	Low	Low	Low	Agitation, photosensitivity, hepatotoxicity
trifluoperazine	High	Low	Low	Low	Headache, fatigue, weight gain, rash
ziprasidone	Low	Low	Very low	Low	QT prolongation , headache, weakness

EPS= extrapyramidal side effects, *risperidone has low risk of EPS if daily dose < 6 mg and moderate risk if ≥ 6 mg/day. Note: all antipsychotics (especially the neuroleptic medications) can cause parkinsonism and hyperprolactinemia. QT = QT segment of electrocardiogram

Name	Therapeutic Uses	Usual Dosage Range	Comments/Side Effects
Benzodiazepines			
alprazolam	Panic disorder	0.25 - 1 mg PO tid prn	**Benzodiazepine side effects:** Sedation, dizziness, anterograde amnesia and physical dependence
clonazepam	Panic disorder with agoraphobia	0.25 - 1 mg PO tid prn	
diazepam	Post-traumatic stress disorder	5 -10 mg PO q6h prn	Risk of benzodiazepine withdrawal syndrome with abrupt discontinuation
lorazepam	Social anxiety disorder	0.5 - 2 mg PO tid prn	
Heterocyclic Compounds			
clomipramine	PD, PDA, PTSD, OCD, SAD, GAD	100 - 200 mg PO qhs	Drowsiness, anticholinergic side effects (dry mouth, blurry vision, constipation, urinary retention, confusion, flushing), tachycardia and nausea
imipramine	PD, PDA, PTSD, SAD, GAD	100 - 200 mg PO qhs	
Selective Serotonin Reuptake Inhibitors			
fluoxetine	OCD	20 - 60 mg PO qd	Anorexia, nausea, most stimulating of all SSRIs
fluvoxamine	OCD	50 - 300 mg PO qd	Nausea, constipation, most sedating of all SSRIs
paroxetine	PD, PDA, PTSD, OCD, SAD, GAD	20 - 60 mg PO qd	Anticholinergic side effects, sexual dysfunction
sertraline	PD, PDA, PTSD, OCD	50 - 200 mg PO daily	Diarrhea
Other Anxiolytics			
buspirone	GAD	5 - 10 mg PO tid	Nausea, headache, dizziness and agitation
propranolol	Performance anxiety	20 - 40 mg PO q12h	Fatigue, bronchospasm, sexual dysfunction
venlafaxine	GAD	75 - 225 mg XR PO qd	Hypertension, agitation, tremor, nausea and HA

PD = Panic disorder, PDA = Panic disorder with agoraphobia, PTSD = Post-traumatic stress disorder, SAD = Social anxiety disorder, GAD = Generalized anxiety disorder, OCD = Obsessive compulsive disorder, HA = headache

PEDIATRIC DRUGS		Age	2m	4m	6m	9m	12m	15m	2y	3y	5y
		Kg	5	6½	8	9	10	11	13	15	19
		Lbs	11	15	17	20	22	24	28	33	42
med	**strength**	**freq**	**teaspoons of liquid per dose** (1 tsp= 5 ml)								
Tylenol (mg)		q4h	80	80	120	120	160	160	200	240	280
Tylenol (tsp)	160/t	q4h	½	½	¾	¾	1	1	1¼	1½	1¾
ibuprofen (mg)		q6h	-	-	75†	75†	100	100	125	150	175
ibuprofen (tsp)	100/t	q6h	-	-	¾†	¾†	1	1	1¼	1½	1¾
amoxicillin or	125/t	bid	1	1¼	1½	1¾	1¾	2	2¼	2¾	3½
Augmentin	200/t	bid	½	¾	1	1	1¼	1¼	1½	1¾	2¼
regular dose	250/t	bid	½	½	¾	¾	1	1	1¼	1¼	1¾
	400/t	bid	¼	½	½	½	¾	¾	¾	1	1
amoxicillin or	200/t	bid	--	1¼	1½	1¾	2	2¼	2½	3	4
Augmentin	250/t	bid	--	1¼	1½	1½	1¾	1¾	2¼	2½	3
high OM dose‡	400/t	bid	--	¾	¾	1	1	1¼	1½	1½	2
Augmentin ES‡	600/t	bid	--	½	½	¾	¾	¾	1	1¼	1½
azithromycin*§	100/t	qd	¼	½†	½	½	½	½	¾	¾	1
(5-day Rx)	200/t	qd	--	¼†	¼	¼	¼	¼	½	½	½
Bactrim/Septra	---	bid	½	¾	1	1	1	1¼	1½	1½	2
cefaclor*	125/t	bid	1	1	1¼	1½	1½	1¾	2	2½	3
"	250/t	bid	½	½	¾	¾	¾	1	1	1¼	1½
cefadroxil	125/t	bid	½	¾	1	1	1¼	1¼	1½	1¾	2¼
"	250/t	bid	¼	½	½	½	¾	¾	¾	1	1
cefdinir	125/t	qd	--	¾†	1	1	1	1¼	1½	1¾	2
cefprozil*	125/t	bid	--	¾†	1	1	1¼	1½	1½	2	2¼
"	250/t	bid	--	½†	½	½	¾	¾	¾	1	1¼
cefuroxime	125/t	bid	½	¾	¾	1	1	1	1½	1¾	2¼
cephalexin	125/t	qid	--	½	¾	¾	1	1	1¼	1½	1¾
"	250/t	qid	--	¼	¼	½	½	½	¾	¾	1
clarithromycin	125/t	bid	--	½†	½	½	¾	¾	¾	1	1¼
"	250/t	bid	--	--	--	¼	½	½	½	½	¾
dicloxacillin	62½/t	qid	½	¾	1	1	1¼	1¼	1½	1¾	2
loracarbef*	100/t	bid	--	1†	1¼	1½	1½	1¾	2	2¼	3
nitrofurantoin	25/t	qid	¼	½	½	½	½	¾	¾	¾	1
Pediazole	---	tid	½	½	¾	¾	1	1	1	1¼	1½
penicillin"	250/t	bid-tid	--	1	1	1	1	1	1	1	1
Benadryl	12.5/t	q6h	½	½	¾	¾	1	1	1¼	1½	2
Dimetapp	---	q6h	-	-	½	½	¾	¾	1	1	1
prednisolone	15/t	qd	¼	½	½	¾	¾	¾	1	1	1¼
prednisone	5/t	qd	1	1¼	1½	1¾	2	2¼	2½	3	3¾
Robitussin	---	q4h	-	-	¼†	¼†	½	½	¾	¾	1
Rondec	---	q4h	-	-	-	-	¼†	¼†	½	½	1
Triaminic	---	q4h	-	¼	¼	¼	½	½	1	1	1
Tylenol w/ Codeine		q4h	-	-	-	-	-	-	-	1	1
Ventolin	2/t	tid	-	-	-	-	½	½	¾	¾	1
Zyrtec	5/t	qd	-	-	-	-	-		½	½	½

* Dose shown is for otitis media only; see dosing in text for alternative indications.
† Dosing at this age/weight not recommended by manufacturer.
‡ High dose (80-90 mg/kg/d) is for otitis media in children at high risk for penicillin-resistant S pneumoniae (age <2 yo, antibiotics within ≤3 months, day care).
§Give a double dose of azithromycin the first day.

The Approach to The Adolescent Patient

- Use every visit as an opportunity for education and risk assessment
- Interview the adolescent patient alone and emphasize confidentiality
- Use an unhurried, non-judgemental approach
- Use open-ended questioning and avoid assumptions
- Remember the BiHEADSS mnemonic
- Key features to these questions is they do not assume anything about the adolescent such as having a family or being heterosexual, etc.
- Always summarize the information and give a follow-up plan

Sample Questions using BiHEADSS

- **Bi - Body Image**
  - ➢ How do you feel about your body and how it has changed recently?
- **H – Home**
  - ➢ Where do you live? Who lives with you?
  - ➢ What happens when people disagree in your house?
- **E – Education/ Employment**
  - ➢ Tell me about your school.
  - ➢ What are you good at? What are you having trouble in?
  - ➢ Where do you go after school?
  - ➢ Do you have a job at the moment?
- **A – Activities/ Accidents/ Ambition**
  - ➢ What do you do for fun?
  - ➢ What do you do with your friends?
  - ➢ Have you ever been injured or injured anyone?
  - ➢ Have you ever been involved in an accident?
  - ➢ What would you like to do later in life?
- **D – Drugs/ Depression**
  - ➢ Many kids your age have experimented with alcohol & drugs. Have you or your friends ever tried any drugs? **or**
  - ➢ When was the first time you tasted alcohol?
    - o **CAGE** questionnaire for affirmative answers
    - o **C** – Have you ever thought about **cutting back** your drug use?
    - o **A** – Do people **annoy** you when they talk about your drug use?
    - o **G** – Do you ever feel **guilty** about your drug use?
    - o **E** – **Eye-opener** - Do you sometimes drink first thing in the morning?
  - ➢ Do you ever feel sad or down?
- **S – Suicidality**
  - ➢ Have you ever thought about hurting yourself?
- **S – Sex**
  - ➢ Have you ever had a sexual relationship with someone?
  - ➢ How are you protecting yourself from AIDS?

Exam, Lab screening and Health Maintenance

- Check blood pressure to rule out hypertension
- Annual pap smear and chlamydia screening for all sexually active girls
- Assure vaccinations are up to date
- Cholesterol screening every 3 years for a family history of heart disease

Adapted from the AMA guidelines for adolescent preventive services. Baltimore: Williams & Wilkins, 1994.

The topics outlined for anticipatory guidance in any one visit are new areas to be addressed and build off the areas discussed during prior visits.

Two Week Check
- Diet: breast milk or formula only. Avoid honey until 12 months old.
- Behavior: hiccups, sneezing, startle response all normal
- Safety: car seat faces backwards, sleep supine, avoid smoke exposure
- Equipment needs: bulb syringe, thermometer, smoke detector
- Family issues: respite care and support for caretaker(s)

Two Month Check
- Diet: upright feeding position, no solids until at least four months
- Behavior: crying is to indicate wants or represents colic
- Safety: crib sides up, sunscreen/hats, bath water temperature
- Stimulation: mobiles, music, reading to baby, talking to baby
- Family issues: father involved. Need time alone for parents

Four Month Check
- Diet: can start rice cereal, no bottle in bed, egg whites or fluid milk products
- Behavior: teething (1st teeth between 4-12 months), drooling
- Safety: falls, choking on small items
- Stimulation: rattles, floor play, encourage vocalizations, sibling play

Six Month Check
- Diet: pureed food, fluoride if breastfed or not in drinking water, limit juices
- Behavior: stranger anxiety, bedtime schedule, fear of separation
- Safety: gates for stairs, latches on cupboards, no walkers, cover all electrical outlets
- Stimulation: rattles, read board books, talking to baby

Nine Month Check
- Diet: introduce infant cup, finger foods, spoon use. Avoid soda pop
- Behavior: bedtime and nap schedules, wear shoes, brush gums/teeth
- Safety: poisons locked away, poison control number (1-800 222-1222), reliable babysitters, climbing hazards, choking danger
- Stimulation: blocks, interactive simple games, reading to baby

One Year Check
- Diet: whole milk and eggs okay, wean bottle, limit sweets and brush teeth.
- Behavior: set limits, consistency in house rules, shoes, no spanking
- Safety: front-facing car seat if child over 20 pounds

Fifteen Month Check
- Behavior: temper tantrums, feeds self, understands "no"
- Safety: doors, choking, sunburn, falls
- Stimulation: introduce body parts, play naming games and read books

Eighteen Month Check
- Diet: avoid junk foods, soda, reinforce dental hygiene
- Behavior: difficulty sharing, independence, sleep fears, self comfort, toilet training readiness (dry naps, can walk and pull pants up/down, can signal when he/she needs to use the bathroom and wants to use a potty chair)
- Safety: street/water safety

Two Year Check
- Diet: encourage regular meals with family and floss teeth.
- Behavior: temper tantrums, defiance
- Safety: knives, electric equipment, constant adult supervision
- Stimulation: peer play, painting, crayons, reading

Three Year Check
- Diet: first dental exam, low fat milk, avoid sweets and soda pop
- Behavior: night fears, fantasy play, better with sharing
- Discipline: time out
- Safety: matches, fire safety, firearms must be locked away, bike helmet
- Stimulation: play groups and preschool, limit television (< 3 hours/day)

Four Year Check
- Behavior: imagination, lying, imitates adults, curiousness
- Safety: avoid adult themes on TV, stranger caution, booster car seat until 8 years **or** > 6 years and at least 4'9" and 80 pounds
- Stimulation: TV alternatives, drawing, outdoor activities

Five Year Check
- Diet: importance of breakfast
- Behavior: school readiness, separation anxiety, importance of sleep
- Safety: knows home address/phone number, sexual abuse
- Stimulation: school activities

Grade school Years
- Behavior: early sex education, chores, manners
- Safety: helmet use, reinforce street/water/fire safety, seat belts
- Stimulation: reading, exercise, after school activities

Middle School Years
- Diet: avoid junk foods, address obesity and eating disorders
- Behavior: sex education, sexually transmitted disease education, drug use and high risk behaviors
- Safety: helmet use, drug use, seat belts, firearms
- Stimulation: encourage goal setting, exercise and after school activities

Clinical Presentation

- Typically begins between 2-3 weeks of age and resolves by 3-4 months.
- Presents as inconsolable crying often accompanied by drawing up the legs or head and gaseous distension.
- Tends to occur in the late afternoon, ≥ 3 hours/day and ≥ 3 days/week
- Rule out other causes of crying and irritability such as infection, hunger, wet diaper or desire to be cuddled.

Potential Contributing Factors

- Formula use
- Swallowing air during feedings (aerophagia)
- Intake of various foods by nursing mothers such as milk products, cauliflower, broccoli, cabbage, eggs, chocolate, wheat, nuts and caffeinated beverages may affect babies.

Parental Education

- Parents need to take a break to avoid the risk of shaking the baby.
  - ➤ Consider a family member, friend or babysitter to watch baby periodically
- Parents must have someone to call if they feel like they might hurt the baby.
- Colic is not an illness.
- Colic is not contagious.
- Colic does not damage the baby in any way.
- Colic is not caused by bad parenting.
- Colicky babies probably have more gas because of aerophagia.

Management of Colic

- Burp baby more frequently while he/she is feeding.
- If the baby is formula fed, can try switching to a soy-based or a hypoallergenic formula.
- Try carrying the baby in a front sling or carrier.
- Try swaddling the baby.
- Can attempt gentle belly massage.
- Can try a warm water bottle lightly applied to the abdomen.
- Lay the infant belly down on your lap and rub his/her back.
- Take the child for a car ride or stroller ride.
- Try a child swing.
- Simethicone drops "not proven effective", but are benign with possible placebo effect.
- Most folk remedies not harmful (e.g., chamomile tea or homeopathic tablets)

Adapted from the North American Society for Pediatric Gastroenterology and Nutrition Clinical Guidelines for Constipation in Infants and Children

Definitions
- Constipation: hard stools passed ≤ 2 times per week for at least 2 weeks.

Evaluation of Constipation in Infants and Young Children
- **History:** duration, diet, toilet training history, pain or bleeding with defecation, withholding behavior, encopresis, delayed passage of meconium (> 24 hours), toileting behavior outside of the home or presence of abdominal pain
- **Family History:** constipation, Hirschsprung's disease, celiac disease, cystic fibrosis, thyroid or parathyroid diseases
- **Exam:** fecal mass on abdominal exam
  - Signs of spina bifida occulta: sacral dimple, tuft of hair or dermal sinus
  - Anal exam: presence of perianal erythema, fissure, fistula or stenosis
  - Rectal exam: presence of fecal mass, anal wink, good rectal tone
  - Complete neurologic exam including cremasteric reflex check
- **Assess for Red Flags:** fever, vomiting, bloody diarrhea, failure to thrive or tight empty rectum on rectal exam
- **Evaluation of Refractory Constipation**
  - Thyroid panel, calcium level, lead level and celiac panel
  - Plain-film abdominal x-ray to assess for fecal mass in colon
  - MRI of the lumbosacral spine if any concern of spinal dysraphism
  - Evaluation for Hirschsprung's disease: anal manometry, barium enema and rectal biopsy looking for the absence of ganglion cells
  - Sweat test if any concern of cystic fibrosis

Management of Functional Constipation in Infants < 1 Year
- **Fecal Disimpaction**
  - Rectal disimpaction with glycerin suppositories
- **Dietary Changes**
  - Increased intake of prune, pear or apple juice
- **Medications**
  - Malt soup extract (i.e., Maltsupex) 15 cc qd/bid mixed with water or juice

Management of Functional Constipation in Children > 1 Year
- **Fecal Disimpaction**
  - Oral disimpaction with mineral oil 15-30 mL/year of age daily **or** magnesium citrate or magnesium hydroxide 1-3 mL/kg/day **or** polyethylene glycol-electrolyte solution (e.g., GoLytely) 20 mL/hr x 4 hours daily
  - Rectal disimpaction with phosphate soda **or** saline enemas (> 2 years old).
- **Dietary Changes**
  - Increased intake of fluids, whole grains, fresh fruits and vegetables
- **Maintenance Therapy**
  - Mineral oil 1-3 mL/kg/day **or** magnesium hydroxide 1 mL/kg/day **or** 70% lactulose solution at 1-3 mL/kg/day divided bid **or** polyethylene glycol powder (e.g., Miralax) 15 cc (or 17 grams) mixed in 8 ounces water daily.
  - Wean maintenance therapy to minimum effective dose

References: Amer. Fam. Physician, 2002; 65: 2283-90 and J. Pediatric Gastro. Nutrition, 1999; 29: 612-26.

Definitions
- **Adrenarche**: increased adrenal androgen secretion associated with maturation of pilosebaceous glands & appearance of axillary and pubic hair.
- **Gonadarche**: Increased gonadotrophin and sex hormone secretion which initiates the development of secondary sexual characteristics.
- **Thelarche**: The onset of breast development

Normal Pubertal Development
- Normal puberty occurs between ages 8-14 years ($\female$) and 9-14 years ($\male$).

Pubertal Milestones in Children					
Tanner Stage*	Female Breasts	Male Genitalia	Pubic Hair	Growth (cm/year)	Other Features
1	• Elevation of papilla	• Testes < 2.5 cm	• Villus hair	• 5-6	• Adrenarche starts
2 (11-12 yr)	• Breast buds • Enlarged areola	• Scrotum reddens • Testes 2.5-3 cm	• Sparse slightly dark hair	• 7-8 ($\female$) • 5-6 ($\male$)	• Clitoral ↑ • Labia darkens
3 (12-13 yr)	• Breast growth beyond areola	• Penis ↑ • Testes 3-4 cm	• Thicker, curlier hair	• 8 ($\female$) • 7-8 ($\male$)	• Voice change($\male$) • Axillary hair • Acne
4 (13-14 yr)	• Secondary mound by papilla + areola	• Scrotum darkens • Penis ↑ • Testes ↑ in size	• Adult-type hair	• < 7 ($\female$) • 9-10 ($\male$)	• Menarche • Voice deepens ($\male$)
5 (14-15 y)	• Adult breasts	• Adult genitalia	• Hair on thighs	• Deceler-ation	• Facial hair • ↑ Muscle

* the age in parentheses is the median age for children entering this pubertal stage

Evaluation of Precocious Puberty
- **Definition**: puberty < 7 ½ years in girls and < 9 years in boys
- **History**: family history of premature puberty or genetic diseases? Child's growth/developmental history and timing/sequence of pubertal milestones.
- X-ray of left wrist for bone age (BA) to compare with chronologic age (CA)
- Labs to consider: serum levels of FSH, LH, estradiol, testosterone, TSH, free T4, hCG and a GnRH stimulation test
- GnRH stimulation test: 100 mcg GnRH administered subcutaneously and FSH and LH levels drawn at 0, 15, 30, 45 and 60 minutes
  ➤ Pubertal pattern is a 2-3-fold rise in FSH/LH levels post-stimulation.

Idiopathic Precocious Puberty
- History, exam, pubertal milestone sequence all unremarkable
- Bone age > chronologic age in idiopathic precocious puberty

TSH = thyroid stimulating hormone, T4 = levothyroxine, hCG = human chorionic gonadotropin, FSH = follicle stimulating hormone, LH = luteinizing hormone and GnRH = gonadotropin releasing hormone

- FSH, LH, sex hormones and GnRH stimulation test will show pubertal levels
- Treatment options: expectant management or use of GnRH analogs* to suppress gonadotropin release (create a prepubertal hormonal milieu).

Benign Premature Thelarche (♀) or Benign Gynecomastia (♂)
- History, exam, pubertal milestone sequence all unremarkable
- Bone age equal to chronologic age
- Growth velocity, FSH/LH + estradiol or testosterone all at prepubertal levels
- Treat with reassurance and expectant management.

Benign Premature Adrenarche
- Appearance of pubic and/or axillary hair and adult-type body odor with no development of secondary sexual characteristics.
- Growth velocity, FSH/LH + sex hormones all in prepubertal range, bone age same as chronologic age
- ACTH stimulation test to rule out late-onset congenital adrenal hyperplasia.

Abnormal Precocious Puberty
- History reveals an abnormal pubertal milestone sequence.
- Red flags: contrasexual development, virilization/hirsutism, visual field deficit, headache or McCune-Albright syndrome triad of precocious puberty polyostotic fibrous dysplasia and café au lait spots
- Evaluation: MRI of brain to rule out a hypothalamic/pituitary lesion
- Labs: TSH/free T4, FSH, LH, sex hormones, hCG levels, 17-hydroxyprogesterone and dehydroepiandrosterone sulfate
- Ovarian ultrasound or high-resolution CT scan of the adrenals to further evaluate any abnormal hormone levels.

Evaluation of Delayed Puberty (No sexual development by age 14 years)
- Search for syndromic features:
  ➤ Turner syndrome -short, hypogonadism, shield chest and webbed neck
  ➤ Klinefelter's syndrome–tall, eunuchoid, small/firm testes + gynecomastia
- Labs: FSH, LH, prolactin, estradiol, testosterone, DHEA-S, TSH, free T4, a GnRH stimulation test and a chromosome analysis if a syndrome is possible.

Disease Processes Associated with Delayed Puberty
- Hypopituitarism
- Anorexia nervosa
- Kallman's syndrome: anosmia and hypogonadotrophic hypogonadism
- Miliary tuberculosis
- Severe cachexia or malnutrition
- Chronic infectious or inflammatory states

Constitutional Delay
- Normal history, exam, growth history
- Bone age < chronologic age
- FSH/LH, sex hormone levels and GnRH stimulation all in prepubertal range.
- Treat with expectant management.

ACTH = adrenocorticotropin hormone, *GnRH analogs include leuprolide injection or intranasal nafarelin and DHEA-s = dehydroepiandrosterone sulfate
Reference: Amer. Fam. Physician, 1999; 60: 209-24

Enuresis

- The involuntary loss or urine that occurs only at night in girls older than 5 years and boys older than 6 years.
  - Affects 10-20% of 1st grade boys and 8-17% of 1st grade girls.
- Primary enuresis if children have never been continent.
- Secondary enuresis if incontinence recurs after ≥ 6 months of continence.

Evaluation of Enuresis

- Complete history and exam (check for abnormal gait + spinal dysraphism)
- Family history of enuresis or Attention Deficit Hyperactivity Disorder
- Check urinalysis and urine culture (rule out diabetes or infection)
- Inquire about encopresis and chronic constipation that can be associated.
- Any diurnal incontinence? (positive answer→ rule out complicated enuresis)
- If complicated enuresis suspected, consider a voiding cystourethrogram to rule out an ectopic ureter in girls or posterior urethral valves in boys.

Management of Enuresis

Family Counseling

- Avoidance of punishment and humiliation
- Improve child's access to toilet.
- Provide good lighting in case fear of the dark a hindrance.
- Avoid fluids for at least two hours prior to bedtime.
- Empty the bladder at bedtime
- Child's participation in morning clean-up
- Encourage parents to keep an enuresis diary.
- Positive reinforcement system for "dry" nights

Conditioning Therapy

- Enuresis alarm systems
  - Best rate of permanent cure (70-75%)
  - The alarm sounds when the child begins to void and eventually trains the child to awake when he/she senses a full bladder.
  - Complete a trial of at least 3-4 months prior to discontinuation.

Pharmacologic Agents

- Desmopressin (DDAVP)
  - 0.2 mg PO qhs titrated to 0.6 mg qhs if needed
  - Very effective but high relapse rate (80-90%) upon discontinuation.
  - Best used intermittently for sleepovers, campouts, etc.
- Imipramine
  - 25 mg qhs (ages 6-8 yrs), 50 mg qhs (8-12 yrs), 75 mg qhs (>12 yrs)
  - Taper dose over 4 weeks when discontinuing therapy
  - Typically for 3-6 months of therapy
  - Acute overdoses are potentially fatal from cardiovascular collapse.

References: Amer. Fam. Physician, 2003; 67: 1499-506 and Pediatrics & Child Health, 1997; 2(6): 419-21.

General Guidelines and Definitions

- **Definition of fever:** rectal temperature ≥ 38°C (100.4°F)
- **Toxic appearance:** lethargic, inconsolable, pale or cyanotic, extreme irritability, and often manifest tachypnea, tachycardia and/or poor perfusion.
- All toxic infants should be hospitalized on empiric antibiotics for a complete sepsis work-up (complete blood count, chest radiograph, blood cultures, catheterized urine culture and lumbar puncture).
- **Older infants** are those children between 3 months and 3 years of age.

Guidelines for Evaluation of Nontoxic Older Infant with Fever < 39°C (102.2°F)

- Exceptions are children with stomatitis, croup, bronchiolitis or varicella who do not need a work-up if they are well-appearing.
- Careful history and exam to identify likely sources of bacterial infection
- If no obvious source of bacterial infection found
  - ➢ No tests or antibiotics needed
  - ➢ Acetaminophen or ibuprofen as needed for fever control.
  - ➢ Re-evaluate in 48 hours or sooner if condition deteriorates.
- If a source of infection is found
  - ➢ Targeted lab tests based on source of infection
  - ➢ Empiric antibiotics to cover likely bacterial pathogens

Guidelines for Evaluation of Nontoxic Older Infant with Fever ≥ 39°C (102.2°F) and No Obvious Source of Infection

- If the child is up-to-date with his/her pneumococcal/Hib vaccinations, the chance of occult bacteremia is probably < 1%.
- Consider a complete blood count (especially in unimmunized children)
- Consider a blood culture if white blood count > 15,000 per mm³ (especially in unimmunized children)
- Catheterized urine culture in all boys < 6 months and uncircumcised boys < 1 year and all girls < 2 years with no other source of infection
- Chest radiograph for cough, tachypnea (> 59 breaths/min. 3-6 months, > 52 if 6-11 months and >42 if 1-3 years), an abnormal pulmonary exam or a white blood count > 20,000 per mm³.
- Stool culture if history of diarrhea and blood or mucus in stool or > 5 white blood cells per high-powered field on stool exam
- Lumbar puncture if history or exam worrisome for meningitis
- Consider empiric antibiotics for white blood count ≥ 15,000 per mm³.
  - ➢ Ceftriaxone 50 mg/kg IM qd for fever of unknown source until cultures results known at 48 hours
- Follow-up in 24 hours if fever persists or 48 hours otherwise

References: Annals Emergency Medicine, 2003; 42: 530-44, J. Pediatrics; 1994; 124: 504-12., Annals Emerg. Med., 1999; 33: 166-73. and American Family Physician, 2001; 64: 1219-26.

Definitions and Miscellaneous

- **Definition of fever:** rectal temperature ≥ 38ºC (100.4ºF)
- **Toxic appearance:** lethargic, inconsolable, pale or cyanotic, extreme irritability, and often manifest tachypnea, tachycardia and/or poor perfusion.
- **Young infant:** less than 3 months of age
- Otitis media should **not** be considered the cause of fever in young infants

Rochester Criteria for Febrile Infants at Low Risk for Bacterial Infections

- Nontoxic appearance
- Full term (> 37 weeks gestation)
- No history of antibiotic use
- No history of unexplained hyperbilirubinemia
- No underlying illnesses
- No focal infections on exam
- Lab data: white blood cell ≥ 5,000 or ≤ 15,000 per mm³, band count < 1,500 per mm³, urinalysis ≤ 10 white blood cells per high-power field and stool analysis with ≤ 5 white blood cells per high-power field (if diarrhea present)
  ➤ Some experts argue that the cutoff for elevated white blood cells should be 18,000 per mm³ in the era of pneumococcus and hemophilus vaccination.

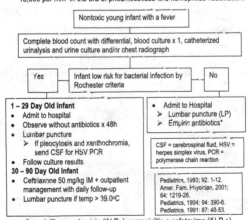

Nontoxic young infant with a fever

Complete blood count with differential, blood culture x 1, catheterized urinalysis and urine culture and/or chest radiograph

| Yes | Infant low risk for bacterial infection by Rochester criteria | No |

1 – 29 Day Old Infant
- Admit to hospital
- Observe without antibiotics x 48h
- Lumbar puncture
  ➤ If pleocytosis and xanthochromia, send CSF for HSV PCR
- Follow culture results

30 – 90 Day Old Infant
- Ceftriaxone 50 mg/kg IM + outpatient management with daily follow-up
- Lumbar puncture if temp > 39.0ºC

- Admit to Hospital
  ➤ Lumbar puncture (LP)
  ➤ Empiric antibiotics*

CSF = cerebrospinal fluid, HSV = herpes simplex virus, PCR = polymerase chain reaction

Pediatrics, 1993; 92: 1-12.
Amer. Fam. Physician, 2001; 64: 1219-26.
Pediatrics, 1994; 94: 390-6.
Pediatrics, 1991: 87: 48-53.

* ampicillin + gentamicin (if LP -) or ampicillin + cefotaxime (if LP +)

Metatarsus Adductus (MA)
- Congenital deformity characterized by medial deviation of the forefoot.
- 10-15% association with developmental dysplasia of the hip
- 85% resolve spontaneously by 12 months of age

Diagnosis
- A line bisecting the heel and the sole of the foot at the arch should cross either the second or third toe in a normal foot.
- This same line will cross the the fourth or fifth toe in a child with MA.

Management
- Teach parents stetching exercises to bring the forefoot to neutral position.
- Rule out club foot deformity and refer for a fixed deformity or for a club foot.
- Consider serial casting beginning ~ 6 months of age and changed every 2 weeks for persistent deformity.
- Consider a metatarsal osteotomy at 12 months of age for deformities refractory to serial casting.

Internal Tibial Torsion
- Caused by medial rotation of the tibia below the knee.
- Tibial torsion is the normal position in newborns. If pronounced, it presents with intoeing at 1-2 years of age when the child is weight bearing.

Diagnosis
- With the child in a sitting position and the legs outstretched, rotate the legs such that the patella are both aligned directly upwards.
- If the lateral malleolus is anterior to the medial malleolus, the patient has internal tibial torsion

Management
- Tibial torsion usually resolves spontaneously by 4 years of age.
- Reassure parents that this condition generally resolves spontaneously.
- Consider supramalleolar osteotomy if the patient has significant ambulation problems at 9-10 years of age.

Medial Femoral Anteversion (MFA)
- Caused by excessive internal rotation of the femur
- Tends to present with intoeing at 3 - 6 years of age (girls > boys).
- Classically, children sit in the "W" position with their feet out to each side.
- Spontaneous resolution occurs in about 95% of cases by 10 years of age.
- Rule out cerebral palsy

Diagnosis
- Assess degree of hip rotation with child in prone position and knees flexed.
- Normal hip internal rotation (IR) for children > 2 years is 30-60°.
- Normal hip external rotation (ER) for children > 2 years is 30-40°.
- Medial femoral anteversion if hip IR > 70° and/or hip ER < 20°.

Management
- Encourage children to sit cross-legged.
- Consider a femoral derotational osteotomy in children older than 10 years with < 10° hip ER and gait problems.

References: Amer. Fam. Physician, 1979; 19(5): 111-7. Curr. Opin. Pediatrics, 1997; 9(1): 77-80.

Differential Diagnosis of a Limp by Age Group		
Toddlers (< 4 years)	**Ages 4 – 10 Years**	**Children > 10 years**
DDH	Legg-Calve-Perthes*	SCFE*
Mild cerebral palsy	Osteomyelitis*	Toxic synovitis*
Trauma +/- Abuse*	Discitis*	Osgood-Schlatter dz*
JRA*	Leg length discrepancy‡	Tumor*
Septic arthritis*	Septic arthritis*	Tarsal coalition

DDH=Development dysplasia of hip, SCFE=slipped capital femoral epiphysis, JRA = juvenile rheumatoid arthritis, ‡ difference > 1 inch may explain limp, * indicates painful conditions, dz = disease

Developmental Dysplasia of the Hip (DDH)
- Screen all newborns with Ortolani and Barlow maneuvers for hip instability.
- Consider a referral to a pediatric orthopedist for all abnormal hip exams.

Juvenile Rheumatoid Arthritis (JRA)
- Diagnosis: objective joint inflammation persisting > 6 weeks, onset < 18 yrs (usually age 1-4 yrs), morning stiffness ≥ 1 hour +/- rheumatoid factor +.
- Subtypes include systemic, polyarticular or pauciarticular JRA

Osteomyelitis/Discitis
- Usually acquired hematogenously
- Technetium-labeled bone scan or MRI scan will be abnormal.
- Exam: decreased range of motion, painful ambulation, fever
- Labs: leukocytosis +/- left shift and elevated erythrocyte sedimentation rate

Legg-Calve-Perthes Disease (LCPD)
- Osteonecrosis of the femoral head between 4-9 years old. Male:Female=5:1
- Clinical features: trendelenburg gait, ↓ hip abduction/internal rotation
- Diagnosis: hip x-rays identify femoral head necrosis

Septic Arthritis
- Presentation: usually child < 2 years, fever, ill-appearing and refusal to walk
- Exam: hip held in flexion and abduction with hip effusion and pain with passive hip range of motion
- Labs: leukocytosis +/- left shift and elevated erythrocyte sedimentation rate
- Diagnosis: arthrocentesis/joint drainage required to identify + treat infection

Slipped Capital Femoral Epiphysis (SCFE)
- Presentation: Male:Female 2:1 and obese child between 8-16 years old.
- Exam: trendelenburg gait and hip usually flexed and externally rotated
- Diagnosis: hip x-rays identifies "a slip" affecting the femoral head.

Toxic Synovitis
- Presentation: usually follows a respiratory infection
- Exam: Non-toxic appearance, limited hip abduction & external/internal rotation
- Labs: usually normal white blood count and erythrocyte sedimentation rate.
  ➤ Consider a hip ultrasound to rule out an effusion if diagnosis unclear

Osgood-Schlatter Disease (osteochondritis of the tibial tuberosity)
- Presentation: progressive anterior knee pain in an adolescent ♂ > ♀ involved in jumping sports. Squatting typically worsens the pain.
- Exam: localized tenderness and prominence of the tibial tuberosity
- Diagnosis: clinical diagnosis and radiographs generally not needed.

References: Pediatrics, 2002; 109 (1): 109-15. Amer. Fam. Physician, 1999; 60: 177-88. Amer. Fam. Physician, 2000; 61 (4): 1011-8 and Current Opin. Pediatrics, 2001; 13 (1): 29-35.

Definition:
- Usually diagnosed in children < 2 yrs whose weight is consistently < 5th % or whose weight crosses & falls below 2 major growth curves within 6 months.

Etiologies of Failure to Thrive (FTT) in Children Two Years or Younger
- **Non-organic causes (vast majority of cases)**
  - Inadequate caloric intake: poor feeding technique, inappropriate food for age or inadequate quantity of food offered
  - Psychosocial problems: dysfunctional relationship between parents and child, emotional neglect or child abuse
- **Organic Causes**
  - Craniofacial: cleft palate, chronic nasal obstruction or adenoidal hypertrophy
  - Neurologic: neuromuscular disorders, hypotonia or cerebral palsy
  - Severe developmental delay
  - Endocrine: thyroid disease or diabetes mellitus
  - Infections: tuberculosis, toxoplasmosis or HIV infection
  - Congenital heart disease
  - Respiratory: bronchopulmonary dysplasia, cystic fibrosis
  - Gastrointestinal: pyloric stenosis, malrotation, intussusception, duodenal atresia, inflammatory bowel disease, gastroesophageal reflux, feeding problems and the delayed introduction of solids
  - Inborn errors of metabolism
  - Lead toxicity
  - Chromosomal anomalies (e.g., Turner syndrome)
  - Renal disease: renal failure or renal tubular acidosis

Work-Up of FTT
- Evaluation of growth curves for height, weight and head circumference
- Birth history: gestational age at birth, birth weight, complications with pregnancy or delivery or any growth restriction
- Detailed nutritional, feeding and stooling history
- Careful developmental assessment
- Psychosocial history: living situation, parental employment and economic status, family stressors, spousal abuse, substance abuse, parental physical or mental illnesses (e.g., postpartum depression)
- Observation: parental-child interaction, developmental assessment, observation of feeding for signs of swallowing dysfunction, infant behavior
- Strongly consider public health nurse visit for home evaluation
- Exam for dysmorphic features, signs of cleft palate or neurologic, cardiopulmonary, endocrine or gastrointestinal disorders
- Labs: complete blood count, urinalysis, urine culture, calcium, electrolyte and renal panel, tuberculosis skin test +/- HIV and stool studies (if history warrants).
  - Other labs based on findings from history and exam

Management of FTT
- Diet: increase caloric intake ~50% (150-160 kcal/kg/day in children < 2 yrs)
  - Limit fruit juices, carbonated drinks and low-calorie foods
- Children to avoid meal distractions (e.g., television or video games)
- Referrals to address the psychosocial problems in the household
- Access to federal assistance programs (food stamps, Women, Infants and Children program) and community services if available.
- Follow-up at least monthly until catch-up growth has been documented.

References: Pediatric Rev., 1997; 18: 371 and Pediatric Rev., 1992; 13: 453.

Adapted from the American Academy of Pediatrics (AAP) Practice Guideline on the Management of Acute Gastroenteritis in Young Children Ages 1 month to 5 years.

Note: The following guidelines apply to acute diarrheal illnesses lasting < 10 days and no signs of failure to thrive.

Evaluating the Degree of Dehydration

Characteristic	Mild (<5%)	Moderate (6-9%)	Severe (>10%)
Heart rate	Normal	Mild increase	Marked increase
Mucous membranes	Normal	Dry	Very dry
Mental status	Alert	Irritable or listless	Lethargic or obtunded
Urine output	Normal	Diminished	Markedly decreased
Skin turgor	Normal	Decreased	Markedly decreased
Fontanelle	Normal	Slightly sunken	Sunken
Eyes	Normal	Sunken orbits	Deeply sunken orbits
Skin	Pink + warm	Capillary refill > 2 seconds	Cool + mottled

Management of Acute Gastroenteritis with Mild or No Dehydration
- Breastfeeding should be continued in breastfed infants
- Continue age-appropriate diets
  - ➢ Rice, wheat, potatoes, breads, cereals, yogurt, fruits and vegetables.
  - ➢ Avoid fatty foods, fruit juices, soft drinks, candy and desserts.
- Mild dehydration should be corrected with 50 mL/kg of an oral rehydration solution (ORS) over 4 hours: examples include the World Health Organization rehydration solution, Rapolyte solution or Rehydralyte solution.
  - ➢ ORS = ½ teaspoon each of baking soda and table salt + 8 teaspoons sugar + 1/3 teaspoon potassium chloride in 1 liter of water
- Lactose-containing formulas/foods can be consumed safely in most children

Management of Acute Gastroenteritis with Moderate Dehydration
- ORS at 100 mL/kg over four hours in a monitored setting.
- Reassess degree of hydration after four hours and continue ORS until patient is adequately hydrated.
- Resume breastfeeding +/- age-appropriate foods as above once rehydrated.
- For vomiting, ORS can be administered in 5 mL aliquot every 1-2 minutes.
- If diarrhea significant, maintenance fluids can be administered at 10 mL/kg per stool using a maintenance solution: examples include Pedialyte, Naturalyte, NutraMax, Infalyte, Lytren or Gastrolyte.

Management of Acute Gastroenteritis with Severe Dehydration
- Intravenous fluid therapy with 20 mL/kg isotonic fluid bolus and repeat isotonic fluid boluses until patient rehydrated.

Antidiarrheal Agents
- The AAP recommends against the use of any antidiarrheal agents including bismuth subsalicylate and adsorbents such as kaolin-pectate and fiber.

Contraindications to Using Oral Rehydration Therapy
- Intractable vomiting, decreased level of consciousness and ileus.

References: Canadian J. of Pediatrics, 1994; 1(5): 160-4 and Pediatrics, 1996; 97(3)

Developmental Milestones (Note: these milestones will occur within a certain time interval and the following ages serve as a rough average within this time period). Refer to Denver Developmental screen for more details

Two Week Check
- Motor: lifts head when prone, regards face, symmetric movements
- Language: startles to loud sounds

Two Month Check
- Motor: lifts head 45° when prone, follows objects to midline
- Language: starting to vocalize, responsive smile

Four Month Check
- Motor: head steady when upright, follows objects past midline, brings hands together, grasps rattle, holds bottle
- Language: laughs, squeals, spontaneous smile, coos, orients to voice

Six Month Check
- Motor: rolls over, sits without support, reaches for objects, bounces and transfers objects between hands
- Language: turns to sound, babbles

Nine Month Check
- Gross motor: crawls or scoots, pulls to stand and bangs 2 cubes together
- Fine motor: feeds self cracker and pincer grasp
- Language: nonspecific paired consonants (baba, mama, dada) and jabbers
- Social: plays peek-a-boo or pat-a-cake and waves "bye bye"

One Year Check
- Gross motor: cruises, walks holding on and drinks from cup
- Fine motor: neat pincer grasp both hands
- Language: dada, mama specific

Fifteen Month Check
- Gross motor: walks well, stoops and recovers and climbs stairs
- Fine motor: scribbles and stacks 2 blocks
- Language: 3 words (excluding dada/mama) & indicates wants without crying

Eighteen Month Check
- Gross motor: walks backwards, climbs onto chair and removes a garment
- Fine motor: feeds self with spoon and stacks 3 cubes
- Language: 7-20 words and points to 3 body parts

Two Year Check
- Gross motor: runs well, throws and kicks a ball, puts on clothing and goes up/down steps alone
- Fine motor: stacks 4 cubes, imitates housework and draws a vertical line
- Language: 20 words, 2 word phrases
- Social: begins playing well with others

Three Year Check
- Gross motor: rides tricycle, dresses with help and broad jumps
- Fine motor: stacks 6-8 cubes and can wiggle thumbs
- Social: can pretend play
- Language: 3 words sentences, knows name & age, 75% of speech intelligible.

Four Year Check
- Gross motor: hops, dresses without help, balances on one foot
- Fine motor: copies a circle & cross, buttons clothes and draws a 3-part person
- Language: 4 word sentences, knows 3-4 colors and speech 100% intelligible

Five Year Check
- Gross motor: skips and can heel-to-toe walk
- Fine motor: draws a person with at least 6 body parts and copies a square
- Language: speaks in simple conversations and knows full name

Seven Year Check
- Gross motor: rides bicycle, climbs well, bathes self
- Fine motor: cuts with scissors, can draw and paste
- Social: participates in school and group activities

Normal Growth of Infants and Children
- In general, infants/children should grow along their individual growth curves
  - Pediatric growth charts available from the Centers for Disease Control at: www.cdc.gov/nchs/about/major/nhanes/growthcharts/clinical_charts.htm

Average Weight Changes at Different Ages
- Regains birthweight (BW) by 2 weeks, doubles BW by 5-6 months, triples BW by 12 months and quadruples BW by 24 months of age.
- 2 weeks-3 months→ weight increases about 1 ounce daily
- 3-12 months→ weight increases about 1/2 ounce daily or 1 pound/month
- 12-24 months → weight increases about 1/2 pound/month

Average Height Changes at Different Ages
- Infants double birth length (BL) by 3-4 years and triple BL by 13 years
- 0-12 months→ average height increase is about 10 inches
- 12-24 months → average height increase is about 5 inches
- 24-36 months → average height increase is about 3 1/2 inches
- 3 years-puberty→ average height increase is about 2 inches/year

Average Head Circumference at Different Ages
- 0-3 months→ head circumference increases about 2 cm/month
- 4-6 months→ head circumference increases about 1 cm/month
- 6-12 months→ head circumference increases about 1/2 cm/month
- 12-24 months→ head circumference increases about 2 cm

Adapted from the American Academy of Pediatrics (AAP) Practice Guideline on the Management of
Hyperbilirubinemia in Term Newborns

Principles of Hyperbilirubinemia in Newborns
- Jaundice in infants < 24 hours of age is pathologic until proven otherwise.
- Direct bilirubin > 2 mg/dL indicates hepatobiliary dysfunction

Common Cause of Newborn Jaundice
- Physiologic or breastmilk jaundice
- Hemolytic anemia
  - ➤ ABO/Rh incompatibility
  - ➤ Congenital hemolytic disorder
- Polycythemia
- Blood extravasation
- Metabolic disorders (e.g., glycogen storage diseases)

Risk Factors for Newborn Jaundice

• Family history of hemolytic disorder	• Prior infant with hyperbilirubinemia	• ABO/Rh incompatibility
• Cephalohematoma	• Breastfeeding	• Gestational DM
• High-risk ethnicity*	• Neonatal sepsis	• Polycythemia
• Excessive newborn weight loss	• Delayed meconium passage	• Congenital hepatobiliary disorder

* Asian or Native American Indian and DM = diabetes mellitus

Labs to Evaluate for Newborn Jaundice
- Total and direct bilirubin
- For ABO or Rh incompatibility obtain a direct Coomb's test
- Complete blood count
- Reticulocyte count & peripheral blood smear exam if hemolysis suspected

Management of Nonhemolytic, Unconjugated Hyperbilirubinemia in Healthy, Term Newborns

Age (hours)	Total serum bilirubin level (mg/dL)			
	Consider photo-therapy	Definite photo-therapy	Exchange transfusion if intensive phototherapy fails*	Exchange transfusion + intensive phototherapy
≤ 12 h	5	6	≥ 12	≥ 20
12-24 h	6	7	≥ 15	≥ 20
25-48 h	≥ 12	≥ 15	≥ 20	≥ 25
49-72 h	≥ 15	≥ 18	≥ 25	≥ 30
> 72 h	≥ 17	≥ 20	≥ 25	≥ 30

Intensive phototherapy consists of double bilirubin lights and use of a fiberoptic bilirubin pad.
* failure of intensive phototherapy if the decline in total serum bilirubin within 6 hours is < 1-2 mg/dL

Miscellaneous
- Continue breastfeeding infants at least every 2 hours
- All jaundiced newborns discharged less than 48 hours after birth should be evaluated within 2 days of discharge

References: Pediatrics, 1994; 94 (4): 558-62 and Amer. Fam. Physician, 2002; 65: 599-606.

Adapted from the 2003 American Academy of Pediatrics recommendations for the routine administration of childhood vaccinations

General Immunization Guidelines
- Check immunization status every visit and immunize whenever possible
- Understand contraindications for the various immunizations
- No need to restart any vaccination schedule
- Catch-up vaccinations are given at least 4 weeks from the last dose with the exception of HBV_3, Hib_4 and PCV_4 for which the wait is at least 8 weeks and $DTaP_4$ and $DTaP_5$ for which the wait is at least 6 months.
- High-risk children include those with sickle cell disease, asplenia, HIV-positive, chronic cardiopulmonary diseases, hematologic malignancies, chronic renal failure, nephrotic syndrome, diabetes, transplant patients or any other immunocompromised state.

Recommended Childhood Immunization Schedule

Age	Vaccinations
Birth	• HBV_1
2 months	• $DTaP_1$, Hib_1, PCV_1, IPV_1, HBV_2
4 months	• $DTaP_2$, Hib_2, PCV_2, IPV_2
6 months	• $DTaP_3$, Hib_3, PCV_3, IPV_3[1], HBV_3[1]
12 –15 months	• $DTaP_4$, Hib_4, PCV_4[2], MMR_1 and Varicella[3]
2 years	• HAV_4 and PPV_i[5]
4 – 6 years	• $DTaP_5$, MMR_2, IPV_4
11-12 years	• dT_6
Yearly	• Influenza[7]

DTaP = Diphtheria + tetanus toxoid and acellular pertussis, Hib = haemophilus influenzae type b, IPV = inactivated poliovirus, PCV = pneumococcal conjugate vaccine, PPV = pneumococcal polysaccharide vaccine, MMR = measles, mumps and rubella, HAV = hepatitis A virus and HBV = hepatitis B virus

- 1 – IPV_3 or HBV_3 can be given anytime between 6 – 18 months.
- 2 – For unvaccinated children 24 – 59 months old: 1 dose of PCV if health and 2 doses ≥ 2 months apart for high-risk children (see above list).
- 3 – 2 doses given 4 weeks apart for children ≥ 13 years
- 4 – Give to children at high risk for acquiring hepatitis A virus infection:
    ➢ Children living in AZ, AK, OR, NM, UT, WA, OK, SD, ID, NV or CA
    ➢ If county has ≥ 20 cases of hepatitis A virus infection/100,000 people/year
    ➢ If child has a clotting factor disorders or cirrhosis
    ➢ Travel to areas with high endemicity.
    ➢ 2nd dose of HAV given at least 6 months from 1st dose and after 30 months of age.
- 5 – 2 doses 5 years apart for sickle cell disease, asplenia, HIV +, or immunocompromised children who have completed the PCV series and only 1 dose for other high-risk children categories listed above.
- 6 – Given at 11 –12 years and every 10 years thereafter.
- 7 – Consider for all children 6 - 23 months and all children with asthma, cardiac disease, sickle cell disease, HIV+, diabetes and household members of adults at high risk. Must give 2 doses separated by at least 4 weeks to children < 8 years receiving the vaccine for the first time.

References: MMWR, 2002; 51 (RR2): 1-36. MMWR, 1999; 48 (RR12): 1-37. MMWR, 2000; 49(RR09): 1-38. or visit the National Immunization Program website at www.cdc.gov/nip

Risk Factors for Neonatal Sepsis
- Intrapartum: prolonged rupture of membranes > 12 hours (minor risk factor) or > 24 hours (major risk factor), intrapartum fever or clinical chorioamnionitis
- Group B streptococcal (GBS)-positive women with inadequate intrapartum antibiotic prophylaxis (IAP) (1 dose less than 4 hours prior to delivery).
- Prematurity, low birth weight, multiple births, fetal tachycardia or male sex
- History of prior infant with Group B streptococcal sepsis

Neonatal exam in Neonatal Sepsis
- Temperature instability, respiratory distress, apneas or bradycardias, cyanotic episodes, lethargy, irritability, poor feeding, vomiting, hypoglycemia, unexplained jaundice, abdominal distension, poor perfusion, seizures, nuchal rigidity or bulging fontanello.

Laboratory Values Concerning for Neonatal Sepsis
- White blood count
  - ➤ < 5,000 or > 30,000 per µL
  - ➤ Immature/total white blood cell ratio > 0.16
  - ➤ Absolute neutrophil count < 7,500 or > 14,500 per µL
- Platelet count < 150,000 per µL
- Chest x-ray with a focal infiltrate
- Positive blood culture
- Lumbar puncture (indicated for symptomatic newborns or if + blood culture)
  - ➤ Cerebrospinal fluid white blood cells > 10/high-powered field, protein > 65 mg/dL and glucose < 50 mg/dL worrisome for bacterial meningitis
- Urine culture (catheterized or suprapubic tap) for late-onset sepsis (>7 days)

Role of C Reactive Protein (CRP) in the Neonatal Sepsis Work-up
- Not indicated for the routine neonatal sepsis screen
- Can help to exclude cases of neonatal sepsis in cases where the mother received intrapartum antibiotics and the infant has negative blood cultures.
  - ➤ Serial CRP levels can be drawn at 24 and 48 hours of life and if both values are < 10 mg/L the likelihood ratio for early-onset sepsis is 0.03.

The Asymptomatic Newborn Whose Mother is GBS+ and Had Adequate IAP
- Recommend close observation in the hospital for at least 48 hours.
- Sepsis work-up only for worrisome clinical signs or risk factors as above.

Empiric Antibiotic Therapy for Neonatal Sepsis
- Cerebrospinal fluid normal
  - ➤ Ampicillin 100 mg/kg IV q12h + gentamicin 2.5 mg/kg IV q12h
- Cerebrospinal fluid abnormal or unobtainable
  - ➤ Ampicillin 150 mg/kg IV q12h + cefotaxime 50 mg/kg IV q12h

References: Pediatrics, 1999; 104: 447-53. Pediatrics, 2001; 108 (5): 1094-8. Pediatrics, 2000; 106 (2): 256-63 and Inf. Dis. Clin. North Amer., 1999; 13 (3): 711-33.

Apgar Scoring

Sign	0	1	2
Heart rate	Absent	< 100	> 100
Respiratory effort	Absent	Slow/irregular	Good/crying
Muscle tone	Flaccid	Some extremity flexion	Active motion
Reflex irritability	No response	Grimace	Vigorous cry
Color	Pale or central cyanosis	Peripheral cyanosis	Completely pink

Newborn Resuscitation

Birth

- Clear of meconium?
- Breathing or crying?
- Color pink, or term delivery?

Yes to all →

Routine care
- Provide warmth & dry
- Clear airway

No

- Provide warmth, position/clear airway
- Dry, stimulate, reposition and provide O₂ prn

- Evaluate respirations, heart rate (HR) and color

Breathing, pink & HR > 100 → Supportive care

Apnea or HR < 100

- Positive pressure ventilation

Ventilating, pink & HR > 100 → Ongoing care

HR < 60 ↓   ↑ HR > 60

- Positive pressure ventilation[1]
- Chest compressions

[1] consider endotracheal intubation if + pressure ventilation ineffective here

- Epinephrine IV/IO/ET/Umbilical vein[1] 0.01- 0.03 mg/kg (0.1-0.3 ml/kg of 1:10,000) q 3-5 min

Pertinent Maternal History

- Gestational age at the time of delivery and adequacy of prenatal care
  - ➤ If born before 34 weeks, did the mother receive 2 doses of steroids?
- Any complications during the pregnancy or intrapartum course?
  - ➤ Preeclampsia, diabetes, hypertension, thyroid disease, collagen-vascular disease, isoimmunization, seizure disorder or infections such as HIV.
  - ➤ Any evidence of chorioamnionitis?
- Any history of maternal tobacco, alcohol, prescription or illicit drug use?
- Group B streptococcus (GBS) culture status
  - ➤ If GBS +, did the child receive adequate intrapartum antibiotic prophylaxis?
- Maternal blood type O or Rh negative?
- Hepatitis B surface antigen (HbsAg), Rubella, HIV and PPD status
- Venereal Disease Research Laboratory test status (reactive or non-reactive)
- Meconium staining during delivery?

The Newborn Exam

- General appearance: healthy or ill? term or preterm?
  - ➤ Is baby small, appropriate or large for gestational age
- Normal vitals: axillary temp. 36.7-37.4°, respiratory rate < 60, heart rate 100-160
- Head: check fontanelles and suture lines, any cephalohematoma, molding or caput succedaneum
- Eyes: check red reflex, corneal light reflex and spacing
- Ears: shape and position (low-set)
- Nose: patency of nares (choanal atresia), any nasal flaring
- Mouth: color of lips, intact palate (cleft lip and/or palate)
- Neck: masses or goiter
- Chest: Pectus deformity, auscultation of lungs (grunting or retractions)
- Cardiac: rate, rhythm, any murmur(s), quality of femoral pulses
- Abdomen: 2 or 3 vessel umbilical cord, any masses or organomegaly
- Male genitalia: testes descended, urethral position, scrotal/groin masses
- Female genitalia: normal external female genitalia
- Anus: Assure patency and normal position
- Extremities: number of digits, Ortolani/Barlow maneuvers (hip stability)
- Spine: any sacral dimple, cysts, sinus tracts, skin defects or tufts of hair
- Skin: color, perfusion, nevi or other rashes
- Neurologic: Moro, grasp and suck reflexes, tone, symmetry of movement, any excessive jitteriness or irritability
- Dubowitz exam if gestational age unknown or in question

Health Maintenance

- 0.5% erythromycin ointment to both eyes (prevents ophthalmia neonatorum)
- 0.5-1 mg Vitamin K intramuscular injection (prevents hemorrhagic disease of the newborn)
- Check baby blood type and Coombs status if mother is blood type O.
- Newborn metabolic/genetic screen after 24 hours of life & before discharge

- Hepatitis B vaccination (and Hepatitis B immunoglobulin if mother HbsAg +)
- Hearing screen prior to discharge

Nutrition
- Encourage breastfeeding and provide tips to moms having difficulty nursing
- For formula-fed infants, the daily caloric needs for a healthy term infant is about 110 cal/kg/day which is approximately 5 ounces/kg/day.
  > Always hold the newborn for feedings. Do not prop a bottle up for feeds.

Miscellaneous
Prior to discharge the baby should have demonstrated the following:
- Passed a meconium stool
- Voided (often happens during delivery)
- Able to thermoregulate in an open crib
- Able to nurse or bottle feed successfully at least twice
- Stable vital signs for at least 12 hours
- No excessive jaundice
- No significant bleeding from the circumcision site (if done)
- Stable blood sugars (if large for gestational age or mother diabetic)

Psychosocial Assessment
- **A public health nurse or social worker should be involved to help assess home safety and assist the family if any of the following risk factors exist:**
  > Have children been taken from their custody in the past?
  > Parental substance abuse
  > Family history of child abuse or neglect or domestic violence
  > Mental illness in a parent or caretaker
  > Unstable parental housing situation
  > Financial or food insecurity

Parental Education
- Keep sick visitors away from the baby for at least the first month of life.
- Avoid smoking in presence of baby
- Rear facing car seat
- Infants should sleep on their back ("Back to Sleep" Campaign).
- Avoid submersing baby in water until the cord has fallen off and always check the water temperature prior to starting any bath
- Soap should not be used on newborns more than every other day.
- Clean cord site with alcohol several times daily.
- Wipe female infants from front to back when cleaning the diaper area.
- No medical indication for circumcision of male newborns
- Parents should be instructed in how to properly use a bulb syringe and how to take a rectal temperature and seek medical care for any temperature>100.4ºF.
- Anticipatory guidance to help siblings adjust to new infant

References: Adapted from the American Academy of Pediatrics Practice Guideline for Hospital Stay for Healthy Term Newborns (Pediatrics, 1995; 96 (4): 788-90.)

- **Candidal diaper dermatitis** – bright red with sharp borders, satellite lesions and involves the intertriginous areas.
  ➤ Antifungal creams
- **Capillary Hemangiomas** – red, elevated nodule comprised of multiple intertwined vessels typically on the face or trunk.
  ➤ Often will enlarge during the first year and slowly regress in size
  ➤ 90% spontaneously regress by age 9 years.
- **Cavernous hemangiomas** – large subcutaneous nodules also comprised of vessels that give the skin a bluish hue.
- **Cutis marmorata** – diffuse reticulated bluish-purple mottling of skin
  ➤ Usually caused by the cold
- **Erythema toxicum neonatorum** – intense erythematous patches with a central yellowish papule
  ➤ Occurs in up to 50% of newborns starting the first 10 days of life
  ➤ Resolves spontaneously during the first two weeks of life
- **Harlequin color change** – differential coloration of dependent half of body when lying down (red) versus the non-dependent half (pale).
  ➤ Most common in low birth weight babies
- **Irritant dermatitis** – generally a red, scaling papular rash of the diaper area sparing the intertriginous area without satellite lesions.
  ➤ Treat with A&D ointment or diaper creams with zinc oxide & keep area dry.
- **Milia** – 1-2 mm whitish-yellow papules on the face from epithelial-lined cysts
  ➤ Present at birth and resolve spontaneously after several months.
- **Miliaria rubra (or "prickly heat")** – 1-2 mm red vesicles at intertriginous areas due to obstruction of sweat flow during hot weather.
  ➤ Minimized with lightweight, loose clothing and avoidance of greasy creams
- **Mongolian spots** – slate grey to blue-black patch located over the lumbosacral area and buttocks
  ➤ Most common in African-american and Asian-american children
  ➤ Typically fades by age 7 years
- **Neonatal acne** – papules and pustules on face of similar appearance as adolescent acne vulgaris
  ➤ Usually develops during the first few weeks of life and resolves by 3 months.
- **Nevus Flammeus** (or "stork bite") – a salmon-colored patch at the nape of the neck, the glabella, forehead or upper eyelids. Fades over the first year.
- **Port Wine Stains** – purplish-red flat hemangioma present at birth.
  ➤ Klippel-Trenaunay-Weber syndrome if associated with hemihypertrophy of an extremity or Sturge-Weber syndrome if the first branch of the trigeminal nerve is involved.
- **Sebaceous Gland Hyperplasia** – 1-2 mm yellowish papules on the nose and cheeks of newborns.
  ➤ Spontaneous resolution by 2 months of age
- **Seborrheic dermatitis** (or "cradle cap") – pink patches with greasy yellow scale on face, intertriginous areas and scalp
  ➤ Use baby oil and a soft brush for scalp lesions
  ➤ Facial or body areas can be treated with hydrocortisone cream
- **Transient Neonatal Pustular Melanosis** – 2-4 mm yellowish pustules most often on the neck, forehead, lower back, abdomen and legs.
  ➤ Rash presents at birth
  ➤ Disappears in 1-2 days leaving light pigmented macules with a collarette of scale that eventually fade over the first 3 months.

Respiratory Distress
Signs: nasal flaring, grunting, retractions, tachypnea and/or cyanosis
Transient Tachypnea of the Newborn: most common respiratory disorder of term infants. Tachypnea occurs soon after birth & resolves in the first few hours of life.
- Chest x-ray may show some hyperinflation with fluid in the fissures.

Meconium Aspiration Syndrome (MAS): amniotic fluid usually with thick particulate meconium. Symptoms will begin in the first couple hours after birth and often worsen with time.
- Chest x-ray with hyperinflation, perihilar infiltrates +/- streaky atelectasis
- Babies at risk for pulmonary hypertension
- Careful DeLee suctioning of oropharynx after delivery of the head ↓ risk.
- Intubation and suctioning of the trachea immediately after delivery is indicated for all depressed babies.

Respiratory Distress Syndrome (RDS): occurs almost exclusively in premature infants < 35 weeks gestation.
- Chest x-ray with "ground glass" appearance and air bronchograms
- Often associated with apnea/bradycardia episodes.

Pneumonia: very rare in newborns
- Risk factors: untreated group B streptococcus-positive mother, chorioamniotis or prolonged rupture of membranes > 18 hours.
- Chest x-ray can mimic the appearance of RDS or MAS

Congenital Heart Disease (CHD)
Clinical presentation: may present with respiratory distress, cyanosis, difficulty feeding, sweating with feeds or poor weight gain (failure to thrive).

Acyanotic with Normal Pulmonary Blood Flow on Chest x-ray
- Bicuspid aortic valve, idiopathic hypertrophic subaortic stenosis, coarctation of aorta and pulmonic stenosis

Acyanotic with Increased Pulmonary Blood Flow on Chest x-ray
- Atrial septal defect, patent ductus arteriosus, ventricular septal defect and anomalous pulmonary venous return

Cyanotic with Decreased Pulmonary Blood Flow on Chest x-ray
- Tetralogy of Fallot

Cyanotic with Increased Pulmonary Blood Flow on Chest x-ray
- Truncus arteriosus, single ventricle, transposition of the great arteries and total anomalous pulmonary venous return
- **Atrial Septal Defect:** fixed split S_2, systolic ejection murmur
- **Ventricular Septal Defect:** harsh systolic murmur at left sternal border
- **Patent Ductus Arteriosus:** differential cyanosis and continuous "machinery" murmur
- **Coarctation of the Aorta:** decreased femoral pulses

Ear/Nose/Throat Problems
- **Choanal atresia:** present with respiratory distress or poor feeding. Babies are pink while crying and cyanotic when calm
- **Cleft lip/palate:** presents with incomplete fusion of the lip and/or palate
  ➤ Referral for reconstructive surgery and speech therapist
- **Nasolacrimal duct obstruction:** presents with persistent tearing from eye
  ➤ Manage with nasolacrimal duct massage. Refer for surgery if lasts > 1 year.

- **Neck mass**: fetal goiter, cystic hygroma or thyroglossal duct cyst
  ➤ Check thyroid studies and refer for surgery if nonthyroidal process.

Gastrointestinal Problems
- **Umbilical cord granuloma**: treat with silver nitrate applications
- **Umbilical hernia**: usually resolves by 4 yrs. Refer for surgery if persistent.
- **Vomiting**: overfeeding, gastroenteritis, reflux or congenital anomaly (e.g., pyloric stenosis or atresia of esophagus or duodenum)
  ➤ **Pyloric stenosis**: intractable, projectile vomiting < 2 months of age
    o Diagnosis is by abdominal ultrasound or upper GI barium study
    o May feel an "olive"-sized mass in epigastric area on exam
    o Labs show a hypochloremic metabolic alkalosis
- **Delayed Passage of Meconium > 2 days**
  ➤ Cystic fibrosis, meconium plug, imperforate anus or Hirschsprung's disease.

Genitourinary Problems
- **Scrotal/groin mass**
  ➤ Inguinal hernia: usually does not transilluminate and involves canal
  ➤ Hydrocele: transilluminates and confined to the scrotum
- **Undescended testes**: wait 12 months before surgical intervention
  ➤ Consider checking a karyotype and refer to a pediatric urologist.

Hematologic Problems
- **Polycythemia**: presents with plethora, acrocyanosis or poor perfusion
  ➤ Diagnosis: Hematocrit > 65% by venous blood draw
  ➤ Treat with partial exchange transfusion.

Metabolic Problems
- **Hypothermia**: rectal temperature < 36.4°
  ➤ Usually from environmental losses and inadequate swaddling, but consider sepsis or congenital hypothyroidism in an ill baby.
  ➤ Treat with rewarming in an incubator.
- **Hypoglycemia**: glucose < 40 mg/dL in a term infant
  ➤ Signs: listless, hypotonia, jitteriness, seizure or poor feeding
  ➤ Prematurity, sepsis, diabetic mom, perinatal hypoxia or low birth weight
  ➤ Treat with frequent feeds or 10% dextrose in water intravenous drip
- **Hypocalcemia**: calcium < 8.0 mg/dL in a term infant
  ➤ Signs: same as for hypoglycemia and tetany
  ➤ Prematurity or mother with diabetes or hyperparathyroidism
  ➤ Treat with 0.5 mL/kg IV/IM 10% calcium gluconate

Neurologic Problems
- **Spinal Dysraphism**: presents as a sacral mass +/- lower extremity weakness (meningocele or meningomyelocele) or as a dimple, dermal sinus or tuft of hair in the sacral area (spina bifida occulta)
  ➤ An ultrasound of the lumbosacral spine is warranted for clinical suspicion

Ophthalmological Problems
- **Leukocoria**: presents as the absence of a red reflex in an eye
  ➤ Congenital cataract or retinoblastoma

Adapted from Centers for Disease Control and Prevention (CDC) and the American Academy of Pediatrics (AAP) Management Guidelines for Otitis Media

Definitions
- **Acute Otitis Media**: fluid in the middle ear or perforated tympanic membrane associated with signs of symptoms of an ear infection.
- **Otitis Media with Effusion**: asymptomatic fluid in the middle ear

Management of Acute Otitis Media (AOM)
- The CDC/AAP guidelines support antibiotic therapy for all AOM

Suggested Initial Empiric Antibiotic Choices for AOM in Young Children
- amoxicillin 80-90 mg/kg/day PO divided bid for high-risk children (< 2 years, daycare or prior antibiotic therapy in the last 3 months
  ➢ amoxicillin 40-45 mg/kg/day PO divided bid for low-risk children
- Penicillin-allergic patients
  ➢ azithromycin 10 mg/kg/day on day 1 then 5 mg/kg/day x 4 days
  ➢ erythromycin ethyl succinate + sulfisoxazole 50 mg/kg/day (based on erythromycin) PO divided qid

Suggested Antibiotics for Initial Antibiotic Failures
- Amoxicillin-clavulanate PO 40 mg/kg/day + amoxicillin 40 mg/kg/day PO divided bid or Augmentin ES 90 mg/kg/day PO divided bid
- Ceftriaxone 50 mg/kg intramuscular qd x 2-3 days
- Cefuroxime axetil 30 mg/kg/day PO divided bid
- Cefdinir 14 mg/kg PO qd
- Cefprozil 30 mg/kg/day PO divided bid
- Cefpodoxime proxetil 10 mg/kg PO qd

Duration of Antibiotic Therapy
- Traditional 10 day course of antibiotics may be excessive, but remains reasonable for high-risk children (those ≤ 2 years, in daycare, with recurrent AOM, immunosuppressed or history of allergies).
- Low-risk, older children can be treated with 7 days of antibiotics

Management of Recurrent AOM (≥ 4 episodes in a year)
- Minimize risk factors: passive smoke exposure, daycare, bottle feeding and allergen exposure in atopic children
- Allergy control with intranasal steroids or antihistamines
- Influenza, pneumococcal and hemophilus influenzae vaccinations
- Chemoprophylaxis: amoxicillin 20 mg/kg PO **or** sulfisoxazole 50 mg/kg PO qd

AOM with Pressure Equalizing Tubes or with Ruptured Tympanic Membrane
- 0.3% ofloxacin otic 5 drops in ear(s) bid (age < 12 yrs) and 10 drops (> 12 yrs)

Management of Otitis Media with Effusion (OME) in Children < 3 years
- Diagnosis made by pneumatic otoscopy or tympanometry
- Hearing evaluation for OME lasting 3 months or longer
  ➢ Bilateral hearing impairment of 20 decibels or worse is significant
- Options for OME ≥ 3 months + significant hearing impairment
  ➢ Antibiotic trial for 10-14 days
  ➢ Bilateral myringotomy with tube placement
- Treatments with no proven benefit for OME
  ➢ Antihistamines or decongestants
  ➢ Systemic steroids
  ➢ Tonsillectomy and/or adenoidectomy

References: Pediatrics Infectious Dis. J, 1999; 18: 1. Pediatrics Infectious Dis. J, 1999, 18: 1152. Pediatrics Infectious Dis. J, 2001; 108: 239. Agency for Health Care Policy and Research clinical practice guideline #12.

Screening History

- History of chest discomfort?
- History of palpitations?
- History of syncope, near syncope or severe exertional lightheadedness?
- History of high blood pressure?
- Have you ever been knocked unconscious or suffered a concussion?
- Have you ever had a seizure?
- Do you ever get out of breath during exercise?
- Do you have any vision problems?
- Have you ever experimented with drugs, alcohol or cigarettes?
- Are you currently seeing a doctor for any reason?
- Are you currently taking any medication including performance-enhancing steroids or supplements?
- Do you have any allergies to medicines or bee stings?
- Is there any family history of sudden death or heart disease?
- Are there any weight requirements for your sport?
- For females: when was your last period and do you have monthly periods?
- Do you have any hearing problems?

Exam

- Blood pressure, height and weight
- Visual acuity
- Cardiovascular: diminished femoral pulses (coarctation of aorta), systolic murmur, irregular heart rhythm, pericardial rub
- Respiratory: wheezing or prolonged expiratory phase
- Abdomen: organomegaly
- Genitourinary: inguinal hernia and undescended testis
- Musculoskeletal: quick exam of joints and back (scoliosis)
- Skin: molluscum contagiosum, herpes simplex, impetigo, tinea corporis or scabies
- Signs of Marfan syndrome: long, thin digits, arm span > height and pectus carinatum/excavatum, hypermobile joints, long, thin face and myopia
- Down Syndrome: rule out atlantoaxial instability

Contraindications to Sports Participation

- Cardiac: active myocarditis or pericarditis, hypertrophic cardiomyopathy, severe uncontrolled hypertension, possible coronary artery disease and uncontrolled ventricular dysrhythmias
- Neurologic: Symptoms of postconcussive syndrome (no contact sports), poorly controlled epilepsy (no swimming, weight lifting, sports at height), recurrent neck and upper extremity dysesthesias/paresthesias (no contact sports)
- Splenomegaly (no contact sports)
- Skin infections as above (no sports with skin-to-skin contact)
- Marfan syndrome (no contact sports)
- Sickle cell disease (no contact or high exertion sports)
- Atlantoaxial instability (no tumbling, diving or contact sports)

References: American Family Physician, 2000; 61: 2683-90.

Adapted from the American Academy of Pediatrics Recommendations for
Preventive Pediatric Health Care

Frequency of Well Child Checks
- Daily newborn care in the hospital
- Clinic visits: at 2 weeks then at months 2, 4, 6, 9, 12, 15, 18 and 24, then at
  years 3, 4, 5, 6 and 8 and then annually from year 10 to 21.

Interval History
- Assessed at every visit
- Interval infections since last visit
- Diet including adequacy of iron and fluoride intake
- Middle childhood: school performance, hobbies, exercise + family dynamics
- Adolescents: as above and involvement in afterschool or community activities,
  use of drugs and alcohol and whether they are sexually active

Measurements
- Height and weight at every visit
- Head circumference at every visit until 2 years of age.
- Blood pressure measurement at every visit beginning at 3 years of age.
- When to initiate interventions or refer

Age (years)	Borderline hypertension	Hypertension
< 8	115-119/75-79 mmHg	≥ 120/80 mmHg
8-12	125-129/80-84 mmHg	≥ 130/85 mmHg
> 12	135-139/85 89 mmHg	≥ 140/90 mmHg

- Childhood obesity if > 95% weight-for-height
  - Nutritional counseling and referral to weight management program
- Malnourished if < 5% weight-for-height
  - Dietary counseling, frequent weight checks, consider visiting nurse or public
    health nurse evaluation of home and social situation
- Short stature if < 5% height for age (unless constitutional based on calculated
  mid-parental height)
  - See section on Short Stature (page 189)
- Failure to thrive if chronic poor weight gain causes the child to cross 2 lines on
  the child's growth curve in a 6 month period.
  - See Failure to Thrive section (page 168)

Vision Screening
- Red reflexes assessed in newborns to screen for congenital cataracts or
  retinoblastomas
- Subjective testing: infants should be able to track to midline by 2 weeks of age,
  track past midline by 2 months and track objects 180° by 4 months.
- Objective visual acuity testing at 3 years of age and repeated each visit until 10
  years of age and if history suggests visual impairment thereafter.
- Strabismus screening: corneal light reflex test at 12 months and cover/uncover
  test or photoscreening at 3 years of age or earlier if history or exam suggests
  strabismus (see section on Strabismus and Amblyopia)
- **When to refer patients to an ophthalmologist:**
  - Any infants with white reflex on fundoscopic exam
  - An abnormal corneal light reflex, cover/uncover or photoscreening test

> Visual acuity of 20/40 or poorer
> 2 line visual acuity difference on the Snellen chart between the two eyes

Hearing Screening
- Universal screening of all newborns for hearing impairment using either evoked otoacoustic emissions or auditory brainstem response testing.
- Repeat screening audiograms at each visit from age 4 to 10 years.
- Referral to an audiologist for
  > All abnormal newborn hearing screens
  > Hearing impairment ≥ 25 decibels at one or more frequencies.

Developmental Assessment and Anticipatory Guidance
- See sections on Growth and Development and Anticipatory Guidance

Immunizations
- See section on Childhood Immunizations

Anemia
- Definition: hemoglobin < 10.5 gm/dL for 6-23 months, <11.5 for 2-12 years
  Prevention & treatment of iron-deficiency should start with dietary changes.
  > Encourage intake of iron-fortified solids by 4-6 months of age
  > Bottle-fed infants should use iron-fortified formulas
  > 2-4 mg/kg/day supplemental iron (up to 15 mg/day) for ex-preterm or low birthweight breast-fed infants starting at 1 month until 12 months of age.
  > No cow's milk, goat's milk or soy milk until at least 12 months of age
  > Limit milk intake to less than 24 ounces/day until the 5 years of age.
- Screen with hemoglobin check at 9-12 months of age
- Children at high-risk for iron-deficiency anemia (low-income families, immigrant children, ex-preemies, breastfed infants with insufficient supplemental iron and children with chronic inflammatory or infectious conditions) should also be screened at 18 months and yearly from 2-5 yrs.
- Interventions initiated once anemia diagnosed
  > Begin with education and use of iron-rich foods
  > Recheck hemoglobin in 4 weeks and desire rise of ≥1 gm/dL.
  > If inadequate rise, start 3 mg/kg/day iron and repeat screening in 4 weeks.
  > If inadequate rise, consider other causes of anemia (e.g., thalassemia, lead poisoning or hemoglobinopathies, GI bleed) & perform appropriate testing.

Metabolic Screening
- Universal newborn screen tests for hypothyroidism, hemoglobinopathies, galactosemia, phenyketonuria and more depending on the state.

Screening Urinalysis
- Screens for proteinuria, glycosuria and pyuria
- Initial test at 5 years of age
- Repeat annually in sexually active adolescent males and females

Lead Screening
- All high-risk infants should have a lead level at 9-12 months +/- 24 months.
- Public health nurse home evaluation for all confirmed high levels.

Screening for Tuberculosis (Tb)
- All children probably should have a PPD placed prior to entering school
- Annual testing for HIV-infected & incarcerated children beginning at 1 year.
- History of BCG vaccination is **not** a contraindication to PPD testing.

PPD = purified protein derivative and BCG = bacillus Calmette-Guerin vaccine

- Testing every 2-3 years for children exposed to high-risk adults beginning at 1 year (adults with documented Tb, HIV-infected, intravenous drug users, homeless, recently incarcerated adults and the children of migrant workers).

Cholesterol Screening
- Screen children with a family history of premature cardiovascular disease, cerebrovascular disease, peripheral vascular disease or hyperlipidemia.
- Initiate screening by checking a total cholesterol as early as 2 years of age.
- If total cholesterol ≥ 200 mg/dL → check a lipoprotein analysis
- Dietary intervention for LDL-cholesterol ≥ 130 mg/dL
  - ➤ Initiate American Heart Association Therapeutic Lifestyle Changes diet
  - ➤ Regular aerobic exercise and weight reduction program
  - ➤ Recheck lipoprotein analysis in 6 months
- Consider drug therapy for children > 10 years with a worrisome family history and LDL-cholesterol ≥ 160 mg/dL despite a trial of diet.
  - ➤ Use bile acid sequestrants (e.g., cholestyramine or colestipol)

Screening in Sexually-Active Adolescent Women
- Annual pelvic exam and pap smears
- Annual screen for chlamydia (even if asymptomatic)

Fluoride Supplementation
- Indicated between 6 months-12 years for children who do not drink fluoridated water or if fluoride content of drinking water is < 0.6 ppm.
  - ➤ 6 months - 3 years need 0.25 mg fluoride daily, 3 - 6 years need 0.5 mg fluoride daily and 6 years -12 years need 1.0 mg fluoride daily

Screening for Scoliosis (see section on Scoliosis)
- Screen each visit for school age children: examine for curved spine, uneven hip or waist crease, uneven nipple line or uneven shoulders.
  - ➤ Scoliosis x-ray series and orthopedic referral for abnormal exam

Injury and Violence Prevention
- Avoid prone sleeping position to prevent (SIDS): "Back to Sleep" initiative
- Advise against spanking as a method of discipline
- Traffic safety: rear-facing car seats until 12 months **and** ≥ 20 pounds, front-facing car seats between 1-4 years **and** ≥ 40 pounds, seat belts and booster seats for kids 4-8 years old until they are > 6 years, ≥ 4'9" **and** ≥ 80 pounds.
- Prevention of falls/accidents: stairway gates, window locks, cabinet latches, outlet guards, fences around pools/spas, poisons and firearms locked away.
- Burn prevention: smoke detectors and water heater set < 130°F
- Safety helmets & protective gear for biking, skateboarding & in-line skating
- Keep Poison Control number (1-800-222-1222) in accessible location
- Sunscreen use
- Screen children for depression
- Discuss with adolescents about drugs, alcohol and driving.

Dental Health
- Dental referral at 3 years
- Avoid bedtime bottle
- Brush teeth and gums daily by 12 months of age

SIDS = sudden infant death syndrome and LDL = low-density lipoprotein

References: Pediatrics, 2000; 105 (3): 645. Pediatrics, 1994; 94 (4): 566-7. Pediatrics, 1998; 101 (1): 141-7. MMWR, 1998; 47 (RR-3): 1-36 and Pediatrics, 1999; 103 (1): 173-81.

Croup (or Laryngotracheobronchitis)
- **Clinical Features**
  - ➤ Affects children with peak ages 6 months to 3 years in fall-winter.
  - ➤ Barky cough, inspiratory stridor, hoarseness, fever and coryza
  - ➤ Causes: parainfluenza 1, 3, respiratory syncytial virus (RSV) or adenovirus
  - ➤ Neck x-rays with subglottic narrowing ("steeple sign") and normal epiglottis
- **Management of Mild-Moderate Croup**
  - ➤ Cool mist humidifier
  - ➤ Steroids: dexamethasone intramuscular injection 0.6 mg/kg **or** 0.15 mg/kg orally bid **or** budesonide 2 mg nebulized daily for 2-3 days total therapy
  - ➤ Racemic epinephrine 0.05 mg/kg/dose (max dose 0.5 mL) in 3 mL normal saline nebulized for moderate-severe croup
  - ➤ Antipyretics
  - ➤ Encourage oral hydration
  - ➤ Clinical improvement after 3 hours of observation for moderate-severe croup can be managed as an outpatient with daily follow-up.

Bronchiolitis
- **Clinical Features**
  - ➤ Fever, coryza, congestion, cough +/- wheezing and feeding difficulties
  - ➤ More severe cases can exhibit nasal flaring, grunting, retractions and apnea
  - ➤ Exam: fine rales, diffuse wheezing +/- and signs of severity as above
  - ➤ Chest x-ray: hyperinflation, patchy infiltrates and/or atelectasis
  - ➤ Causes: RSV, parainfluenza, adenovirus, mycoplasma and influenza B.
  - ➤ Risk Factors: prematurity, low birth weight, crowded living conditions, day care, passive smoke exposure, bottle fed infants, ill contacts, winter-spring.
  - ➤ Rule out foreign body aspiration especially for focal findings on exam/CXR.
- **Prevention of RSV infection**
  - ➤ palivizumab (monoclonal antibody) 15 mg/kg monthly from October to April for high-risk infants: ex-preemies < 35 weeks, history of chronic cardiopulmonary disease and immunodeficiency.
- **Management of Bronchiolitis**
  - ➤ Hospitalize for respiratory distress, hypoxia, dehydration or high-risk < 6 mo.
  - ➤ Nasopharyngeal swab for RSV antigen if hospitalized for isolation purposes
  - ➤ Apnea monitoring indicated for moderate-severe bronchiolitis
  - ➤ Contact isolation and careful handwashing for all close contacts.
  - ➤ Albuterol 0.15 mg/kg/dose benefit equivocal. Can use if clinical response.
  - ➤ Racemic epinephrine 0.05 mg/kg/dose benefit of equivocal benefit.
  - ➤ No role for steroids in most cases (unclear benefit for the intubated infant?)
  - ➤ Ribavirin limited to high-risk infants with severe bronchiolitis.
  - ➤ Mainstay of therapy is hydration and supplemental oxygen (if needed).

Upper Respiratory Tract Infections in Children
- **Clinical Features**
  - ➤ Cough, rhinorrhea (frequently mucopurulent) and low-grade fever
  - ➤ Exam: non-toxic, no increased work of breathing, unremarkable exam
- **Management**
  - ➤ Educate parents that antibiotics are not indicated for the common cold
  - ➤ Bulb syringe to suction out nose, may use a humidifier near the bed
  - ➤ The use of decongestants and antitussives (codeine or dextromethorphan) for symptomatic relief for infants > 6 months of questionable benefit.

References: J. Pediatrics, 1999; 135(2): 45-50. Pediatric Clinic North Amer., 1999; 46 (6): 1167-78. NEJM, 2001; 344 (25): 1917-28. Ped. Inf. Dis. J., 2002; 21: 873-8 and Pediatrics, 2001; 108(3): 52.

Definition
- Lateral curvature of the spine as measured by the Cobb angle > 10 degrees usually accompanied by some degree of vertebral spine rotation.

Classification of Scoliosis
Idiopathic Scoliosis
- Infantile form: 2 months - 3 years, left sided thoracic, male predominance
- Juvenile form: onset between 3-10 years of age, high risk of progression.
- Adolescent form: onset after 10 years of age (80% of all scoliosis cases)
Secondary Scoliosis
- Systemic disorders: Ehlers-Danlos or Marfan syndromes or homocystinuria
- Neurologic syndromes: tethered cord, syringomyelia, neurofibromatosis, muscular dystrophy, cerebral palsy, poliomyelitis, Friedreich's ataxia, Riley-Day syndrome or Werdnig-Hoffman disease.

Evaluation of Scoliosis
- Red flags: significant back pain or marked spine stiffness, a left thoracic curve, an abnormal neurologic examination, sudden rapid progression in a previously stable curve and onset before 8 years of age.
  ➢ These patients (and those with infantile or juvenile scoliosis) should be referred to a pediatric orthopedist & have a MRI study of the spine
- Routine scoliosis screening with an Adam's forward bending test should begin by 8 -10 years and end at 16 years.
  ➢ The Adam's forward bending test screens for a rotational deformity.
- A scoliometer placed in the midline at the vertebral level of maximum rib prominence measures the angle of spine rotation.
  ➢ An angle of thoracic rotation > 5-6 degrees requires a work-up.
- Tanner staging should be determined once scoliosis identified.
- A standing posteroanterior spine radiograph to measure the curve using the Cobb method and to determine the Risser stage for all abnormal exams.

Risk of Spinal Curve Progression

Cobb angle (degrees)	Risser Stage	Risk of progression	Referral/Management
10 - 19	2 - 4	5 – 15%	x-ray every 6 months
10 - 19	0 - 1	15 – 40%	x-ray every 6 months
20 - 29	2 - 4	10 - 30%	Refer if curve > 25°
20 - 29	0 - 1	40 - 70%	Refer if curve > 25°
29 – 40	2 - 4	40 – 70%	Refer
29 – 40	0 - 1	70 – 90%	Refer
> 40	0 - 4	Not applicable	Refer

Management of Scoliosis
- Patients with spinal curves < 25° can be followed with serial scoliosis x-ray series every 6 months.
- Controversy exists about the benefit of bracing children with moderate curves between 25 – 40°.
- General consensus that surgery should be performed for curves > 40°.

References: Amer. Fam. Physician, 2001; 64: 111-6 and Amer. Fam. Physician, 2002; 65: 1817-22.

Febrile Seizures Definition
- Simple febrile seizure: A generalized seizure lasting < 15 minutes in a febrile child between 6 months and 5 years old who is neurologically normal and has no evidence of meningitis, metabolic disturbance or recent trauma.
- Complex febrile seizure: duration > 15 min., focal or recurrent within 24 hrs.

Management of Febrile Seizures
- Airway, Breathing, Circulation
- Benzodiazepines indicated for prolonged seizures (> 15 minutes)
  ➢ Lorazepam 0.05-0.1 mg/kg intravenous push or
  ➢ Diazepam 0.5 mg/kg per rectum
- Antipyretics
- Search for underlying source of infection and treat accordingly
- No lumbar puncture needed for **simple** febrile seizures with a normal neurologic exam, hemodynamically stable, no petechiae and no nuchal rigidity.

Long-term treatment of children after a simple febrile seizure
- The American Academy of Pediatrics recommends against both continuous or intermittent anticonvulsant therapy in children with simple febrile seizures.
- Antipyretics may be given to a febrile child to increase their comfort, but these have never been shown to decrease the chance of a recurrent febrile seizure.

Evaluation of the Child with a First Nonfebrile Seizure
- Applies to children ages 1 month to 21 years of age
- No history of epilepsy, trauma, signs of meningitis or metabolic disturbance
- Exclusion of breath-holding spells, syncope, gastroesophageal reflux, pseudoseizures, complex migraines, night tremors or micturitional shivering
- Laboratory tests: electrolytes, renal panel, complete blood count, glucose, calcium, magnesium, pyruvate, lactate, ammonia, serum amino acids, urine organic acids +/- urine drug screen (if toxic exposure in question).
- Lumbar puncture: no role unless patient has a focal neurologic exam, nuchal rigidity, is a child< 6 months or has an altered state of consciousness.
- Electroencephalogram should be performed in every child in awake and sleep states and with hyperventilation and photic stimulation.
- Neuroimaging
  ➢ An emergent CT scan for children with a prolonged Todd's paralysis (postepileptic hemi/monoplegia) or prolonged postictal state x several hours.
  ➢ A nonurgent MRI scan for any child with an abnormal neurologic exam, a focal seizure history, children under 1 year of age and those with an abnormal electroencephalogram that does not have the pattern of benign partial epilepsy of childhood or primary generalized epilepsy.

Treatment of Children after a Nonfebrile Seizure
- Antiepileptics can reduce the risk of a seizure recurrence by about 50%.
  ➢ The first-line antiepileptics (phenobarbital, phenytoin, valproic acid and carbamazepine) have unacceptable side effects 20-30% of the time.
- Long-term prognosis for seizure remission same whether antiepileptics are started after the first or second unprovoked seizure.
- Antiepileptic treatment does not decrease the risk of developing epilepsy.
- Safety issues: bicycle on sidewalk, use helmet, swim only with a partner, avoid bathtubs, no driving unless seizure free for 2 years, avoid activities where a fall from height is possible.

References: Pediatrics, 1999; 103(6): 1307-9. Neurology, 2000; 55: 516-23 & Neurology, 2003; 60: 166-75.

Definition: short stature is defined as height below the 3rd percentile for age.

Projected Adult Height Based on Mid-Parental Height:
- Girls: projected height = [mother's height + (father's height – 5")] / 2
- Boys: projected height = [(mother's height + 5") + father's height] / 2
- If a child is progressing along a growth curve that is consistent with the projected mid-parental height, there is no cause for concern.

Causes of Short Stature
- **Normal causes of short stature**
  - Familial short stature
  - Constitutional delay in puberty
- **Pathologic causes of short stature**
  - Growth hormone deficiency
  - Diabetes mellitus
  - Hypothyroidism
  - Hypopituitarism
  - Skeletal dysplasias (chondromalacia or rickets)
  - Chronic inflammatory conditions
  - Genetic syndromes (e.g., Turner syndrome and Prader-Willi syndrome)
  - Severe malnutrition
  - Precocious puberty with early closure of epiphyseal plates

Exam
- Examination of Tanner stage, nutritional status, stigmata of syndromic conditions and for disproportionately short limbs (i.e., dwarfism)
- Height less than 3 standard deviations below the mean typically pathologic
- Follow height velocity carefully: a child age 2-9 years should stay on the same growth curve. Crossing channels during this period is abnormal.
- If a decreased height velocity suggests a pathologic condition, check the weight-for-height ratio. Short, thin kids tend to have a systemic disorder and short, obese kids tend to have an endocrinopathy.

Laboratory Tests
- Complete blood count, electrolytes, renal panel, erythrocyte sedimentation rate (evidence of chronic inflammatory states), thyroid panel, liver function tests, calcium, phosphorus, alkaline phosphatase and urinalysis
- Consider a karyotype in girls (Turner syndrome)
- Screen for growth hormone deficiency by checking serum levels of insulin-like growth factor I and II (IGF-I and IGF-II) + IGF-binding protein (IGF-BP).
  - Growth hormone deficiency: growth hormone during insulin-induced hypoglycemia→ growth hormone < 5 mcg/L = growth hormone deficiency

Radiographic Tests
- Left hand and wrist x-rays for bone age
  - Delayed bone age seen in constitutional delay, Turner syndrome, hypothyroidism, hypopituitarism and chronic inflammatory states.
  - Familial short stature has a normal bone age and normal growth velocity

Approved uses for Growth Hormone Therapy in Children with Short Stature
- Growth hormone deficiency
- Chronic renal insufficiency before renal transplantation
- Turner syndrome or Prader-Willi syndrome
- Infants born small for gestational age who have not achieved catch-up growth by 2 years of age

Contraindications to Growth Hormone Therapy
- Pseudotumor cerebri and proliferative diabetic retinopathy

References: Endocrine Practice, 2003; 9(1): 65-76.

Recommended Ages for Attempting Ocular Alignment Screening Tests

- **Age 6-24 months**: Hirschberg corneal light reflex test. The reflection should fall in the same location in the cornea of each eye.
- **3-4 years**: cover/uncover test
- **5-6 years**: Snellen visual acuity test

Indications for Referral to an Ophthalmologist

- Visual acuity ≤ 20/40 or two-line difference between the two eyes in children older than 6 years.
- Any eye movement seen on the cover/uncover test suggests strabismus.
- Any child with a white reflex behind the eye (leukocoria).

Strabismus

- **Definition:** constant (tropias) or intermittent (phorias) eye deviation that causes malalignment of the visual axis and dysconjugate gaze.
  - ➢ Deviation lateral (exotropia), medial (esotropia) and vertical (hypertropia)
  - ➢ Intermittent deviations are respectively exophoria, esophoria + hyperphoria.
- **Pathophysiology:** the brain suppresses the visual input from the strabismic eye to allow for a clearer image beginning at ≥ 3 months of age.
- If this preferential suppression of visual input persists for years, people will develop monocular vision loss (amblyopia).
- Strabismus surgery **before age 6** once the visual acuity goal is reached.

Treatment of Accomodative Strabismus

- Optical correction of astigmatism or hyperopia (farsightedness) with glasses results in ocular convergence and thus corrects accommodative strabismus.

Amblyopia

- **Definition:** visual loss not related to any structural abnormality of the eye or visual pathway.
- **Strabismic Amblyopia** – secondary to strabismus (most common subtype)
  - ➢ **Treatment**: patch the "good eye" for all but 1-2 waking hours every day which forces the strabismic eye to improve its visual acuity.
  - ➢ Treatment of amblyopia is more urgent than treatment of the strabismus (surgical realignment of the visual axis).
- **Anisometropic Amblyopia** – related to farsightedness or astigmatism
  - ➢ **Treatment**: corrective lenses needed for anisometropic amblyopia.
- **Deprivation Amblyopia** – caused by a congenital cataract, ptosis, hyphema, nystagmus or retinoblastoma
  - ➢ **Treatment**: surgical correction of the underlying problem (excision of a congenital cataract, drainage of a hyphema or correction of ptosis).

References: American Optometric Association, 1997. Care of the patient with amblyopia. 2nd ed.: 57.
Pediatrics, 1996; 98(1): 153-7 and Amer. Fam. Physician, 2001; 64: 623-8.

Index

Index

Page left blank for notes

Page left blank for notes

Ordering From Tarascon Publishing

INTERNET	FAX	PHONE	MAIL
Credit card orders at www.taras-con.com	Fax credit card orders toll free to 877.929.9926	For phone orders or customer service, call 800.929.9926	Mail order and check to: Tarascon Publishing, PO Box 517, Lompoc, CA 93438

	Price/Copy by # of Copies Ordered				# Ordered	Price
TARASCON POCKET PHARMACOPOEIA®	1-9	10-49	50-99	≥100		
Classic Shirt-Pocket Edition	$9.95	$8.95	$7.95	$6.95		$
Deluxe Labcoat Pocket Edition	$17.95	$15.25	$13.45	$12.55		$
PDA software on CD-ROM, 12-month subscription*	$29.95	$25.46	$23.96	$22.46		$
PDA software on CD-ROM, 3-month subscription*	$3.97	$7.62	$7.18	$6.73		$
OTHER POCKETBOOKS & MAGNIFIER	1-9	10-49	50-99	≥100		
Tarascon Primary Care Pocketbook	$14.95	$13.45	$11.94	$10.44		$
Tarascon Pocket Orthopaedica®	$11.95	$9.90	$8.95	$8.35		$
Tarascon Pediatric Emergency Pocketbook	$11.95	$9.90	$8.95	$8.35		$
Tarascon Adult Emergency Pocketbook	$11.95	$9.90	$8.95	$8.35		$
Tarascon Internal Medicine & Critical Care Pocketbook	$11.95	$9.90	$8.95	$8.35		$
How to be a Truly Excellent Junior Medical Student	$9.95	$8.25	$7.45	$6.95		$
Sheet magnifier – fits in any book to make reading easier!	$1.00	$0.89	$0.78	$0.66		$

*Palm OS or Pocket PC; download the software directly from www.tarascon.com for an approximately 10% discount!

					Subtotal	$
SALES TAX - California only					California Sales Tax (7.75%)	$

CHOOSE SHIPPING METHOD: cost based on subtotal →	≤$10	$10-29	$30-75	$76-300		
☐ Standard shipping	$1.00	$2.50	$6.00	$18.00	Shipping	$
☐ UPS 2-day air (no post office boxes)	$12.00	$14.00	$16.00	$18.00	TOTAL	$

Name	Card number
Address	☐ VISA ☐ Mastercard ☐ AmEx ☐ Discover
	Expiration date
City / State /Zip	CID# (if available) Signature
	E-mail and phone

Page left blank for notes

Page left blank for notes